Controversies in Queer Theology

The Controversies in Contextual Theology Series
Series Editor: Lisa Isherwood, University of Winchester

Controversies in Feminist Theology
Lisa Isherwood and Marcella Althaus-Reid

Controversies in Political Theology
Thia Cooper

Controversies in Body Theology
Edited by Marcella Althaus-Reid and Lisa Isherwood

Trans/formations
Edited by Lisa Isherwood and Marcella Althaus-Reid

*Through Us, With Us, In Us: Relational Theologies in the
Twenty-first Century*
Edited by Lisa Isherwood and Elaine Bellchambers

Controversies in Interreligious Dialogue and the Theology of Religions
Paul Hedges

Controversies in Contextual Theology Series

Controversies in Queer Theology

Susannah Cornwall

scm press

© Susannah Cornwall 2011

Published in 2011 by SCM Press
Editorial office
13–17 Long Lane,
London, EC1A 9PN, UK

SCM Press is an imprint of Hymns Ancient and Modern Ltd
(a registered charity)
13A Hellesdon Park Road
Norwich NR6 5DR, UK

www.scm-canterburypress.co.uk

British Library Cataloguing in Publication data

A catalogue record for this book is available
from the British Library

978-0-334-04355-3

Typeset by Regent Typesetting, London
Printed and bound by
CPI Antony Rowe, Chippenham and Eastbourne

Contents

Acknowledgements

Any book is a team effort, regardless of whether or not its author acknowledges it as such. It is inevitable that I have absorbed and assimilated other people's ideas along the way, and any failure to acknowledge them adequately should be taken as a compliment to those concerned – though I have, of course, done my utmost to credit them wherever possible. Nonetheless, I would like to give especial thanks to all my erstwhile teachers, and my colleagues and students at the University of Exeter, for the gentle and collegial way in which they have contributed to the crucible in which my theological ideas have formed.

Specific thanks are due to Patrick S. Cheng, Stuart Macwilliam, David Nixon, Adrian Thatcher and Andrew Worthley for their comments on early ideas for this book, and for reading (and perspicaciously remarking on) drafts along the way. Patrick's, Stuart's and David's own expertise in queer theology and critical theory made them invaluable interlocutors. Thank you too to the series editor Lisa Isherwood, and Natalie Watson at SCM Press for all their support and enthusiasm with this project and other work.

Thank you to all the participants in the Queer Theology discussion group at the 2009 conference of the European Society of Women in Theological Research in Winchester, whose comments and opinions were stimulating and insightful: Ulrike Auga, Pilar Yuste Cabello, Teresa Forcades i Vila, Bärbel Fünfsinn, Martina Heinrichs, Janie Hope, Karin Hügel, Lisa Isherwood, Sylwia Kupczyk, Angelika Ritter-Grepl and Hanna Strack. I am also grateful to Julie Clague, Vicky Gunn and One Glasgow for enabling me to visit the University of Glasgow in 2009 to give a lecture in the Queer Meets Faith series, where some of these ideas were first aired. Discussions following my paper 'Queering Susanna(h)' at the 2010 Society for the Study of Theology conference at the University of Manchester also helped me to clarify my thinking in certain areas, and I am grateful to the SST committee for providing a bursary which allowed me to attend, and to all who took part in discussing issues raised by the paper on that occasion.

Many thanks to Morwenna Ludlow and Piers Ludlow for inviting me to Princeton in Summer 2009 and for all their hospitality there. Kate Skrebutenas at the Princeton Theological Seminary Library kindly gave me help with finding microfiches of North American theses. The assistance of staff at the British Library and the Cambridge University Library was also much appreciated. Much of this manuscript was written in the solace of the children's literature room at the University of Exeter's Haighton Library, and so I also have to thank its book-bound inhabitants for their welcome presence. The works of Richard Adams, Lucy M. Boston, Aidan Chambers, Susan Cooper, Antonia Forest, Jane Gardam, Alan Garner, E. Nesbit, Graham Oakley and Robert Westall are among the faithful friends that helped to spark theological questions in me long ago, and continue to provide timely distraction of the sort that turns out to be intellectually and spiritually invigorating more often than otherwise.

I am grateful for more directly stimulating conversations (both virtually and face to face) about queer theology and other matters to Gemma Burnett-Chetwynd, Rebecca Catto, Patrick S. Cheng, Julie Clague, Frances Clemson, Dom Coad, Grace Davie, Siobhán Garrigan, Julie Gittoes, Brutus Green, David Grumett, Vicky Gunn, Symon Hill, John Hughes, Lisa Isherwood, Louise Lawrence, Morwenna Ludlow, Stuart Macwilliam, Jon Morgan, Noel Moules, Rachel Muers, Philippa Newis, David Nixon, Francesca Stavrakopoulou, Jacqui Stewart, Adrian Thatcher, Andrew Thomas, Samuel Tongue, Jim Walters, Lewis Ward, Alexandra Wörn, Andrew Worthley and Mark Wynn.

Thanks go to my family for all their love, hospitality and support: to my parents, Geoff and Jenny Cornwall; and to Vici Cornwall, John Cornwall, Judy Cornwall, Charlie Cornwall, Jack Cornwall, Hayley Fox, Nigel Fox, Nathaniel Fox, Charis Fox, Elias Fox, Tirzah Fox, John

Abbott and Andrea Rosenfeld (what an unusual joy it is to have a Jewish godmother!) Most of all, I am privileged to share my life with Jonathan Morgan, an outstanding theologian who endures more of my under-developed and incoherent ideas than anyone else and whose incisive and creative input colours so much of what I do.

While I am pleased to share the credit with all these people and so many others, the blame is mine alone. Any errors or omissions in this manuscript are entirely my own responsibility, and I would be grateful (if not exactly pleased) to be alerted to them.

Introduction

In this book I seek to give an overview of work of the major scholars working in queer theology and queer biblical studies since the 1980s. There are certain questions which arise over and over again when considering the nature and utility of queer theology: questions about how to hold together ambivalent identities, about the extent to which any identity category is exclusive and essentialist, and about whether theology and biblical criticism informed by queer discourse represents a break with the Christian tradition or is in fact representative of a strand already existing within Christianity. Unsurprisingly, therefore, controversies in queer theology echo controversies in theology more broadly, especially those to do with who has the authority to make and disseminate theological assertions.

However, there is an additional complication to bear in mind: whereas some Christian theologies have sought to be normative and assimilationist and have asserted that theirs represents the most true or perfect understanding of a particular element of human talk about God, queer theologies have often rejected their own finality or incontrovertibility, because of a suspicion of absolutism or conceptual imperialism. Marcella Althaus-Reid characterized this as 'a queer theological praxis which by definition has the instability of a becoming and not the certainty of an arrival' (Althaus-Reid 2008, p. 109). This means that queer theologies are, almost by definition, less self-aggrandizing and less evangelical (with a small 'e') than some of the theological methodologies they seek to resist. To acknowledge the huge diversity and disagreement even between those whose theology and biblical criticism falls under the queer umbrella, as this book seeks to do, might seem to erode the utility or persuasiveness of such an ambiguous trope. However, it is important to note from the outset that queer theology is, in some sense, an outsider discourse, and always stands in a difficult relationship to the ecclesiastical and academic mainstream even where it is not actively opposed. Even if it has been done largely by those whose university or seminary context renders them relatively cushioned and privileged, both economically and physically, in comparison to those who work 'on the ground', queer theology has sometimes been a dangerous label with which to be associated.

Many Christians consider themselves and their religion unproblematically to have succeeded, fulfilled or superseded the Judaism in which their own faith is rooted. However, Christian reflection on the Hebrew Bible is greatly indebted to both historical and contemporary Jewish research. Where I draw on Jewish scholarship, I do so with the acknowledgement that this cannot unproblematically be woven into a web of Christian discourse and with grateful thanks for the way Jewish theological discourse and biblical criticism help to show up for Christianity its mixed, jumbled and heterogeneous history. Although the remit of this present volume is to reflect upon controversies in queer *Christian* theology, it is worth mentioning recent exploration of the 'queer non-space' that is existence between religious categories, as well as across religious and secular queer theories. This is the context of Frederick Roden's 2009 edited volume, *Jewish/Christian/Queer*, in which the 'queernesses' of all three identities are read together: Christianity, a sometimes uneasy synthesis of Jewish and Greek thought; Judaism, simultaneously a religion and a race, and abjected by later Christian anti-Semitism; and queerness, marginalized by socio-sexual conservatism in some strands of both Judaism and Christianity. Roden argues that

> [Q]ueer theology's strength is in its use of metaphor to authorize and explain difference rather than to make accommodations between past and present . . . I call for a similar stance towards history in order to release limits of fixed identity politics for both Jewishness and Christianity. (Roden 2009b, p. 7)

Roden suggests that the fact that both Judaism and Christianity contain queer theological strands in their traditions, but that these are much more often outrightly named as queer in Christian theology, is evidence of the way in which *all* Judaism is always already considered queer and other in a normatively Christian world (Roden 2007b, p. 7). The New Testament itself shows Paul struggling with questions about whether a Christian need also be a Jew: Paul the Jew suspects in Romans 1 that Gentiles are easily led into sexual temptation, drawn to queer desires that are 'against nature'; yet even God somehow transcends the natural order by including Gentiles in the fold of salvation in Romans 11 (Rogers 2009, pp. 19–21, 25). The religious and sexual queernesses of being a Gentile are themselves overturned by God's excessive soteriological performance. (For further essays on the associations between Judaism and queerness – and reflection on Judith Butler's ambivalent relationship with her own Jewish heritage – see Boyarin, Itzkovitz and Pellegrini 2003.)

The field of queer Muslim scholarship is younger and less well-established, but, as in Jewish and Christian queer theologies, Muslim women and people with non-heterosexual sexualities have come to claim that their own experience is a valid source of knowledge about God and human sex. Queer Muslim interpretation, in common with Jewish and Christian queer theology and biblical criticism, draws on particular scriptural texts as especially important or significant for finding queer precedent in the tradition. For example, the Qur'anic story of Lut (known as Lot in the Hebrew Bible), and his interactions with the people of Sodom and Gomorrah, is reframed by Scott Sarij al-Haqq Kugle as a condemnation of greed and oppression rather than of homosexual activity (Kugle 2003, p. 214), and has become an important site of discourse in queer Muslim scholarship (Rouhani 2007, p. 173; Kugle and Chiddy 2009, pp. 143–4) – just as its counterpart in the book of Judges has for Christians and Jews who have identified the real 'sin of Sodom' as inhospitality. Amreen Ebrahim analyses the 14 terms used in a condemnatory sense in the Qur'anic Lut narrative and concludes, 'Same-sex indiscretions are . . . put on the same ethical plane as all sorts of inappropriate opposite-sex and non-sexual activities' (Ebrahim 1997,

p. 95); homosexuality is barely mentioned in the Qur'an in comparison to adultery, suggesting that it is rather unimportant (Ebrahim 1997, p. 99). Such progressive Muslim thought and activism are grounded, claims Omid Safi, in 'the Divine injunction to enact the justice *('adl)* and goodness-and-beauty *(ihsan)* that lie of the heart of the Islamic tradition' (Safi 2003b, p. 1). As such, queer Muslim reframings are identified not as discontinuous with the will of Allah, but merely discontinuous with some of its distortions through the tradition. Queer Muslim identity is complicated by a need to query and, in some cases, hold together the apparently conflicting matrices of homosexuality, religious devotion, social obligation grounded in religious ideology and questions of citizenship and resistance to Western imperialist hegemonic discourses of both sexuality and capitalism (Rouhani 2007, pp. 173–5; Safi 2003b, p. 2). This is heightened by the fact that many Muslims consider homosexuality as peculiarly Western and not something which properly exists in Muslim societies (Kugle and Chiddy 2009, p. 146; Siraj 2009; Yip 2004; Habib 2010a). Queer Muslims thereby have to balance yet another possibly conflicting element of identity.

Queer Muslim theology and interpretation is moving away from apologetics toward proactively queer reading, grounded in activism: Ibrahim Abraham notes the work of the Muslim group Queer Jihad, whose members read the Qur'anic and Hadithic *mukhannath* (effeminate men) and *khasiyy* (eunuchs) as proto-queer figures (Abraham 2007, p 4.6), and of other queer Muslim activist movements such as Al-Fatiha in the USA and Imaan in Britain (Abraham 2007, p. 4.2). For more recent reflections on specifically queer Muslim experience, see Shah 2010, Kelly 2010, Musić 2010, Khan 2010, Abraham 2010, Yorukoglu 2010, Atay 2010.

I have utilized more direct referencing, and longer quotations, in this book than are standard in a work of academic theology. This is done consciously, as a way in which to allow more voices than my own to remain audible. It is not possible to engage with every author as fully as I would like, and it would be unrealistic to expect every reader of the present book to be already familiar with those theologians and theorists to whom I can give only a superficial treatment. Dealing in breadth sometimes means compromising depth, and it is inevitable that glossing an argument sometimes elides its sense; there are times at which only hearing someone's original words will do. I hope my readers will be encouraged to go back to the original texts from which I can only quote snippets and fragments, and to interrogate and celebrate them further. If there are moments when I have unwittingly misunderstood or misrepresented an argument or a motivation, then I can only apologize and hope that those I have wronged, or their advocates, will do me the privilege of letting me know so that this conversation might be a multivocal and ongoing one.

There is another important reason for letting the voices of those who have worked on questions of queer theology over the last few decades speak for themselves. I myself am a heterosexual woman, married to a heterosexual man. As far as each of us knows, we are female and male respectively. The chapters below will show that there is much debate over the extent to which a heterosexual person can be considered queer or can speak about queer theologians. Some people believe that a heterosexual can only ever be an ally to queer people rather than claiming queerness themselves; others say that queering is about a rejection of more than heteronormativity and that it is the responsibility and task of heterosexual married people just as much as others to queer discourses of regulatory race, class, gender and sexuality. I do not claim a right to speak on behalf of others: rather, I seek to speak *with* them, reflecting on how queer theology implicates and interrogates all Christians, whatever their sex, sexuality and gender identity. Nonetheless, I am aware that the society in which I live grants me certain privileges not afforded to those whose gender, sexuality and 'race' are often deemed non-normative or non-ideal. It is not my intention to patronize, misrepresent or equivocate about anyone else.

The theologians and biblical scholars whose work I draw upon come from a range of Christian (and some Jewish) traditions, and hold a range of identities. Many identify as lesbian or gay, others as heterosexual and some simply as queer. One of the things which queer theology has done so effectively, in common with feminist, postcolonial and other postmodern theologies, has been to highlight the importance of individual location and context in formulating theology. That non-heterosexual people's experience qualifies them to respond differently, and legitimately, to the Bible, was one of the foundational assumptions in early lesbian and gay theology. A person's sexual orientation is often a fundamental part of the way in which they encounter and interpret texts. Even so, I have chosen not to segregate or, at times, identify queer, LGBT (lesbian, gay, bisexual and transgender) and heterosexual scholars, for I suggest that this risks reinscribing stereotypes about each group: rather, I have chosen to utilize their work thematically, in terms of its implications for queer theology. Grouping together scholars who (for example) critique white bias via queer theology, despite the fact that they themselves have diverse sexualities and identities, may be deemed naïvely to perpetuate an unhelpful universalism. Nonetheless, I believe that it would be just as naïve to suppose that knowing someone identifies as gay rather than heterosexual, or bisexual rather than lesbian, tells us everything about their allegiances and intellectual assumptions.

It is my privilege to reflect in this book on long theological careers, and theological work which has spanned several decades and is still ongoing. However, this also presents certain challenges. Some of the established scholars who have come to be so important in the field of queer theology, like Robert E. Goss and Elizabeth Stuart, started out by characterizing what they were doing as gay or lesbian theology, only latterly coming to utilize the queer label. For this reason, it will be important for the reader to note carefully the dates of work cited. I have attempted to draw special attention to work published prior to the mid-1990s, since it is possible and indeed likely that scholars' ideas, allegiances and even identities may have shifted in this time, and that they may no longer stand by opinions expressed some years ago. However, it is of course possible that ideas can change even over a much shorter period of time. Readers should be aware that I cite work important and influential at a given time, but this does not mean that its author still necessarily endorses it exactly as it was.

Ringing in my ears during the preparation of this book have been two things: the television-mediated noise of the vuvuzela trumpets blown in celebration at the 2010 (Association) Football World Cup in South Africa; and the words of Elizabeth Stuart, describing the symbolic 'football match' taking place between groups of Christians seeking to claim authoritative pronouncement on homosexuality and Christian ethics, while gay and lesbian Christians are confined to the sidelines 'watching scholars tackling each other for the ball of our lives' (Stuart 1995, p. 1). The fundamentalist and the conservative Christian, says Stuart, kick the ball into goals marked 'homosexuality is a perversion' and 'homosexuality is not chosen but is still condemned' respectively. The liberal dithers around with the ball, kicking it up and down the field, stands with it in the middle, makes a lukewarm pronouncement about homosexuality falling short of an ideal, and eventually 'scuttles off the pitch before the crowd and players can get him' (Stuart 1995, p. 1). Finally, the radical, who is well-versed in feminist theology and biblical criticism, suggests that lesbian and gay people, *too*, are well able to make serious commitments, and that lesbian and gay people, *too*, should be allowed to marry – as though this reflection of heterosexual relationship were the highest and most desirable mode of human love imaginable. It would be fair to say that the debate has moved on since 1995, with more overt support for non-heterosexual Christians from their allies and less commitment to heterosexual marriage as an ideal to which all must aspire. Nonetheless, those who reflect on issues of queer theology from a position of 'outsiderhood' – as I do myself – will do well to keep in mind Stuart's words as she concludes, devastatingly:

> [The radical] awaits the adoration of the crowd but the only sounds are of splatters of rage coming out of the fundamentalist and the conservative, and the anxious perspiring of the liberal in the changing-room. The radical cannot understand it: he is hurt, he has risked his reputation, even his career, to speak out for lesbian sisters and gay brothers. He turns to the crowd: 'What *do* you want then?' he shouts in exasperation. And with one voice the answer booms: 'Can we have our ball back please?' (Stuart 1995, p. 2)

The queer theologies of recent decades, while not unproblematically an expansion of liberation theologies (for reasons we shall see below), have served and continue to serve a vitally liberative function in the lives of queer Christians and others who have found themselves and their modes of life and love written out of signification. That queer theology has proven tenacious and vigorous enough to generate its own controversies and debates is testament to the commitment of those who have refused to let themselves be erased from theology's and biblical criticism's past and present. For all of those whose work is discussed and cited herein and for those whose theological exploration has never made it into writing but which has nonetheless been part of a groundswell of queer human–divine relationality, I give thanks.

1

What is Queer?

The minute you say 'queer' you are necessarily calling into question exactly what you mean when you say it. There is always an implicit question about what constitutes 'queerness' that attends the minute you say the word. (Harper, White and Cerullo 1993, p. 30; quoted in Walters 1996, p. 838)

When we come to think about or analyse something – an idea, a phenomenon, a movement – we usually like to know a few basic things about it, in order to sketch out its limits and to help us contextualize it among all our other, existing knowledge. However, when we are dealing with queer theology or indeed the broader queer theory with which it is associated, things are not so simple. As we will see throughout this book, many of the controversies surrounding queer theology stem from attempts by various groups to say that the thing *they* do is queer theology, in a way that the things done by others are not – while simultaneously querying whether queer is something that can or should be defined at all. As such, the question 'what is queer theology?' is an open-ended one, which will be examined and re-examined throughout this book. But the very concept of queer has built into it from the start an idea of elusiveness, uncertainty, non-fixity, and a resistance to closed definitions. It is therefore extremely difficult to set out what exactly queer *is*.

Indeed, 'queer', an odd term which serves the treble function of noun, verb and adjective, is often characterized as being more a critique of the concept of identity or definition than an identity or definition in its own right. It is almost impossible to give a neat breakdown of queer with which to start our journey. This elusiveness is significant in itself, as we will see. Nonetheless, it is possible to give some hints or pointers to the kinds of ideas addressed and encompassed by queer theologies and broader queer theories.

For some older speakers of English, the main connotation of the word 'queer' may still be a sense of oddness or strangeness, with a possible hint of wrongness attached. Indeed, in recent history, until the 1960s or thereabouts, this was the way the word was usually understood. 'Queer' first appeared in the English language in the sixteenth century (possibly borrowed from the German *quer*, meaning odd or oblique), carrying with it a sense of being across or against something. Phrases such as 'queer fish', used to mean an eccentric or unusual person, still exist and do not carry the specifically sexual implication that queer has latterly come to have.

During the early decades of the twentieth century, 'queer' came to be used as a derogatory slang term for a homosexual person or his/her activity. For many people, this sense is still the prevailing one. Why, then, we might ask, have an entire critical theory and, subsequently, a theological movement, arisen around what is basically an insult? It is not possible to pinpoint with any certainty when the term queer first started to be reclaimed by homosexual people as an empowering term, but it is evident that this trend was well underway by the 1980s, and was catalysed by the formation in the late 1980s and early 1990s of lesbian, gay and bisexual activism groups such as Queer Nation (which used the slogan 'We're here! We're queer! Get used to it!').

Queer critical theory has often been especially concerned with exploring the reasons why homosexuality is considered abnormal or perverse in many societies, and seeks to uncover or demystify the ways in which heterosexuality is made normative. In these terms, 'queer' is used to suggest that non-heterosexuality is, indeed, 'abnormal', but that 'normality' is not necessarily an unproblematically good or positive thing. Queer theology sometimes borrows terminology and methodological background from queer theory, resisting and interrogating heteronormativity (that is, the notion that heterosexuality is the best or only way for every individual and for societies) in specifically theological terms.

10

As we will see, however, this does not necessarily mean that queer theology equals lesbian and gay theology. For some people, queer and LGBT are basically synonymous; for others, queer's ability to question and resist various normativities is not just about sexuality, but about all kinds of dimensions of life and theological concern. Queer theology has been variously characterized as a theology of resistance to social norms (as by those who parody or reclaim the term historically used as an insult); a theology pertaining in particular to sex; a theology for lesbians and gay men, which seeks to justify their lifestyles; a theology accepting or endorsing a range of sexualities and genders; a successor to feminist and liberation theologies; a theology of deconstructionism; and a cynical attempt to 'twist' the 'biblical truth' about human sexuality. Queer theology is informed to varying extents by the underlying background work done in secular queer theory, though queer theologians and biblical scholars exhibit a wide range of familiarity and agreement with its tenets. This can be confusing: when one reads a theologian utilizing the language of queer, one might assume they are drawing on Judith Butler, Michel Foucault and other figures, whose work is significant within queer theory, but this is not always the case. For example, the theologian Elizabeth Stuart remarks of Robert E. Goss' writing in 1993's *Jesus Acted Up* that

> his use of the term 'queer' may give the superficial impression that he has taken on board the full implications of a Foucauldian approach but in fact he uses the term as a short hand for gay and lesbians [sic] acting in transgressive coalitions. (Stuart 2003, p. 86)

Moreover, as we will see, theologians fall into different camps in terms of whether or not they consider queer a break with the Christian tradition. As Rachel Muers notes, some theologians who have utilized queer theory, such as Eugene F. Rogers, consider there to be a close affinity between queer hermeneutics and classic theological concepts such as participation in the Trinity. In this way, says Muers, Rogers and others consider that 'queer theology becomes more "orthodox", and more sympathetically engaged with a wide range of theological thought, than

11

the gay and lesbian theologies that preceded it' (Muers 2005, p. 445). By contrast, she says, other theologians such as Marcella Althaus-Reid consider queer theology basically deconstructive of theological orthodoxy, believing that it has generally been used to reinscribe oppressive norms of heteropatriarchal authority. Discussion of this tension and difference, shown to be simultaneously troubling and generative, will appear throughout this book.

In the following chapters I focus on some of the major themes arising in discussions of queer theology: is queer theology synonymous with gay theology? Is queer theology inherently white or Western? Is the Bible or the Christian theological tradition queer? Should queer Christian people, in all good conscience, remain affiliated with the Christian tradition at all? First, however, in this opening chapter, I outline some of the problems and ambiguities surrounding the use of the very word 'queer', particularly as this relates to theology. I address tensions surrounding the fact that queer as a movement has often refused to submit to categories of identity and explore whether this ontological aloofness renders queer too inherently 'slippery' to be theologically useful. The first half of the chapter covers some of the major ideas within queer theory that are important to understanding queer theologies; readers who are already familiar with the background and terminology of queer theory, or who are less interested in it, may wish to skip ahead. The second half of the chapter begins to focus on queer theologies specifically.

Theoretically queer

De/finitions

David M. Halperin, the critical theorist, famously described queer as

> by definition, *whatever* is at odds with the normal, the legitimate, the dominant. *There is nothing in particular to which it necessarily refers* ... 'Queer' ... demarcates not a positivity but a positionality vis-à-vis the normative – a positionality that is not restricted to lesbians and gay men. (Halperin 1995, p. 62)

Halperin's 'definition' of queer is distinctly strange, in that it is entirely provisional. If queer is *whatever* is at odds with the dominant, then perhaps different things must be considered queer at different times and in different places, depending on what is dominant at those times and places. It is therefore not surprising that this book focuses on the areas of theology where 'queer' is shown most starkly to be indefinable, and to be used in many different ways, by its proponents. Alexander Doty gives a slightly narrower account of queer than Halperin's; for Doty, 'Queerness . . . is a quality related to any expression that can be marked as contra-, non-, or anti-straight' (Doty 1993, p. xv; quoted in Walters 1996, p. 835). This is, perhaps, a less unexpected picture of queer, identifying it as concerning sexuality in particular. However, as we will see below, for Doty (as for some other critics), being 'anti-straight' does not necessarily imply non-heterosexuality. Opposing heteronormativity (discussed in more detail below) is more subtle and complex than that.

Another famous portrayal of queer comes from Eve Kosofsky Sedgwick, who suggests that queer can refer to 'the open mesh of possibilities, gaps, overlaps, dissonances and resonances, lapses and excesses of meaning when the constituent elements of anyone's gender, or anyone's sexuality aren't made . . . to signify monolithically' (Sedgwick 1993, p. 7). In other words, queerness concerns not just a homosexual resistance to heterosexuality, but a deconstruction of an unquestioned heteronormative picture even by those who are themselves attracted to people of another gender. In Sedgwick's account, knowing that someone is female does not mean we can also assume that they are feminine or that they desire sexual relationships with men. This multiplicity and openness is echoed in the many ways in which queer is claimed and characterized theologically, as we will see. Queer theology is not only controversial in contrast to a theological 'mainstream', if such a thing exists, but is also controversial internally, because it contains a plethora of interior arguments and contradictions.

Importantly, however, we must be aware from the outset that the existence of this difference in dissent does not point to the *failure* of queer theory or queer theology. Indeed, in some accounts, it is precisely the existence of dissent and uncertainty which gives queer its very vibrancy and potential, since it is not fixed or static. Donald E. Hall, after Sedgwick, has noted that the etymology of the word queer, from the German and Latin *quer*, 'adverse', implies being *across* or *athwart* several categories, traversing several at once (Hall 2003, pp. 12–13). In this account, the very concept of queer resists definition, and refuses to be limited to just one category or just one classification: like the concept of God in apophatic theology, it is not possible to say quite what queer is, but much easier to recognize what queer is not. There is not a total consensus about what queer actually is, either from its proponents or its detractors. Nonetheless, at various times the term queer has been used more 'content-fully' than at others, which means (as we shall see in more detail below) that some people understand queer theology as basically synonymous with lesbian and gay theology, while others understand it quite differently.

Judith Butler

One of the most significant theorists whose work has been seminal to queer theory more broadly is Judith Butler, the author of texts such as *Gender Trouble* (1990) and *Bodies That Matter* (1993) which have become foundational in gender studies and critical theory. Like Teresa de Lauretis and others, Butler has expressed ambivalence about the efficacy of the actual terminology of queerness, in part because of the ways in which it can be misused. Using similar logic to that later expressed by Halperin, Butler insisted in 1993 that 'queer' could not be an identity in the same way as 'woman' or 'homosexual' were identities, even if it had begun to be seized upon in this way by some gay men at the time. Rather, it was a profoundly shifting, contingent term, and this was, in fact, important to its efficacy:

> If identity is a necessary error, then the assertion of 'queer' will be necessary as a term of affiliation, but it will not fully describe those it purports to represent. As a result, it will be necessary to affirm the contingency of the term: to let it be vanquished by those who are excluded by the term but who justifiably expect representation by it. (Butler 1993a, p. 230)

In other words, says Butler, failure, inadequacy and obsolescence are built into queer from the start: as soon as it is defined or claimed by one group to the exclusion of others, it loses part of its capacity to critique and resist normativity. Rather, queer anticipates and holds within itself its own destruction, which is a tenacious denial of absoluteness. This, however, is what makes queer so profoundly *itself*:

> That it can become . . . a discursive site whose uses are not fully constrained in advance ought to be safeguarded not only for the purposes of continuing to democratize queer politics, but also to expose, affirm, and rework the specific historicity of the term. (Butler 1993a, p. 230)

Butler believed that 'queer' had become essentialized in its usage by some of its proponents (as white, as lesbian and so on), and that this had enforced 'a set of overlapping distinctions' (Butler 1993a, p. 228) rather than uncompromisingly resisting definition. Butler was already aware that she and other theorists were being accused of 'depoliticizing theory' by resisting identity-based politics, which had been so important since the 1960s and 1970s in terms of black civil rights, gay civil rights, and second-wave feminism. Nonetheless, she insisted that critiquing the queer subject was 'crucial to the continued *democratization* of queer politics' (Butler 1993b, p. 19) since it meant no one's claim could be final and no one group could appeal to having been more excluded than others.

This notion of queer as opposed to identity has often been repeated and is often considered foundational to queer discourse. Queer's 'aggressive impulse of generalization' (Warner 1991, p. 16) has made it unpopular in some quarters, especially from those for whom identity politics based in sexuality has been an important locus of community. In fact, however, Butler herself was not as strongly anti-identity as she is often portrayed. Rather, Butler believed that queer ought not to be used to 'paralyse' the efficacy of claiming identities, *as long as* such identities were held in a resisting way that was profoundly aware of the problematic nature of power, and of the tendency of identities to be both prescriptive and exclusive (Butler 1993b, p. 20). Queer, she asserted, could never be 'owned' exclusively, but 'always and only redeployed, twisted, queered from a prior usage and in the direction of urgent and expanding political purposes, and perhaps also yielded in favor of terms that do political work more effectively' (Butler 1993b, p. 19) – and probably in unanticipated ways. Despite its distinction from gay identity, then, queer could not finally reject identity categories altogether; to do so would itself be undemocratic and too prescriptive. Nonetheless, some critics felt that Butler herself essentialized some phenomena – such as transgender, linking it too unequivocally with a capacity to queer heterosexuality (see for example Prosser 1998). Controversially as far as some lesbian and gay critics were concerned, Butler asserted that queer could be a discursive rallying-point even for anti-homophobic heterosexuals (Butler 1993a, p. 230).

Indeed, in her later work, such as the 2004 book *Undoing Gender*, Butler showed more explicitly that queer theory does not oppose identity claims themselves, but rather *regulatory* identities, which exclude some people from certain spheres of politics (which is why even heterosexual people can be queer activists) and unproblematized or 'unmarked' identities. Butler owned that self-determination in performing and maintaining gender identity relies on the existence of 'a social world that supports and enables that exercise of agency' (Butler 2004, p. 7). Identity cannot be entirely done away with; particularly, perhaps, for people claiming a more than typically 'unusual' gender identity, like those who have publicly transitioned gender, 'a livable life does require various degrees of stability . . . A life for which no categories of identity exist is not a livable life' (Butler 2004, p. 8). Indeed, Butler argued that these identities are how we come to recognize one another, since bodies become intelligible via continually 'citing', or bringing to mind, certain familiar norms (just as drag queens might cite – and exaggerate – 'feminine' tropes such as elaborate hairstyling and the use of bright or glittery make-up).

What is most expedient in queer, then, suggests Butler, is not a wholesale rejection of identity and normativity, but a conscious and ongoing engagement with *undoing* them: Butler's 2004 book title, *Undoing Gender*, implies an unknotting of constricting categories of binary gender; a playful 'revealing' of what, if anything, lies inside the seductively bright wrappings of the gender parcel; and an acknowledgement that gender is something both done (performed by an act of choice) and un-done or not-done (imposed from outside, not chosen). However, to acknowledge our constitution by norms not of our making, says Butler, does not mean such norms always have a 'final or fatalistic control' over us (Butler 2004, p. 15); desire and identity exceed their regulation, play with it, resist it and cede to it in turn.

It is this conscious and unconscious interplay which stops them from becoming static and which, says Claudia Schippert, 'leads to the queer theoretical project of attempting to expand the realm of what can be imagined – and what can become thus livable' (Schippert 2005, p. 92). Annamarie Jagose, in her introduction to queer theory, suggests that queer 'ceaselessly [interrogates] both the preconditions of identity and its effects' while itself being 'not outside the magnetic field of identity' (Jagose 1996, p. 132). Donald E. Hall concurs that queer theorizing necessitates temporary moments of becoming in which identity *is* solidified, followed by regular times of 'unbecoming' in which it is shown, once more, to be inadequate (Hall 2003, p. 109). As in Butler's account, this reproduces the provisionalities and uncertainties bound up in how queer is understood and how it projects itself.

Foucault, subjectivity and power

Butler, Halperin, Sedgwick and other influential queer theorists all draw on mid-twentieth-century work by poststructuralist philosophers such as Jacques Derrida and (most frequently) Michel Foucault, particularly his *The History of Sexuality* trilogy. Poststructuralist thought holds that, rather than being stable, discrete subject-selves, humans' subjectivities are constructed by the meshes and layers of power and discourse taking place all around them. For Foucault, power should be understood not simply as the overt juridico-legal kind of power which publicly imposes itself on citizen-subjects, but as what he describes as 'power-knowledge' and what Antonio Gramsci had called hegemony. Ideas circulate (and are resisted) not in an authoritative, top-down way, but multiply and cyclically. It is power-knowledge which regulates discourse, and its effects are imposed subtly and insidiously rather than overtly. Human subjects are thus profoundly produced and maintained by whatever is going on in a given culture or society. In this account, the concept of the subject-self is claimed to be incoherent and fictive. Rather, humans exist as many different, sometimes conflicting dimensions, all of which affect the way they interact with and interpret their surroundings. This is significant because it means that concepts like 'woman', 'lesbian', the 'heterosexual subject', the 'male subject' and so on are problematized: such identities are unstable and fuzzy, rather than something irreducible. No one facet of identity is primal or essential to the self; they are all contested, and it is *through* this uncertainty and looseness that human subjectivity emerges. Performativity is an effect of power-knowledge. This is picked up particularly strongly in the work of Butler, who insists that gender is performed rather than being something which supervenes in any definite way on sex (which is also contestable).

Both Butler and Foucault seek to show that the heteronormative is fictive, by denying the authenticity and incontrovertibility of historically privileged sexed and gendered roles. Foucault's analysis of 'the homosexual' as a nineteenth-century construction that is mutually dependent on the concept of 'the heterosexual' (the one cannot exist conceptually in the absence of the other), and of sexuality as having become so discursively significant that it is now understood as a fundamental category of personality, underpins subsequent scholarship seeking to question the incontrovertibility, naturalness or permanence of heterosexuality. Although he distanced himself from the poststructuralist label, Foucault's work is often recognized as part of a poststructuralist canon which asserts that the subject-self is not a coherent or stable entity so much as a palimpsest written and overwritten by social discourse and interrelation. Texts, historical figures and other entities are read multiply and uncertainly, influenced by the position and perception of the interpreter. 'Truth' is therefore polyphonic, existing and arising in and through multiplicities of interpretation. In terms of sexuality, this entails reframing sexuality as something produced and influenced by power dynamics, rather than something innate or unmarked. Foucault argues that sexual identity, in common with other aspects of identity, is socially constructed via discourse. Since discourse is continual and contested, sexuality is constantly redefined. Schippert explains,

> Viewing sexuality not as a natural attribute of a person, but rather as (one of) the constellations that give rise to the meaningful and intelligible construction of a modern self in the first place, queer theoretical scholarship moves away from strategies of liberating the oppressed or repressed part of an inherent sexuality, to placing greater significance on the critical examination of the discursive productions of sexual identity in its connection to other categories of meaning. (Schippert 2005, p. 91)

Foucault's analysis of power, especially in *Discipline and Punish* (Foucault 1979) and *The History of Sexuality, Volume 1* (Foucault 1990), is particularly significant for queer studies, since it sets out a notion of power as arising from multiple sites and continually contested. This disturbs some of the binary tropes entrenched in structuralism, such as sign/signified and (importantly) heterosexual/homosexual and male/female. If power arises from everywhere, there is always the possibility that it can be transformed and redeemed. Power can generate as well as repress. This interpretation is not unproblematic: even the process of transformation involves exercising power and might thereby be understood as itself in thrall to systems of control. Liberation from social and conceptual imprisonment can therefore never be as simple as a 'good' oppressed person overthrowing a 'bad' oppressor. A continual re-examination of discourses of empowerment and emancipation is necessary, in order to identify elements which are themselves becoming oppressive – a process which occurs cyclically as queer theory and queer theology interrogate narratives of identity and culture.

Other tropes often picked out from Foucault and Butler, and held up as particularly important in queer studies, include the concept of queer as a critique of norms. Critiquing norms does not necessarily mean simply resisting them, though this will be important at times; rather, critiquing implies reflection on one's own relationship to norms and the ways in which one refuses and/or reproduces them. Foucault identifies critique as the process of subjects questioning the mutual interrelations in the productions of power and of truth. Simply to reject a particular norm is not enough, for this alone does not begin to interrogate *why* and *how* norms are produced and maintained. All this is important in considering the relationship of queer theory to the dominant cultural discourse and of queer theology to 'mainstream' theology: using this kind of logic, queer can never be a simple rejection of heteronormativity[1] (for example), but must also be self-critical and self-interrogative, giving space to query normativity itself and reflect on the ways in which all motives are mixed and all structures of power are dubious

Problematizing queer

At least in the English language,[2] the term 'queer' has a history of being used as a derogatory insult for those who are homosexual, its etymologies including difference or oddness, suspiciousness, strangeness and being questioning or ruinous. In recent years, it has been 'reclaimed' by some of those people against whom it was formerly used as an insult, who have rejected the idea that *they* are wrong or illegitimate, but have said that what they do expressly seek to 'spoil', 'ruin' or 'jeopardize' is the heterosexual matrix and the imposition of solely heterosexual norms. Queer is often therefore now considered a positive and empowering term. This reclaiming or turning of the term queer might be considered a kind of appropriation, or catachresis, a term used in postcolonial discourse (especially by Gayatri Chakravorty Spivak) to denote 'the process by which the colonized strategically appropriate and redeploy specific elements of colonial or imperial culture or ideology. As such, it is a practice of resistance through an act of usurpation' (Moore 2006, p. 37; cf. Spivak 1991, p. 70). Indeed, I will show later that postcolonial theories of hybridity and resistance might be useful tools for queer theology to think with. However, Rebecca Alpert comments, 'For some of the wilderness generation, the term queer often has negative associations. They are not comfortable using a term in self-reference that has been used by those who have oppressed them . . . It is not easy to forget the

problems of the past' (Alpert 2006, p. 67). This is of particular importance to understanding the complex interrelations and overlaps between
the term queer and the term gay as used by homosexual people. Queer
is often understood as a more militant term, but Farhang Rouhani notes
that it is problematic to characterize gay merely as mainstream and queer
merely as radical in terms of politics. Rouhani says,

> The implications of such a distinction are that gay politics capitulate
> and are inauthentic, while queer politics resist and are thus authen-
> tic. Such a valorisation of queer politics is simultaneously useful and
> deeply problematic . . . The politics of differentiation and authentic-
> ity in such a construction runs the risk of withholding the possibility
> of a critique of queer complicities. (Rouhani 2007, p. 169)

Knowing that people call themselves queer or belong to a queer group
does not automatically mean they are more socially or politically extrem-
ist than people who identify as gay instead. Indeed, they may not be
homosexual, but bisexual, heterosexual or something else.

The elusive nature of queer, then, is not a coincidence and has in
fact been deemed ideologically crucial. As we have seen, it is, in some
respects, problematic to conceive of claiming a 'queer identity', since
queer upsets the very concept of identity-as-concrete even if it has also
been linked to various identities at various times. Iain Morland and
Annabelle Willox, for example, argue that it was the rise of HIV/AIDS in
the early 1980s which transformed queer from what had basically been
a gay-synonymous identity into a newly political strategy. Identity politics, which had been so important during the 1970s, proved irrelevant to
the virus: although initially called a 'gay disease',[3] it soon became clear
that people of diverse sexualities and gender identities were vulnerable.
Morland and Willox suggest, 'Queer activism's necessity and urgency
lay in its challenge to the notion that identities could classify people,
keep them safe, and keep them alive' (Morland and Willox 2005b, p.
2). The boundaries of political identity were exposed by HIV/AIDS as
weak or meaningless: identifying as heterosexual did not prevent one
from being vulnerable to the virus. Anyone could contract it, regardless

of whether they considered themselves homosexual. This became crucial to the subsequent queer political movement which, while acknowledging the legitimacy of multiple sex, gender and political standpoints, also attempted to find 'a cultural diversity that surpasses the notion of identity' (Morland and Willox 2005b, p. 3). To 'be' queer, or even to speak of 'queer people', is, therefore, in this account, inadequate or at least ironic, for to do so fails to recognize queer's profound distinction from other political identity movements, as something which disturbs identity – or is even, for some commentators, *post*-identity.

Of course, this refusal to be tied down by categories of identity is a double-edged sword: while acknowledging the inadequacy and provisionality of political designations, as Halperin says, queer's lack of specificity 'has also become its most serious drawback' (Halperin 1995, p. 64), since some commentators argue that this might lay it too readily open to appropriation by people who do not find themselves in a marginalized position in society. Queer theory might, in other words, become yet another weapon in the hands of those who already have a whole arsenal of legitimacy, tradition and power on their side, rather than being 'reserved' solely for those who want to query the reality and hegemony of grand narratives and the norms reproduced through them. Moreover, some have argued that, without a clear identity or definition, queer might be used simply as a cipher for any non-normal sexual practice and might, as Sheila Jeffreys, Suzanna Danuta Walters and Elizabeth Grosz fear, be used to encompass phenomena such as paedophilia with no sense of moral judgement attached (Jeffreys 2003, p. 34; Walters 1996, p. 838; cf. Isherwood and Althaus-Reid 2004, p. 9). Grosz, for instance, claimed in 1994,

'Queer' is capable of accommodating, and will no doubt provide a political rationale and coverage in the near future for many of the most blatant and extreme forms of heterosexual power games. They too are, in a certain sense, queer, persecuted, ostracized. Heterosexual sadists, pederasts, fetishists, pornographers, pimps, voyeurs, suffer from social sanctions: in a certain sense they too can be regarded as oppressed. (Grosz 1994, p. 113)

This, however, is to ignore queer's frequent appeal to justice and freedom in sexual relationships, where freedom for all participants necessarily entails informed consent. Moreover, it is to misunderstand queer's lack of attachment to any one ideology. To resist and question a given norm does not mean endorsing its opposite norm. Rather, queer is about new and creative forms of morality which engage critically with all kinds of behaviour without giving trite, glib, pat answers about the way forward.

Many commentators argue that it is not desirable or possible to think about queer outside the context of lesbian and gay history, since, although queer usually resists regulatory identity, it is in opposition to heteronormativity and heterosexual identity specifically that queer has proven most incisive and resistant. Late-adopters of the concept may, it is argued, come to it too naïvely, not cognizant of its loaded history which is profoundly bound up with struggles for justice and safety (cf. Loughlin 2008, p. 149). As Alpert notes, 'The term queer resonates differently for people who lived through a time when everyone was hiding and when being labelled queer meant something much more threatening than the current generation could imagine' (Alpert 2006, p. 67). Yip and Keenan suggest, from a slightly different angle, that 'queering is about the mobilisation of lesbian and gay experiences ... to counter heterosexist hermeneutics' (Yip and Keenan 2009, p. 94). Here, we might understand queering, activities which make or enact queerness, as having a necessary *grounding* in the biographies of those who have resisted or queried heteronormative theologies because of their own sexualities, but as *not* necessarily being limited either to sexual issues or to utilization only by those who identify as homosexual. Indeed, Schippert notes that queer resists all dominant discourses, of which heterosexuality is only one kind (Schippert 2005, p. 91). Once the hegemony of heteronormativity has been cracked by appeals to lesbian and gay life-stories, its stranglehold on other areas also begins to be loosened. This is reinforced in Butlerian terms by the assertion that, although gender is always operative within human relationships, it operates in different ways when these relationships are expressed via queer sexualities. The characterization of all men as sexual predators and all women as prey, for example, is thus grossly inadequate, and Butler rejects Catharine

MacKinnon's account of gender as 'the congealed form that the sexualization of inequality takes' (Butler 2004, p. 53).

Queer theory is highly conceptual, and has sometimes been criticized for being too intellectual and divorced from grassroots activism (a criticism also levelled at queer theology, as I discuss below). Its strong emphasis on deconstructing normativity – in all areas of discourse but particularly with regard to resisting essentialist conceptions of sex and gender – is grounded in highly analytical critical theory which may be somewhat opaque for those not versed in this style of intellectual discussion. Interestingly, queer theologians have often not engaged explicitly in their writing with Butler, Foucault and the other theorists whose work underlies queer theory. In some cases this lack of acknowledgement of critical theory may be motivated by a desire to make queer theology more accessible than queer theory has often been, even while retaining its emphasis on praxis (albeit not always realized) and resistance. However, it also seems that the use of the term queer within theology is much broader than within queer theory itself, and that in fact not every queer theologian is even familiar with queer theoretical discourse. This represents both a positive expansion of the ways in which the term is used and understood theologically, and a possible problem: if queer theologians do not use the term in the same way that queer critical theorists do, this may make queer theology less credible as an intellectual discourse and may limit the extent to which queer theology can credibly critique secular queer theory. This should be borne in mind both throughout the rest of this chapter, where I begin to set out some specifically theological queer concerns, and throughout the book in its entirety.

Queering theology

More than sexuality

As we have already seen, queer theology carries over from queer theory a certain absence of definition, a resistance to being neatly contained. Nonetheless, it is possible to point to some of the ways in which queer theology has been rolled out, and some of the especial areas of concern associated with it. It is important from the beginning to note that queer theology has been treated with suspicion by theologians of many different stripes, not just those who might be considered particularly likely to oppose homosexuality. Marcella Althaus-Reid notes,

> Disconcertingly, queer theologies have been criticized from opposite ends of the spectrum, from historical liberation theologians to conservative evangelicals . . . The historical feminist liberationists . . . have not even yet completely come to terms with gender issues beyond the equality paradigm. For them sexuality tends to be seen as a frivolous distraction from issues of social justice and women's rights in the Church. In a sense they see queer theologies as a luxury which only privileged women in academia can afford to pursue. At the other end of the theological spectrum conservative evangelicals view queer theologies as a source and consequence of all the evils and corruption in society. (Althaus-Reid 2008, p. 106)

Althaus-Reid makes clear that sexuality is a crucial element, under-analysed in classic liberation theologies, which queer privileges. However, this has sometimes been overstated, to the extent that one common conception is that queer theology is only or inevitably to do with sex. Within queer religious writing, comments Mark D. Jordan, queer often 'seems to cover any topic somehow connected with sex, gender and sexuality' (Jordan 2007a, p. 568). In the recent sociological collection *Contemporary Christianity and LGBT Sexualities* (Hunt 2009a), there seems to be a reiteration of the association of 'queer' with 'sexual', even if not exclusively *homo*sexual; Hunt suggests that the shift within queer theology specifically has been from justifying LGBT desire and behaviour and 'towards the exploration of wider theological themes arising from these communities' (Hunt 2009b, p. 15), and it is significant that the volume in question contains several essays on bisexual and transgender Christianity (Toft 2009; Yip and Keenan 2009) as well as those on homosexuality.

To take another example, Thomas Bohache, in a 2003 essay, figures queer people as 'those identifying as gay, lesbian, bisexual, transgendered, intersexual, supportively heterosexual or a combination thereof' (Bohache 2003, p. 9). Almost every possible sexual orientation is covered, so one might assume that almost every *person* is covered – which makes it slightly odd that Bohache chooses to categorize them according to sexuality at all. The fact he does not figure queer people as 'those identifying as black Caribbean, black African, Asian, Chinese, another ethnic group, supportively white or a combination thereof'[4] (even though this would *also* cover everyone) is important, since it demonstrates that Bohache (and he is far from alone) understands queerness to map onto sexuality and gender identity more profoundly than onto other kinds of identity. To what extent this is problematic is discussed in much more detail in Chapter 3.

Indeed, even leaving the question of race aside for a moment, I have noted elsewhere (Cornwall 2010b) that many people with intersex conditions (for instance) have expressed strongly that they do *not* wish to be aligned with queer or to claim this as a political identity, and indeed that intersex is not an issue of sex, sexuality or gender identity at all, but is simply to do with having a specific medical condition. Similarly, many homosexual people are deeply suspicious of queer. It is therefore not possible unproblematically to imply that queer encompasses all or only those people whose 'difference' is marked out via categories of sex, sexuality and gender variation. Jordan notes that the overwhelming majority of early queer religious criticism – as represented in Comstock and Henking's 1997 anthology, mostly comprising work produced between 1984 and 1996 – does *not* use 'queer' in the sense being hammered out within the secular queer theory of the time (that is, of a project of resistance to and querying of normativities of all kinds, even if gender performance is a common motif), but in a narrower sexual sense (Jordan 2007a, p. 568).

I will show in the following chapters that the use of queer theory within theology has come latterly to address more issues than specifically sexual ones, but that its image problem – the assumption or *perception* that queer theology is just to do with sex or, even more narrowly, just to do with homosexuality – may present a potential obstacle to its utility for theologians. This may occur because those who assume from the outset that homosexuality is sinful, unbiblical and wrong are unlikely to be persuaded to take seriously a methodology or hermeneutic which they perceive to be inherently 'about' or 'for' homosexual people. They are therefore also unlikely to be convinced by gay-friendly apologetics or reading strategies if these are also presented through a queer theological or critical lens. Although it is positive and right that queer theology has been such a significant tool in reclaiming and emphasizing the goodness of the corporeal and the sexual as sites of God's grace and interaction with human beings, it may be that queer theology needs to emphasize all the modes and arenas in which it speaks to *more than* the sexual, in order to be taken seriously as a methodological tool by less liberal Christians or those for whom a querying of sex and gender norms is too disturbing a way into hermeneutical suspicion. Conversely, however, it may be that to do so would be to undermine the very core of queer's resistance, difference and outsiderhood, and that queer theology simply never will be acceptable or mainstream; this might in itself be considered methodologically and hermeneutically significant.

Affinities between theology and queer theory

Mary Elise Lowe identifies six 'insights' that she believes queer theologies have taken on from secular queer theory. These are: a deconstructionist methodology; an assertion that all meaning is constructed; a concept of gender as performance; a belief in the instability of identity; an understanding of individuals as shaped by discourse; and a claim that the process of becoming *a* subject, and becoming subject *to* the norms disseminated via such discourse, occur simultaneously (Lowe 2009, p. 52). These affinities notwithstanding, theology's relationship with queer theory and interpretation might seem rocky at best, especially given secular queer theorists' sometimes vocal rejection of religious discourse and religious authority.

However, suggests Mark D. Jordan, there is a sense in which theological and queer theories do have profound likenesses, whether their respective adherents like it or not. Theology, he says, 'lives at the boundary between theory and practice, speculation and advocacy'

(Jordan 2007a, p. 569). He goes on, 'Queer theology does come after queer theory by successful hybridization. It was also there all along inside queer theory – and, indeed, before queer theory, as its competing parent, its disciplinary root and rival' (Jordan 2007a, p. 573). Like theology, he suggests, queer theory is inevitably a *mixed* discipline, incorporating both critical analysis and activist praxis. Queer theory is in some sense theology's successor, having taken over some of the linguistic analysis which was historically theology's province – but queer theology also continues, standing contemporaneously with queer theory and persisting as a discourse which will not go away, since theological language and imagery will also not disappear from talk about bodies and sexes, however much atheist and secularist commentators might wish it would (Jordan 2007a, p. 573). This means that those who tread a tightrope between queer theory and theology will not necessarily, perhaps, experience quite as much cognitive dissonance due to these allegiances as might be supposed.

Gerard Loughlin also suggests that there are close family resemblances between queer theory and theology. He engages directly with Halperin's understanding of queer as identity without essence, and comments, '[Gay's] range is often limited, as in "gay culture" or "gay rights". Queer, on the other hand, seeks and arguably has no such limits' (Loughlin 2008, p. 145). In part, this is because, as Kathy Rudy, Deryn Guest and others have noted, queerness is not inherently coincident with homosexuality but rather concerns a commitment to challenging multiple norms (see for example Rudy 1996a, p. 83, Guest 2005, p. 45). Anyone, therefore, can be queer. If this sounds dangerously universalistic, like a particularity subsuming everything within itself and eliminating difference and variation, then the danger may be mitigated by Loughlin's explanation that theology is inherently queer even and *especially* in its status as a discipline often deemed marginal or unimportant in the modern world. In actual fact, its grand-sounding 'unlimited' reach may look rather paltry in practice. Theology's current relative lack of influence, lack of authority and lack of reach in comparison with certain other times in its history is itself queer. Theological queerness, for Loughlin, is therefore not simply a question of queer theology disrupting 'mainstream' theology: rather, *all* theology is somehow simultaneously strange, weak and marginal, and potently disruptive of a mindset which says it is possible to comprehend (or encompass) all the mysteries of the universe. Loughlin comments,

> Even when theology was culturally dominant it was strange, for it sought the strange; it sought to know the unknowable in Christ, the mystery it was called to seek through following Jesus. And of course it has always been in danger of losing this strangeness by pretending that it has comprehended the mystery, that it can name that which is beyond all names. (Loughlin 2008, p. 144)

This danger, the danger of idolatry, is never far away; but the sense of mystery and haziness comes through in Christian history, most clearly in the apophatic tradition and the writings of the mystics. Loughlin holds that just as all we can properly say about God is that *God is*, so all we can say about queer is that *queer is* (Loughlin 2008, p. 151). Any closer definition risks tying God, or queerness, into small boxes or human-made distortions.

There are affinities with Loughlin's analysis in work by Cheri DiNovo, who suggests that because the Cross is somehow always 'over' Christians, to be a Christian is also to be 'under' a cross. Christians are thereby 'crossed out', *X*-ed out, and are by definition what-they-are-not, since they are always in a process of becoming. DiNovo figures this as particularly queer, and for her it is significant that Christ himself is also '*X*-ed out', obliterated (at least temporarily) by a cross – and made profoundly 'indecipherable' because of the significance of his life and manner of his execution (DiNovo 2007, pp. 4–6). Christ himself, sometimes abbreviated to *X*, has a body which exists 'to give itself away to the other, for the other' (DiNovo 2007, p. 14). The Body that is the Church thereby becomes marginalized while siding with queer bodies which are also marginalized (DiNovo 2007, p. 18), but this '*X*-ing out' is yet more inherent to Christianity. There are clear echoes here of Derrida's concept of erasure, whereby a word or idea cannot stand without calling upon a 'trace' of its opposite, the word or idea it contradicts. The hint of this opposite constantly destabilizes the authority of the original concept: unhappiness only makes sense in light of happiness, and happiness (at least for anyone over the age of three) always comes with a bittersweet realization of its transience. Typographically, this erasure is symbolized by writing a word and crossing it out but letting both the word and the crossing-out remain legible. The strikethrough actually draws attention to the 'missing' word (see Derrida 1976, p. 7).

Of course, queerness itself has not always quite succeeded at such self-extenuating or 'crossed-out' apophasis: queer might well seek to 'outwit identity' and prescription, but even so, 'It can turn all too quickly from a positionality into another positivity, another identity' (Loughlin 2008, p. 149). This might be seen in such instances as the early 1990s activism group Queer Nation San Francisco, where queer was very clearly understood as another political identity both internally and by the media – which, argues Mary L. Gray, ultimately led to the group's downfall, since the adoption of a new fixed identity category did not adequately disrupt the stability of identity per se (Gray 2009, pp. 216–8; see also the final chapter of this volume). For Gray, Queer Nation San Francisco would have done better to resist media attempts at definition and to have allowed the meta-project of questioning the *concept* of difference – rather than of simply organizing around one *element* of difference – to set its agenda (Gray 2009, p. 230).

Marcella Althaus-Reid insists that queer theology, too, must be 'stubborn' in its refusal to become stabilized or fixed (Althaus-Reid 2008, p. 110). This built-in instability can seem frustrating, but what it means is that queer discourse has internal limits, a 'safety-valve', on its finality. Teresa Hornsby suggests, using the Butlerian notion that it is often all but impossible to tell the difference between the power one promotes and the power one opposes, that it is actually not possible to undertake a project or employ a methodology which is not somehow complicit in oppression even as it liberates: 'No doubt, as I write to dismantle, to deconstruct, to liberate, I also write to edify, to construct, and to oppress. Next year someone will be writing an article naming all the ways that this present project reinforces dominant destructive ideologies. Thank you, Judith Butler' (Hornsby 2006a, pp. 72–3). For Loughlin, the safety-valve on queer discourse means that these potential problems for queerness are not insurmountable: queer might congeal around a given identity or ideology for a time, but it can also soften and flow again. Moreover, he suggests, even if it does have a propensity to 'solidify into a substantive identity' from time to time, it is still novel, different and 'outside' enough to be able to destabilize the heterosexual theological norms to whose contingency it most classically attests (Loughlin 2008, p. 150).

Loughlin's identification of theology as inherently and historically strange is picked up by Ninna Edgardh, who uses it to argue that queer theology is thereby a means by which to redetermine which stories are told about one as a community, and the stories one projects from one-self too (Edgardh 2009, p. 46). Building on this, and on Jane Shaw's and Elizabeth Stuart's essays in *Queer Theology: Rethinking the Western Body*, Edgardh builds an analysis of the political posturings surrounding the 2008 Lambeth Conference, from which the gay Episcopalian bishop Gene Robinson, of New Hampshire, was excluded – ironically, on the grounds of preserving the unity of the Anglican Communion, since not all the other bishops agreed that Robinson should be there (Edgardh 2009, p. 44). Edgardh concludes that queer theology provides tools for a radical reinterpretation of categories of identity, so that they are not to be rejected out of hand but rather understood (after Stuart) as sacramentally gifted, and interpreted rather than unchanging (Edgardh 2009, p. 48; Stuart 2007, p. 75; see also Valentine et al 2010).[5] In this way, she suggests, the Christian Churches might come to a place where they can hold together their unity-in-disunity as a testimony to the ways in which Christianity is an exemplar for how humans can live together in peace (Edgardh 2009, p. 42).[6] Edgardh's work represents a recent instance of queer theory and queer theology mutually reframing one another, where queer theology in its language of gift and sacrament is able to help critique queer theory's solidifying drift – even if the language of 'sacrament' as used by Stuart is sometimes so loose and imprecise as to fail to describe anything specific at all.

Queering normativity: Queer theological discontinuity

In the next chapter I will discuss some of the tensions surrounding the extent to which queer theology and LGBT theology supervene. It is important to note here, however, some reasons why queer's *discontinuity* with lesbian and gay theology might be considered so important. Claudia Schippert criticizes the early work of the theologians Robert E. Goss and J. Michael Clark for using 'queer' synonymously with 'gay', for in doing so, she says, 'conceptions of power are elided' (Schippert 1999, p. 52). In other words, she holds, in this early work insufficient account is taken of why and how gay theology might have ignored the specific concerns of lesbians, transgender people or people of colour – which is not necessarily helpful in reflecting on how queer theology might avoid the same pitfalls. Queer theory might seek to interrogate and demystify power relations, but that does not mean it is entirely immune from abusing power. Swapping 'gay' for 'queer' does not sufficiently disturb gay male hegemony if queer theology is made no more interrogative and self-critical than Schippert understands gay theology to have been. She comments,

> Within the field of religion, a number of recent texts appropriate the term 'queer' – without too many troubling thoughts and more as a replacement for 'gay and lesbian' or maybe 'gay, lesbian, bisexual, transgender, etc.' However, foregrounding the promise of queer's lack of specificity regarding (gender-) identity, these approaches often elide the challenges 'queer' might pose to the methodologies or textual-political strategies employed. (Schippert 1999, p. 51)

Schippert goes on to claim that of the two main books with which she engages, Clark's *Defying the Darkness: Gay Theology in the Shadows* (1998) and Jeffrey Weeks' *Invented Moralities: Sexual Values in an Age of Uncertainty* (1995), both fail to properly deal with the *uncertainty* bound up in queer, a concept Schippert considers central to a truly radical notion of queerness. Weeks, she suggests, tries to contain it, and Clark merely sidesteps it (Schippert 1999, p. 51). It might be countered that both these authors, but particularly Weeks writing in the early days of queer theological discourse, were simply focusing elsewhere than on theoretical queerness specifically. Nonetheless, for Schippert, Clark's idea of 'acting queerly' does not go far enough – perhaps because Clark and his partner's model of 'defiance to death' looks very much like an average middle-class, suburban, monogamous lifestyle, complete with mortgage, pets, garden and neighbourhood watch rota (Clark 1997, pp. 5-6). Clark, claims Schippert, merely integrates 'queer' into an existing liberation theological framework, but without properly working through the implications – that is, the sense that if queer is a rejection of normativity then it might have to be a rejection of (ethical) norms as well, since even liberal ethical imperatives can indurate into something static rather than remaining ever in process. Even a 'good' norm 'can be liberating in one context, [but] can also be used as tool of domination in the same or another context' (Schippert 1999, p. 48).

If this argument is right, suggests Schippert, then queer cannot be tacked onto or absorbed into gay, feminist and liberationist ethics, but must deconstruct and query these normativities just as much as it does everything else, including everything more ostensibly oppressive (Schippert 1999, pp. 50-1). Queer theory – and, by association, queer theology and queer biblical studies – is actually profoundly *discontinuous from* and *incommensurate with* the liberationist methodologies and hermeneutics with which it is often linked. (This is an important criticism and I will return to it throughout this book.) Goss and others also meet with Schippert's criticism for the same reason, since in texts such as Goss' *Jesus Acted Up*,[7] 'possible tensions and differences vis-à-vis "liberation" and conceptions of power are elided' (Schippert 1999, p. 52). Schippert's objections to queer 'normativity', and her assertions that queer does not 'succeed' liberation theology, are discussed in more detail in the final chapter of the present volume. It is enough simply to note at this point the problematizing of a forward trajectory from feminist and liberation theologies through to queer ones.

Indeed, queer theology's shared history with feminist theology might be just as problematic for its future as its shared history with gay theology, since (argue Marcella Althaus-Reid and Lisa Isherwood) feminist theologies have tended to focus too much on questions of equality, which, they claim, are inclined to solidify into a bland glossing-over of difference and thereby fail to challenge the heteronormativity at theology's heart (Althaus-Reid and Isherwood 2007, p. 306). While feminist theologies 'have traditionally seemed to imply the continuation of a process of evolution from a patriarchal ideological interpretation of Christianity' (Althaus-Reid 2008, p. 108), the move from feminist to queer represents more of a *dis*continuity, a rupture, since queer theologies – as understood by Althaus-Reid – seek to disrupt and overturn the existing paradigm rather than redeem it largely unchanged. In this account, just as women's theology cannot be an unproblematic 'continuation' of liberation theology, since liberation theology has taken insufficient account of the reality of minority sexual lives, so queer theology cannot roll out unproblematically from feminist and womanist theologies (Althaus-Reid 2008, pp. 108–9). Feminist theologies have not represented enough of a break with traditional patriarchal modes of writing and discourse (Althaus-Reid 2008, p. 113), but queer theologies must do.

A thought experiment: queering death

Queer theology, like secular queer theory, has often focused on issues of sex and gender. As we have seen and will see further, this might be deemed problematic, especially if issues such as race and class are thereby elided. However, this does not mean that queer theology must be sequentially univocal, considering only one area at a time. Indeed, more recent criticism makes clear that it may queer sex and other phenomena all at once. Several theologians have explored the concept of queering death theologically, and a brief reflection on this topic shows us that the deep affinity between Christianity and queerness goes beyond matters of sex, even though sexuality can never be erased from the circumstances out of which humans relate to God and to one another. Christianity's queer stream might be picked up in its concern with the miraculous and its unwillingness to accept that anything is impossible with God (as per Matt. 19.26).

Elizabeth Stuart's queer reading of the Johannine resurrection account appeals to an event which is at once the end of sex and gender as we have known them, and the end of death:

> The scene repeats with critical difference the creation of male and female and the bonds of marriage in Eden. Here in a different garden, the man does not return to dust but returns from dust to life, here male and female do not cleave unto one another but let go of one another. (Stuart 2004, p. 59)

By failing to live in this transformation, by clinging to static patterns of gender and sexuality, however, says Stuart, Christianity has 'found itself out of step with its foundational rhythm of death and resurrection' (Stuart 2004, p. 60). Death is necessary for Christianity because it is this which is the gateway to the afterlife, the 'space beyond heterosexuality and homosexuality' (Stuart 2004, p. 61), which precludes our present structures of sexual relationship and family life from being claimed as absolute. (Indeed, this is evident from the wider attestation of Scripture: there is to be no marrying or giving in marriage in heaven.) This analysis is clearly influenced by a Butlerian model of queer as a disruption of regulatory identities. But Stuart takes it further, beyond a resistance to heterosexual hegemony: in a Christian understanding, *death itself* is interrupted and subverted; at the very centre of Christianity is a profound queering of the discontinuity between life and death, the ontological and epistemic separation between God and God's creatures. Stuart says,

> Whatever death now involves it does not herald the absence of God, the source of life, for there is now no place where God is not. Death is not in dualistic relationship to life any more than male is to female; in fact both death and life are deconstructed in the blaze of resurrection. (Stuart 2004, p. 62)

As she asserted in an earlier essay on sex, death and eschatology, 'Perhaps the time has come to focus . . . more on sex in the next days, which is a profoundly Christian methodology. Christianity is as much about dangerous futures as it is about dangerous memories' (Stuart 1997b, p. 204). It is about asserting a hope in the belief that death is not the ultimate divider, but something that will be and has been conquered, so that we are not in fact forever divided from those we have lost (Stuart 1997b, p. 197). Queer people are already particularly well-versed in imagining and hoping for a life after oppression and fear, and Stuart suggests that these 'visions of "life after" resonate with and stir up some dangerous memories from the Christian tradition which together challenge so much theo-sexual orthodoxy' (Stuart 1997b, p: 198). Biblical assertion about the absence in heaven of anything that looks very much like nuclear families, marriages or monogamous couples is only one example.

But death is not only an end-of-life event, stresses Stuart: the symbol of baptism means that 'Christians are sacramentally united with Christ and the performance of his death and resurrection is repeated upon their own bodies' (Stuart 2004, p. 63). Christians are at once already dead and resurrected to life in the new creation, and still living through the dyingness of this world; and, crucially, 'The Church is mandated as the body of Christ to live out this new reality in the midst of a world still being born into it' (Stuart 2004, p. 67). Christians, then, should live as people who are already freed *both* from the melancholy of gender and from the melancholy of death (Stuart 2004, p. 69). There is no longer any need to cling to ossified categories or tired typologies of gender and sex, not only because queer discourse has undermined them, but also because the Christian hope of a new creation and a life-beyond-death *has built into it* an obsolescence and a provisionality for existing regulatory identities. In this kind of thinking, as for Jordan and for Loughlin, queer is not something 'new', but a resisting strand which has been inside Christianity all along.

Importantly, this can be traced even in those theologians who have often been identified as part of the theological bastion which reinforces tired hegemonies of sexuality and gender. It can be seen, for example, in the project of resistance to human ideology inherent in the work of the famously gender-complementarian Karl Barth. For Barth, no human ideology can ever be final or ultimate because all human activity occurs in a sphere already encompassed in (and therefore secondary to) the love and work of God:

> Since [God's] sign-giving stands in the closest possible connexion with objective revelation, like that revelation it must be regarded as a divine act . . . The given-ness of these signs does not mean that God manifest has Himself as it were become a bit of the world. It does not mean that He has passed into the hands or been put at the disposal of men gathered together to form the Church. On the contrary, what it does mean is that in Christ the world and man have fallen into the hands of God. It means the setting-up of God's lordship, not of a sacral human lordship. (Barth 1956a, p. 227)

This has the advantage of removing God from any ideology or hegemony which might claim to be the sole and unique official mouthpiece of the deity – from a 'sacral human lordship' – leaving God's freedom always unmarred by the limitations of the fallibility of human amanuenses (as Barth also stresses in *The Epistle to the Romans,* his assertion that God cannot be subsumed into human culture or dogma). It is not unimportant that Barth and his translators chose to refer to God as 'He', nor that this strongly gendered view of God and humanity – and the anthropology he pins onto it – is where Barth has since met with some of his fiercest criticism (see for example Fiddes 1990, Blevins 2005, Cornwall 2010b). This, in fact, demonstrates a significant shift, namely the way in which gender norms and assumptions have become part of what is 'uncovered' and problematized in theological discourse over the eighty or so years since Barth's work was first published. Barth's account, and the language in which it is couched, has itself been shown to be a provisional and partial version of the story even as it testifies to God's over-againstness in relation to human ideology. In other words, Christianity's queerness (as a reflection or echo of God's queerness) is so profound and so irrepressible that it can break through even where it appears to be used in the service of maintaining limiting normativities. Like death, modes of discourse from which exception and difference have been written out are shown to be less than absolute.

Indeed, Grace M. Jantzen argues that it is exactly by queering such a seemingly inescapable and insurmountable problem as death that it is possible to conceive of a creative yet inchoate 'queer language' which, by focusing on natality and life rather than resignation to death and sinfulness (Loughlin comments that 'the trope of second birth – being "born again"– only occludes our first birth or natality' – Loughlin 2007b, p. 26), might be a site for a real remaking of categories of sex and gender too (Jantzen 2007, pp. 252–3). Where even the inescapability of death is diminished by its contextualization as a moment in eternity, human categories of sex and gender are shown up even more effectively as at least partial artifice. The subversion of sex-gender structures and the subversion of death, in Stuart's and Jantzen's accounts, occur simultaneously and are in some way inextricable. This is but one example of queer theology speaking to more than just sex, sexuality or gender, albeit by scholars whose grounding in theologies and philosophies informed by feminist and lesbian criticism has placed them well to query grand narratives and recognize discursive penultimacy (even if, in Stuart's case at least, a mainstream doctrinal and confessional commitment is retained). When grand narratives are questioned and resisted, every arena of human life and experience is interrogated.

Conclusion

There is an important duality here: queer has been shown to be something which cannot be categorized or satisfactorily defined, yet it is at the same time claimed, especially by some recent queer theologians, as something whose reach is unlimited.[8] As this opening chapter has made clear, there is not a stable, unproblematic definition of queer with which we can work. However, we have noted that queer is often figured as a phenomenon or methodology in a state of *opposition to regulatory normativities*. We noted, too, that although queer theology should not necessarily be considered synonymous with lesbian and gay theology (for reasons made clear in the next chapter), historically and currently it is strongly associated with questions of gender and sexuality, particularly as these pertain to *non-normative (and often non-heterosexual) gender and sexuality.* For this reason, much of the subject matter addressed by queer theology and biblical studies has been sexual. However, as we have begun to see and as we explore in more detail later, queer theological methodologies should not be considered relevant to sex alone. Indeed, we saw in the work of Jordan, Loughlin and others that all aspects of theology might be understood as somehow queer, since they stand over against mainstream human ideology and (claims Loughlin) refuse to be subsumed by it.

We noted that queer has sometimes been called an ethically empty referent, since it rejects any static link between signifier and signified, and seeks to resist and critique regulatory discourse, including normativity. The question of whether it actually is ethically empty – and whether or not this is a problem – is discussed in more detail in Chapter 7. However, it will be salient to bear in mind a suggestion and two questions. The suggestion is this: if queer is suspicious and interrogative of all human ideology and regulatory identity, then queer might have to be considered something more devastating and more of a break with the past than its apparent close relatives, gay, feminist and liberation theologies. Although queer theologies might be considered liberating for queer people, queer theology is not simply another kind of liberation theology. The questions are these: have the queer theologians writing over the last decade in particular been any more successful than those of the 1980s and early 1990s at negotiating queer in its definitional recalcitrance rather than freezing it into another regulatory identity? Has queer shown itself in practice to be a truly different methodology for theologians, or simply one cut from the same basic cloth as feminist and liberationist theologies and perhaps, therefore, unable adequately to critique or interrogate them?

As we move toward considering in more detail some of the controversies surrounding queer theology, then, I aim to show that this field is still in flux, and to begin to explore the implications of employing queer methodologies across theological work. To be queer is to be contested as well as to contest, since queer insists that all identity and ideology is provisional and unfinished. Throughout the volume, then, I deal not in certainty but in suggestion, and try to show that controversies in queer theology are evidence of dynamic movement which is highly creative and fecund. The fact that there are so many voices at this table demonstrates the breadth of theologians and other commentators invested in querying metanarratives based in exclusion and demarcation, even if this does not always play out in identical ways. Queer theological discourse is still in its genesis, and much exciting and important work remains to be done.

Notes

1 It is important to note from the outset that heteronormativity implies not merely heterosexual eroticism, but the assumption that heterosexuality is the only or most legitimate form of sexual relationship or social structure. Cultural critics Lauren Berlant and Michael Warner describe heteronormativity as 'the institutions, structures of understanding, and practical orientations that make heterosexuality seem not only coherent – that is, organized as a sexuality – but also privileged. Its coherence is always provisional' (Berlant and Warner 1999, p. 355).

2 Although 'queer theology' is now discussed in other languages, including Dutch and German, the term is usually 'borrowed' from the English. The 'new' use of queer in these languages does not always have a built-in sense of 'crossing' or being 'athwart' or 'against' as in English. See Cornwall 2010a, pp. 24–5.

3 Before the AIDS designation became widespread, the condition was some-times called GRID, gay-related immune deficiency (see for example Zimmerman and Zimmerman 1996, pp. 200, 202–3; Hall 2003, p. 51).

4 These are the racial categories usually used in my own British context; the US categories would read something like 'American Indian or Alaska Native; Asian; Black or African American; Native Hawaiian or Other Pacific Islander; White; some other ethnic group, or a combination thereof' (see for example http://www.census.gov/population/www/socdemo/race/racefactcb.html). This varies further in other countries depending on their racial and ethnic demographics.

5 Valentine et al's sociological analysis of the interactions of pro-LGBT groups (such as the Lesbian and Gay Christian Movement (LGCM), Changing Attitude, Integrity, and the Inclusive Church Network) and anti-LGBT groups (such as Anglican Mainstream) at Lambeth 2008 shows the ways in which nego-tiations of group identity feed back into the Church of England's and Anglican Communion's broader understandings of themselves. Valentine et al comment that LGCM's strategy of handing out rainbow ribbons in the conference 'Market-place' was designed to visibly mark out supporters, but that 'it was evident that a number of the wearers had accepted them without recognizing their symbolism'

(Valentine et al 2010, p. 931). This might be figured as an ironic echo of hetero-sexual normativity, parodically 'colonizing' non-supportive bodies as visible sites of outward endorsement; or it might be understood as an undermining of sym-bolic tokens of support since these can be reinterpreted and have their meanings elided. Importantly, suggest Valentine et al, 'the LGCM sought to mobilize its supporters by forcing them to "come out" symbolically by wearing the ribbon, as well generating a wider perception of numerical significance through the tactic of indiscriminate ribbon distribution' (Valentine et al 2010, p. 931). Note that the pro-LGBT groups sought to distinguish themselves not only from anti-LGBT groups but also from one another, especially where one group's tactics were con-sidered too oppositional or confronting (Valentine et al 2010, p. 934).

6 However, it is significant that, a year after Lambeth 2008, Rowan Williams, the Archbishop of Canterbury, expressed regret that the Episcopal Church in the USA had ignored a three-year moratorium on appointing openly gay bishops by the election as bishop in 2009 of the lesbian priest Mary D. Glasspool in Los Angeles. Williams suggested that Canon Glasspool's appointment would shatter the agreed 'period of gracious restraint in respect to actions which are contrary to the mind of the Communion' (http://www.archbishopofcanterbury.org/2650), and it seemed for a time that this would finally lead to the Episcopalian Church in the USA formally seceding from the Anglican Communion. However, Glasspool was consecrated as a bishop in May 2010. Philip Giddings and Chris Sugden, convener and secretary of the conservative Anglican Mainstream group, issued a statement calling for the Episcopal Church to withdraw or be excluded from the Anglican Communion's representative bodies (www.anglican-mainstream. net/2010/05/15/statement-from-anglican-mainstream-following-the-consecration-of-mary-glasspool-as-suffragan-bishop-of-los-angeles-usa/). Although their theological and hermeneutical sympathies are in many respects very different, it is likely that Williams was still feeling the legacy of his last-predecessor-but-one, Robert Runcie, who stated during the debate over Revd Tony Higton's Private Member's Motion on sexual morality to the General Synod in 1987 that to pro-vide a less-than-united message on sexuality was dangerous. Runcie said, 'I do not deny, and cannot, that homosexual acts are condemned in the biblical and Christian tradition. It is our duty to teach the Christian ideal to our children and not to confuse them with options' (audio archived by London Broadcasting Company/Independent Radio News at http://radio.bufvc.ac.uk/lbc/index.php/segment/0014600163007). Higton's original motion had asserted that 'fornica-tion, adultery, and homosexual acts are sinful in all circumstances', but the motion eventually passed by 403 votes to 8 had been softened by Malcolm Johnson's amendment to state that, like fornication and adultery, 'homosexual genital acts fall short of [the] ideal and are to be met by a call to repentance and the exercise of compassion'. Rowan Williams wrote the following year that the Synod had been

'simultaneously cajoled and panicked' into passing the resolution: 'Well-meaning "liberals", equally afraid of the harshness of the original motion (about which the less said the better) and of getting involved in a genuinely theological debate on sexuality, joined hands with some of the most disturbing elements in the contemporary Church of England, those who are determined to make it an ideologically monolithic body, to produce a vote which has, in practice, delivered much of what the original motion aimed at. This shabby compromise has been held up by bishops as representing the "mind" of the Church, and accorded something like legislative force' (Williams 1988). Much frustration has been expressed in recent years at Williams' apparent stepping-back from his formerly open liberal views on homosexuality in order to preserve the unity of the Anglican Communion.

7 The title cites the political activist organization ACT UP, the AIDS Coalition To Unleash Power, founded in New York in 1987.

8 However, even if this broader understanding of queer as going beyond sexual (and especially homosexual) concerns is happening in theology per se, it is not necessarily happening in queer critical reflection on religion more broadly, from disciplines such as literary criticism. Even in recent volumes such as 2007's *Catholic Figures, Queer Narratives* (Gallagher, Roden and Smith 2007), 'queer' basically equals gay and lesbian. There is a distinct absence here of some of the names familiar from and central to secular queer theory (de Lauretis, Halperin, Butler et al) with whom Althaus-Reid, Goss and other queer theologians and biblical scholars engage. In part, this is because the *Catholic Figures* writers are consciously drawing on historical literary sources instead, reflecting on novels by authors such as Oscar Wilde, James Joyce and Radclyffe Hall; however, it is also significant that any 'classic' queer theoretical underpinning is either so far assumed as to go without saying or else absent altogether. Although the focus of the volume is literary rather than critical-theoretical, the fact that the term 'queer' can be used therein without explicitly outlining its genealogy is an important testament to the term's new broader application.

2

Is Queer Theology Synonymous with Gay Theology?

The totality of the meaning of queer will always be more or less than or different from its synonymity with lesbian/gay, and . . . its force, in fact, resides in the way it can be both conflated with lesbian and/or gay and used to disrupt that conflation or deconstruct lesbianness and/or gayness. (Barnard 2004, p. 10)

We want a world where gays are not only tolerated, but where the practices and sensibilities of gay and lesbian communities can be associated with long-standing goods of the Christian tradition. We want a world where gay and straight are not significant terms, especially in relation to theology. Why then, I ask, write a book about gay and lesbian identity projects? And why name it *Gay and Lesbian Theologies* when what is really desired is something like post-gay and lesbian theologies, or post-identity Christian politics? (Rudy 2004, p. 109)

Queer's genealogy in gay liberation theology

I showed in Chapter 1 that queer theory's genealogy in lesbian, gay, bisexual and transgender (LGBT) political movements is considered by some commentators to be an irreducible and ineluctable aspect of its characterization. This is also true of queer theologies, as I will explore in more detail in this chapter. Many of the writers who have subsequently come to categorize themselves and their theologies as queer started out by doing what they identified at the time as gay liberation theology, drawing on pioneering writers in the area of gay theology. Some held tenaciously to LGB, LGBT or similar group identities.[1] In this chapter I explore in more detail the reasons why some commentators insist that specific LGBT identity cannot and should not be eradicated from queer theology, and contrast this assertion with the notion that queer theology is something profoundly different in kind from gay theology and that this is crucial to its ongoing outworkings.

Stuart (2003, pp. 17–26) provides a helpful overview of the work of writers such as Malcolm Macourt, William R. Johnson, Sally Gearhart and John J. McNeill, summarizing this early history in the 1970s (see also Macourt 1977; Gearhart and Johnson 1974; McNeill 1976; Perry 1972). These writers sought to show the non-pathology of homosexual orientation (sometimes by appeal to the new psychiatric and psychological scholarship emerging at the time), and to re-read and re-interpret the biblical passages which seemed to address homosexuality directly. Some, like McNeill and Perry, strongly emphasized that they had been born gay, and that this was the way God had created them and meant them to be. This was, as Daniel T. Spencer comments, a largely reactive and apologetic stance which sought to justify the place of queer people in the church (Spencer 2001, p. 195). There was already a recognition, as by Sally Gearhart, that lesbian theology could not simply be done as an adjunct to gay theology, and that gay men could not unproblematically speak on behalf of all homosexual people (Hunt 1996, p. 298). However, not everyone shared Gearhart's insight – as I discuss below.

Mary E. Hunt paints a basically chronological picture of the development of queer theology, painting it as having succeeded lesbian/gay/bisexual theology, which in turn succeeded homosexual theology, in a three-stage process. She fixes dates on these phases: the 'homosexual' era from 1972–82, the 'LGB' era from 1982–92, and the 'queer' era from 1992 onwards (Hunt 1996, pp. 298–9). However, I suggest that, while these labels might be useful shorthand, the development of queer theology has not occurred on such a simplistically forward trajectory as all that. Understanding queer theology as a linear *evolution* of these earlier forms risks both ignoring the appeals of queer theologians to strands within Christianity that predate this timeline by many hundreds of years,

44

and negating the fact that some writers prefer to understand their work as lesbian theology or gay theology without considering this a prior or less developed stage than queer theology. It would also not be entirely fair to say that issues of female and bisexual experience only began to be acknowledged after 1982.

Mary Elise Lowe describes parallels between the early work of gay theologians, like Robert E. Goss, and that of earlier liberation theologians, identifying contextual hermeneutics, an emphasis on embodiment, and a strong strand of solidarity with oppressed people, as central elements common to both movements (Lowe 2009, p. 51). In Lowe's account, these, in turn, became the underpinnings of queer theologies and hermeneutics. However, in some respects, Lowe's distinctions between gay and lesbian theologies and queer theologies are too simplistic – like her assertion that the early gay and lesbian theologians did not have adequate methodological tools to be able to understand biblical texts as constructed and contextual but queer theologians do (Lowe 2009, p. 57), or the claim that gay and lesbian theologians were sex-essentialists but that queer theologians agree with Butler that sex is social construction (Lowe 2009, p. 58). The latter assertion leads Lowe to caricature *all* gay and lesbian theologians as calling for full inclusion within churches on the grounds of solidarity, and *all* queer theologians as embracing bisexual and transgender people in a way that gay and lesbian theologians do not (Lowe 2009, p. 58). This slightly naïve analysis is not quite fair in either direction. Lowe does say that she has not intended to pit these theologies in opposition or to make them an either/or choice, but her analysis risks doing so (Lowe 2009, p. 59).

Much gay liberationist work, written as it was in the late 1970s and 1980s, was inevitably coloured by the escalating AIDS crisis – the calamitousness arising as much from social fear expressed as homophobia as from the syndrome itself. J. Michael Clark notes that when his book *A Place to Start* was written during 1987 and 1988, 70 per cent of diagnosed HIV/AIDS cases were in gay men, which had led to a redoubling of homophobia and violence against them.[2] Indeed, the whole book is set in the context of AIDS, of absent friends who had already succumbed to the virus, and of an increasing gay 'exile' from mainstream society because of the little-understood epidemic which marked out gay men as 'death-bringers' (Clark 1989, p. 47). Clark reports, in a later book, that all of his theology was done in the context of actual and threatened death, particularly the many AIDS-related deaths of gay friends and the HIV-positive status of himself and his partner. In fact, he claims that his career as a theologian and the incidence of AIDS in the gay male community were 'simultaneous, intertwined from their beginnings' (Clark 1997, p. 28). Schneider comments that, for Clark, 'life is ineradicably tragic but worth living even more fully as a result' (Schneider 2000, p. 10). Clark chooses to 'defy the darkness' of this perpetual presence of death, via an aggressively tenacious emphasis on ethics, praxis and right relationship. In fact, he comes to believe that, although AIDS is a tragedy, gay men must also take responsibility for the ways in which their lifestyle choices may have helped to perpetuate its spread (Clark 1997, p. 42). This is not anathema to his 'defiance', but rather ties in with a desire to affirm life and mutual accountability. However, Rollan McCleary, who prefers to appeal to gay spirituality rather than to queer, suggests that Clark's focus on the tragic and grave is likely to be unpalatable to most gay men, and that since religion has already been so hurtful to many gay people, it should consciously 'make a few joyful amends' rather than majoring on tragedy (McCleary 2004, p. 103).

Gay theology's contextualization by the chronology of the diagnosis of and public attitude toward HIV/AIDS is crucial to understanding the way in which it developed and the ongoing importance of political identity for many gay men (as well as lesbian allies and others). Queer theology evidently comes 'after' this history in some respects; however, Elizabeth Stuart believes that 'queer theology came too late in the AIDS crisis to be motivated to respond to the articulation of life after death among those dying' (Stuart 2003, p. 102). In other words, while specifically gay-identified theologies like Clark's may have had a distinctly life-affirming thrust, they were not sufficiently conceptually equipped to show how binary gay–straight identity mapped onto a death–life polarization, or to resist this division. We saw above how Stuart and Jantzen subsequently sought to show how queer theology might reframe death and dying. It remains to be seen how queer theology will engage with the fact that new HIV/AIDS cases now occur with disproportionate frequency among women (often married women) in the Global South and their children.

Queer and the male homosexual bias

In asking to what extent queer theology supervenes on gay theology, we must contrast gay not only with 'heterosexual' but also with 'lesbian'; 'gay' is emphatically not unproblematic shorthand for 'male homosexual', but has often had a specifically masculine implication to it. Stuart notes the perceived problem, raised by Gearhart and others, that too much early gay liberation theology was done by gay men who unproblematically believed they could also speak on behalf of lesbians because both groups rejected heterosexual partnerships (Stuart 2003, p. 15). Too little account was taken by some male gay scholars and activists of the specifically female exclusion faced by lesbians.

Stuart suggests that, if queer theory represents a 'takeover' of gay discourse without rooting out and problematizing questions of gender hierarchy, queer may not represent any better an option for women than male-biased gay theology does. She comments, 'Queer theory . . . has been accused of patriarchal terrorism boring its way into gender politics and erasing the hard fought identities of women and gay men in the name of liberation' (Stuart 2003, p. 103). The identities of women in particular, it is suggested, may have been threatened, rather than recognized, by an incoming queer grand narrative which has been more interested in the overarching than the particular.

This has been keenly expressed by some writers: words like homosexual and queer 'mean men unless women are explicitly included', claims the lesbian political scientist Sheila Jeffreys (Jeffreys 2003, p. 34). For biblical critic Deryn Guest, queer theology and queer biblical interpretation specifically may be of limited use for lesbians if they do not challenge and resist the male bias she perceives not only in heteronormativity but also in (male) gay discourse even in the twenty-first century. She acknowledges that there are problems and limitations associated with specifically lesbian or specifically gay criticism. Nonetheless, this does not necessarily imply that it would be better to jettison them in favour of queer discourse. In fact, says Guest, there is still much potential in expressly lesbian biblical hermeneutics, and 'there need not be a wholesale move to queer terminology if our definition of "lesbian" can be organized in such a way that resists the rigidity of sexual identity labels' (Guest 2005, p. 48). Even if keeping the label 'lesbian' risks separatism and a reification of lesbian identity, believes Guest, this might be a necessary price to pay for ensuring that lesbian concerns, and women's concerns more broadly, are not elided. Guest is concerned that it may, in fact, be *too soon* to use a catch-all label like queer, since there has not yet been enough time and dedicated space for specifically lesbian biblical criticism (Guest 2005, p. 50). This argument clearly draws on Walters' 'concern over the implicit and explicit marginalization and demonization of feminism and lesbian-feminism' (Walters 1996, p. 837), which underpin her hesitation over the language of queerness: 'If queer becomes the new reigning subjectivity for hip activists and intellectuals alike, what kinds of politics and theories then become "transcended", moved through and over in the construction of the queer hegemony?' (Walters 1996, p. 837).

It is not clear whether or not Guest would consider queer an *eventual* appropriate successor to lesbian criticism within biblical studies and theology: she is certainly not convinced that it is a necessary category (or an expedient one for lesbians) as yet. In this account, the public 'voice' which purported to represent all homosexual people in the 1970s actually had an inbuilt male bias, failing to acknowledge adequately the ways in which lesbians were doubly marginalized in society, because of both their status as women (with the concomitant jeopardy associated with the low-waged, low-status jobs disproportionately done by women) and their status as homosexual people. The fact that women have been especially negated in some strands of Christianity, it was believed, added another layer of exclusion, and meant that theological protest voiced by gay males alone was likely to elide the specific additional problems faced by lesbians.

If queer is painted as basically a *successor* to gay, rather than something different in kind despite an undeniable shared genealogy, then lesbian women and transgender people might (as Guest makes clear) still find or perceive themselves to be excluded. This might particularly be the case for those persuaded by Suzanna Danuta Walters' argument – glossed by Sheila Jeffreys – that the triumvirate of poststructuralists so beloved by queer theorists, namely Foucault, Derrida and Lacan, symbolically rode up on big white horses and declared that gender was nothing but performance anyway and gender politics was therefore 'silly' and a waste of everyone's energy (Walters 1996, p. 844; Jeffreys 2003, p. 34). In so doing they 'came to the rescue and showed how meaningless and unnecessary . . . lesbian feminism was. Queer politics, then, was created in contradistinction to lesbian feminism' (Jeffreys 2003, p. 35). Jeffreys argues that barely had lesbians succeeded in gaining specific recognition alongside gay men – becoming the L in LGB – when 'the tables were turned and lesbians were buried again under queer' (Jeffreys 2003, p. 36). The broadness hidden within the terminology of queer, argues Jeffreys, meant that lesbians were lumped together with bisexuals, transgender people and sadomasochists whose interests are – she says – in direct opposition to those of lesbian women (Jeffreys 2003, pp. 36–7) and represent societal self-harm.[3] Even if this picture takes too little account of the role of Butler, Sedgwick and the authors of other foundational queer texts,[4] it represents a real felt resentment on the parts of some lesbians.

Moreover, Jeffreys is unhappy that queer is so often figured as a 'politics of outsiderhood' (Jeffreys 2003, p. 37) – because, she believes, this account repeats the experience of gay *men* who have understood themselves to have been marginalized and excluded – whereas lesbian feminist politics has profoundly been about inclusion, and is *not* therefore 'queer' in the sense of inherent abjection. She says,

Lesbian feminism does not see lesbians as representing a transhistorical minority of one in ten or one in twenty at all. The experience of the 1970s, in which hundreds of thousands of women in the Western world chose to re-create themselves as lesbians, is living proof of the falsity of such an understanding. Lesbian feminists have maintained that 'any woman can be a lesbian', since the lesbian represents political rebellion against male supremacy, and is the very model for free womanhood. (Jeffreys 2003, p. 37)

It is perhaps ironic, then, that Jeffreys' brand of lesbian feminism has itself been accused of marginalizing and rejecting women: namely, those who were not born as women – those who have transitioned gender, with or without sex reassignment surgery – and, through its biological essentialism, some intersexed women. It is *not* the case that 'any woman can be a lesbian', if in order to be 'authentic' a woman must have a vulva, clitoris, vagina, breasts, uterus, ovaries and XX chromosomes.

The point stands, though, that the name 'queer' is by no means a magic bullet which easily overcomes categories of exclusion or oppression. Even if it consciously seeks *not* to be an identity like any other, it has sometimes been shown to be vulnerable to annexation and appropriation by some people to the exclusion of others. Queer is still working out *how* to be queer, and how to walk the talk of living out non-prescriptive modes of discourse and behaviour.

Queer theology and the locatedness of specificity

Robert E. Goss notes the potential of queer theology to move beyond 'ghettoized gay theology' (Goss 1998, p. 195). However, like Guest, he says that a queer theology which purports to be all-inclusive – which purports to go beyond contingency, perhaps – might also be dangerous. Just as some early gay male theologians tended to elide specifically lesbian concerns by propounding a universalizing homosexual politic, so queer theologians who consider queer a comprehensive catch-all term may unwittingly gloss over difference and diversity. This might result in 'false inclusion of the voices of translesbigays with various shades of contextuality' (Goss 1998, p. 195). Even in 1998, when queer theological discourse was far more strongly associated with gay and lesbian theology than it has subsequently become, Goss appreciated the multiplicity emerging within it: queer womanist theology, queer lesbian theology, queer bisexual theology, queer theologies from different ethnic contexts, and so on. In particular, Goss believes that queer theology has the potential to overcome the exclusion of bisexual and transgender concerns – as sometimes played out in lesbian and gay theologies which have understood lesbian and gay identity in distinction from, or even opposition to, these other categories (Goss 2002, p. 224). In the intervening years, although questions about the pros and cons of queer's all-encompassing bent have continued, it has also become clear that there is, even hermeneutically, space for difference and variety in the queer family of theologies that may historically have been less welcomed within the heteronormative Western theological mainstream.

Ken Stone, discussing the concept of queer preaching, notes the objection that, since queer is often associated exclusively with LGBT, queer questions will be 'too narrow', focusing too exclusively on LGBT experience. As a result, he says, they are thus 'frequently dismissed as being relevant . . . for only a tiny segment of the population that the preacher must address' (Stone 2007, p. 161). Courses in lesbian and gay studies, which may be the only places in which queer theory is deemed relevant or appropriate (at least in the US seminary context in which Stone writes), 'are sometimes misunderstood as nothing more than opportunities for the encouragement of lesbians and gay men' (Stone 2007, p. 163). However, he counters, such specificity is unavoidable, because the nature of rhetoric is always to be situated somewhere particular. So the fact that 'queer reading often takes its point of departure from reflection on specific experiences and contexts' (Stone 2007, p. 162) should not be understood negatively, and should not detract from its capacity to speak into different contexts even while being grounded in a specific one. The interrogation of norms surrounding gender and sexuality might therefore be a 'way in' to using queer analysis to interrogate broader normativities in confessional contexts; but, if this is to occur, priests and scholars who utilize queer methodologies in their preaching and teaching *must* engage with queer's capacity to disrupt more than sex, gender and sexuality, and acknowledge the ways in which these operate in broader matrices of power.

Even if LGBT and queer are equated for a time, then, it seems likely that this will only be temporary. Queer's suspicion of regulatory identity means that, even where it celebrates specificities and particularities of bodily experience, it will not be limited by them. In fact, queer's propensity to resist all kinds of normativities means that it often exceeds the bounds of LGBT-sited discourses, even where it is perceptibly rooted in them. In fact, this might be understood positively, showing that queer's reach is extensive, and something which should be promoted further. This might entail building on existing 'resisting' methodologies and strategies, such as postmodern hermeneutics, and exploring their affinities with queer criticism. This will help to demonstrate that queer criticism is not only, or always, that done by or for homosexual people, and thereby resist the cordoning-off of both queer theology and queer individuals.

However, specifically LGBT experience is still sometimes understood as an *exceptionally* important locus of queer criticism. Elizabeth Stuart suggests that queer reflection on theology might be particularly compelling *precisely because* LGBT people are still so often dismissed as not being 'really' Christians or 'really' able to reflect on God at all. By actively privileging the voices of those who have formerly been quashed, queer theology might undermine Christianity's too-easy alliance with heterosexual hegemony. LGBT people using queer theological discourses might be especially able to critique some of the ways in which Christianity has been allied to heteronormativity, precisely because they are all too aware of the fact that this can be exclusive and hurtful. Heterosexual people can, of course, also critique Christianity's bond to heteronormativity; but their experience as being endorsed rather than condemned by it may give them less incentive to do so and less inducement to utilize specifically queer analysis. Being situated in a particularity of experience always presents limitations as well as advantages, and experience-based theologies might be dismissed for being focused too much on human beings and not enough on a transcendent God. Stuart acknowledges that many people might deem an LGBT-focused and authored book such as *Religion is a Queer Thing* unnecessary, and too overtly grounded in a particularity of situation. Christianity as such, claim the objectors, is nothing to do with specific social or physical circumstances, and so should not be read through such a skewed lens. However, she says,

This is a clever argument because not only does it immediately separate God from issues of racism, sexism, poverty and so on and make
them purely human concerns, but it also identifies Christianity with
the theology of those who have not found themselves economically
or socially disadvantaged. In the name of a God who did become
involved in the mess and power battles of human life and stood with
the losers, queer Christians are among those who destabilize the
notion of what constitutes Christianity and a Christian by refusing
to accept on trust that a white, straight, male Christianity is the sole
Christian truth. (Stuart 1997a, p. 5)

For Stuart, then, queer theology is not necessarily synonymous with gay
theology, *but* the specific experiences of gay and lesbian people might
be particularly effective in showing up anti-hegemonic strands in some
areas of Christianity and critiquing others as unjustifiable.

The suggestion seems to be that queer theology *must* start from and
always refer to a given rootedness or specificity of history *exactly in order
to become more broad in its implications*. Indeed, as Stuart notes, it is
exactly by maintaining a *diversity* of viewpoints in all their 'mess and
muddle' that queer theology might be able to 'escape the danger of being
a self-serving ideology masquerading as theology and become a theology
which has the potential to transform not just queer people but all men
and women' (Stuart 1997a, p. 4). Importantly, respecting and engaging
with a multiplicity of viewpoints does not mean ignoring their differences
or pretending that they are all the same – which is to do a disservice to
their diversity. Queer theology is not just 'for the queers', not just for
people who might have had this epithet hurled at them as an insult in the
past: Stuart notes that 'a significant number of heterosexual people also
wish heterosexual normativity to be fouled up', and that their own perspective is also 'important to the development of queer theology' (Stuart
1997a, p. 5). If this is to be more than just a heterosexual colonization
of an arena in which homosexual agency has been at the fore, though, it
will be necessary to ensure a continual re-checking and re-balancing of
all the voices at the table, with an appreciation that a gay or transgender
person can speak about gay or transgender experience in a way that a

heterosexual or non-trans person cannot (cf. Walters 1996, pp. 840–1).[5] That said, there might be a particular queer imperative to show that, rather than being about one thing and one thing only, the texts are sites of multiple and liminal meanings. Moreover, suggests Stone,

> Perhaps the biblical texts that queer readers need to emphasize are not texts that construe religious identity in polarized terms or draw clear borders between insiders and outsiders . . . Ultimately, a 'safer' biblical interpretation, and a 'safer' religious practice, may need to work instead at dissolving those very boundaries between 'inside' and 'outside'. (Stone 2005, pp. 66–7)

Queer heterosexuality

This kind of idea is picked up by Calvin Thomas and others in the 2000 collection *Straight with a Twist,* in which the trope of heterosexuality in popular culture and literature is explored. Thomas suggests, after Michael Warner and Alexander Doty, that it is possible to be both heterosexual and queer. This would take place through a process of resistance to the notion of desire as constructed ideally, or necessarily, along binary lines with the 'other' as one's stereotyped 'opposite'. Thomas says,

> Such a questioning could in and of itself qualify as queer. Indeed, . . . straights, who would be definitionally barred from the terms gay, lesbian, or bisexual, could not be excluded from the domain of the queer except by recourse to the very essentialist definitions that queer theory is often at pains to repudiate. (Thomas 2000b, p. 14)

However, notes Thomas, this should not occur at the expense of writing out self-identified lesbian and gay people from association with queer, or constitute some kind of 'straight takeover'. In the same volume, Clyde Smith describes his own journey of coming to identify as a 'queer heterosexual', suggesting that the expansion of the queer community to encompass heterosexual people, though positive, should also not elide difference or, where appropriate, boundaries between groups (Smith

2000). Importantly, 'queer heterosexuality', in several accounts, is not merely the state of being a heterosexual ally to non-heterosexual people (Schlichter 2004, p. 544); rather, it implies taking on or claiming a sexuality or gender expression which is *itself* non-normative. This might include involvement in polyamory, kink/BDSM,[6] or other 'niche' sexual practices (ct. Walters 1996, pp. 861–2);[7] or it might entail a simple refusal to endorse a division of labour along stereotypically gendered lines in household or kinship arrangements.

For Doty, the queerness of heterosexuality is less clearly defined. He seeks merely to point out 'the queerness of and in straights and straight cultures, *as well as* that of individuals and groups who have been told they inhabit the boundaries between the binaries of gender and sexuality' (Doty 1993: pp. xv–xvi, quoted in Walters 1996, pp. 835–6; my emphasis). To relegate 'queerness' to those who are bisexual, transgender or otherwise 'non-normative' is, for Doty, to negate the difference and variety built in even to what is sometimes represented as a monolithic phenomenon, heterosexuality. To figure heterosexuality as always inherently non-queer is to reinforce both an unhelpful binary opposition, and fixed identity politics.

The fact that there is no consensus about what one might have to do to be considered a queer heterosexual leaves the notion open to critique, as from those who suggest it is too easy a label to take on in order to appropriate queer discourse for heterosexual purposes (see for example Walters 1996, p. 863). However, this resistance to definition is only the same as the problem attached to broader queer theory. As Annette Schlichter notes, queer heterosexuals are in some senses analogous to male feminists and white anti-apartheid activists and might, similarly, be understood as either positively supportive or negatively usurping of the concerns of others. However, the situation of the queer heterosexual is also different from these, precisely because queer *interrupts* identity politics and identity claims rather than just introducing new ones (Schlichter 2004, p. 545). (In this respect, it is more like postcolonial discourse, which seeks to retell and reframe the stories of *both* the colonized and the colonizers, showing that a postcolonial understanding recontextualizes imperial history in its entirety, not just the formerly silenced parts of it.)

In fact, queer analysis and further reflection on queer heteronormativity might help to make a creative way through the somewhat monolithic and stereotypical representation of heterosexuality and heterosexuals some-times evident in lesbian and gay discourse (Schlichter 2004, p. 549). In short, suggests Schlichter, 'the queer straight becomes a troubling figure that is instrumental in maintaining the fluid and self-critical character of the queer production of knowledge as a democratic project' (Schlichter 2004, p. 555).

The 'queer heterosexual' has thus far been even less visible in queer theological texts than in secular ones, though with a notable exception evident in Marcella Althaus-Reid, who notes that queering 'T-theological' discourse and practice (which she understands to mean theology grounded in a particular heteronormative and capitalist worldview) is necessarily done by heterosexual people as well as lesbian, gay, bisexual or transgender ones. This broader understanding of queer recurs elsewhere: for example, Rachel Muers characterizes queer theology simply as 'a critical and constructive rereading of established categories of sex and gender from a Christian theological perspective' (Muers 2007, p. 200). On this reading, too, queer theology is not only or exclusively to be concerned with or done by homosexual people – even if reframing and refiguring homosexuality (a category which some might say was set up by Christian commentators especially so that they could then shoot it down)[8] will inevitably be a major part of it. However, queer theology does not solely repeat the early work of Gearhart and others: indeed, if queer theology is understood to necessitate a fundamental refiguring and rejection of exclusion, prejudice and social privilege *even more radical* than that done by gay theology, then it has the potential to go further than gay theology could, in undermining normativities and regulatory identity structures. Queer is unrelenting in its belief that *any* identity claim can become exclusive and elitist, even if it is an identity claim which has formerly been (or continues to be) written out of signifi-cation and might therefore be characterized as marginal or subalternist.

This makes any project of queer resistance to normative identity poli-tics far from easy or neat, and might cause pain or bemusement to those who feel their political agency as a specifically gay man or lesbian woman (for example) has been hard-won and must not be lightly ceded. However, as we have seen, Butler herself does not anticipate or endorse a thoroughgoing move away from all kinds of identity claims. Indeed, comments Stuart Macwilliam, the accusations of anti-feminism, conservatism and an undermining of lesbian concerns that are sometimes levelled at queer theory may arise from 'a misleading antithesis' (Macwilliam 2002, p. 387). To set up an opposition between gay and lesbian liberationist proponents on the one side and 'the insouciant, irresponsible identity dissidents' on the other is, suggests Macwilliam, artificial (Macwilliam 2002, p. 387). While it is true that queer theorists are critical of identity categories, he says, this 'hardly amounts to denying that the categories exist or that they can be and have been useful platforms for achieving progress in the practical struggle against oppression. But queer theory argues a case not only for understanding the nature of contingency but also for attempting, however uncertainly, to go beyond it' (Macwilliam 2002, pp. 387–8). This is clearly grounded in Butler's assertion that, even if queer is a problematic term and tends to fall prey to essentialism, critiquing and thereby expanding the term might 'open up new possibilities for coalitional alliances that do not presume that these constituencies are radically distinct from one another' (Butler 1993a, p. 229).

Queer theology and variant sex/gender

Sean Gill (Gill 1998, p. 176) makes the claim that queer dissolves 'all received conceptualizations of gender and sexuality'. In weighing up this statement, it is important to reflect on the recent theologies which have stemmed from variant gender as well as from variant sexuality – namely, those focusing on transgender and intersex experience. As we saw in the previous chapter, this is a divisive area. It is important to remember that many people with intersex conditions do not consider their states have anything to do with gender identity at all, but are merely specific medical conditions affecting them as a male or as a female. However, given that many people who underwent corrective genital surgery as babies or children do feel that they were assigned to a gender which did not fit them because of prior binary constraints, and given that there is also a small but significant number of intersexed individuals who state that their gender is neither masculine or feminine but liminal or 'third', it is certainly important to consider how queer theologies and intersex theologies might interplay and mutually inform each other. Similarly, although many transgender people feel unambiguously members of their new sex and gender and do not wish to be recognized as anything other than an unremarkable man or woman, others wish to embrace a queerer aspect to their journeys. Some female-to-male transsexuals, for example, have had surgery or hormone therapy to enlarge their penises, but have also chosen to retain their vaginal openings. It is thus possible for them either to penetrate or to be penetrated during sexual intercourse, and to participate in a range of sexual roles and behaviours. This might be understood as a refusal to close off one kind of binary-gendered behaviour in favour of another – thereby inhabiting a liminal identity site which might be deemed queer.

So to what extent are transgender and intersex concerns visible in queer theologies, how far is queer theology even useful for people who identify as transgender or intersex, and can these phenomena be said to be 'part of' queer theology as much as lesbian and gay testimony has been? Victoria S. Kolakowski, a transgender woman, states, 'I find it ... ironic that the most compelling ... argument for gay and lesbian affirmation in the Christian Scriptures may come from teachings about the transgendered eunuchs, because transgendered people are second-class citizens in the Queer Christian community' (Kolakowski 1997, p. 49). The term 'queer' is useful, she suggests, because it recognizes that lesbian, gay, bisexual and transgender people are 'all bound together in a common oppression, because we're all breaking the same social rules' (Kolakowski 1997, p. 49); 'queer' as a catch-all helps to avoid the over-emphasis on the differences between homosexual and transgender concerns which have excluded trans people. It is important that homosexual people recognize that transgender people are not just a tiny minority for whom they should feel sympathy and to whom they should be kind (which is simply patronizing, suggests Kolakowski). It is also necessary that homosexual people do not write transpeople out of their common history by 'taking over' all non-normative figures in the

Christian tradition as proto-gay. The biblical eunuchs are *transgender* ancestors, *not* homosexual ones, says Kolakowski; for gay people to 'appropriate' them is to elide their specific trans-ness (Kolakowski 1997, p. 47; Kolakowski 2000). In contrast to those, like Guest and Walters, who fear that queer is too broad to take sufficient account of the concerns of lesbians or women, Kolakowski believes that it is exactly by emphasizing their similarity to other non-heterosexual or gender typical people, and by using 'queer' as an umbrella term, that transgender persons' specificity *as* transgender can be given space to exist – since, in discouraging partisan identities, there is room for multiplicity, which will include small voices as well as more strident ones. In this account, it is not necessary for everyone to have their own distinct letter in the LGBTI-strand, if there exists a term which inherently has built into it a sense of diversity and open-endedness. Queer might be such a term. The problem comes when Q-for-queer is appropriated to mean something closed, rather than retaining its sense of assertive indeterminacy.

Some writers on transgender in theological perspective have drawn on queer theologies more readily than others. Lewis Reay coins the term 'trancestors' in a 2009 essay identifying (like Kolakowski) eunuchs as the biblical forerunners of today's transgender people, and claims that Jesus himself is a 'trancestor' because he queers gender by overturning normative patriarchal social structures (Reay 2009, p. 157). Reay draws on work by Althaus-Reid, Bohache, Goss, Wilson, West, Mollenkott and others from the queer theological canon and does not acknowledge any potential tension in utilizing queer in the service of transgender. Of course, part of this may be pragmatic: if much of the existing work finding 'trancestors' in biblical texts has happened in a volume called *The Queer Bible Commentary*, then those seeking such figures will probably engage with it whether or not they consider transsexualism and transgender people to be socially queer phenomena.

Transgender people have often been accused of reinscribing unhelpfully binary gender norms. Personal testimonies are not competitions to be recognized as queerer-than-thou; nonetheless, there might be something profoundly queer about statements (like that by Siân Taylder) that, at least for some persons, transgender itself is a *conscious* rejection of one's gender of rearing. To transition gender by *choice* and not because one feels one has to in order to survive might be considered queer in a different way. Taylder says,

> I took to paganism and a romantic notion of the Earth Goddess; the more I wanted to be a woman, the more my religious leanings reflected the eternal feminine. I say 'wanted to be a woman' because that's how it was, plain and simple. I didn't consider myself to have been born in the wrong body, I didn't accuse any divine being of making an almighty mess of things . . . and I'm certainly not going to claim that God intended me to be a woman. I hated being a man, as simple as that; I found it increasingly hard to relate to being a man and so, at the relatively tender age of 27, I decided to 'become' a woman – inasmuch as one can 'become' a woman. I did it because I was actually quite good at it, I did it because it made me feel a lot more comfortable with myself and I did it, believe it or not, . . . as an act of rebellion. (Taylder 2009, pp. 83–4)

Such a journey might be figured as one of *pragmatic transition:* Taylder herself admits that there are aspects of femaleness she will never experience, and that transitioning from one binary gender to the other does little to question the 'prison of gender' per se; nonetheless, she suggests, 'I'm a socially and surgically constructed woman, but as far as I'm concerned that's better than not being a woman at all' (Taylder 2009, p. 84). For Taylder, her self-identification as a traditionalist Roman Catholic (who nonetheless holds decidedly heterodox views such as the belief that Jesus' conception was a lesbian event) is also queer, since, she suggests, both conservative Catholic traditionalists on the one side and radical feminist dissidents on the other, would prefer to remain distinct from each other, rather than meeting and mingling in a figure like herself (Taylder 2009, p. 85). Taylder's self-identification as simultaneously transgender and as someone who has, to some extent, *chosen* her transgender state, might be considered to position her in opposition with those who assert strongly that to be transgender, to have a sense of gender dysphoria, is an involuntary state. The concept of queerness might help to articulate some of the tensions bound up with various lived expressions of transgender, rendering it profoundly apophatic. It is important to note that Taylder herself is sceptical about the necessity for queer theology, though in her case, this stems from an assumption that its major goal would be sexual liberation, and that this can just as well be undertaken by feminist theology (Taylder 2004, p. 368).

It is somewhat contentious that transgendering and transvestism have sometimes been used as metaphors for Christ without any close engagement with the actual lives or experiences of transgender or trans-vestite people (see, for example, Heschel 1997 and McLaughlin 1993). I fear these particular reframings do not go far enough, for while they destabilize binary gender as mapped onto essentialist sex, they still represent *crossing* phenomena rather than truly liminal ones,[9] and do not adequately disrupt sex itself or the ways in which Christ's personhood and divinity have been pinned on it. More interesting and fruitful is Tricia Sheffield's suggestion that queer reading might provide a new way to analyse Christ's body alongside real transgender narratives – even if she repeats Virginia Ramey Mollenkott's problematic trope of considering intersex a kind of transgender, and believes that dominant Christianity has made Christ's body one that 'participates fully in the realm of patri-archy' (Sheffield 2008, p. 243) in a way not entirely justifiable.

For Sheffield, Christ's body as constructed in Chalcedonian belief is 'trans', since it is simultaneously human and divine – and thereby 'poly-morphous' and 'transmutative' – with both natures preserved. (Cheng characterizes this as 'hybridity', as I discuss elsewhere.) Since Christians participate in this Christic body as well as helping to constitute it, the queerness of Christ's body might be a particularly important site of solidarity and hope for transgender people. Sheffield believes that, too often, Christ's two natures as human and divine have only come to bear doctrinally in consideration of his exceptional death and resurrection, not his earthly life prior to death. However, she suggests, more attention could usefully be given to the tensions of experiencing two natures in one body, which Sheffield believes is analogous to the tension of the two 'natures' in transgender people:

Jesus' body must be seen as being fully human and fully divine in his living and not just in his suffering and death. This understanding of life in an ambiguous body can help address the problem of what it means to *live* and perform as a transgendered person when such lives are pathologized by dominant society. (Sheffield 2008, p. 242)

Transgender people, suggests Sheffield, might recognize in this queer Christ a figure whose dual natures are not erased but held together despite their apparent mutual exclusivity (just as transgender people might be said to hold together both a sex and its 'opposite' gender identity, or both a repetition and a rejection of gender as binary). Sheffield's argument is not a perfect one – as noted above, there are plenty of transgender people who do not feel they have two natures which need to be held together, but simply just one rather unusual nature; and many intersexed people reject the notion that their conditions are a matter of sex-gender identity at all. Nonetheless, Sheffield's appeal to transgender testimony is valuable, since it avoids using transgender as an abstracted and unproblematized metaphor without reference to real trans testimony (as Heschel and others have done).

Indeed, for the reasons just outlined, plenty of people with intersex conditions resist alliance with 'queer' political and activist movements. Nonetheless, I have argued elsewhere that there might be a sense in which intersex is *theologically* queer even if it is not politically queer for all people falling under the intersex umbrella. The existence of intersex means that the male–female binary is not a stable or universal one. This presages a further implication: theological norms grounded in binary maleness and femaleness, and masculinity and femininity as superimposed on them, cannot be absolute or incontrovertible. As Althaus-Reid has shown, while heterosexual-capitalist norms might have been convenient bedfellows for Christianity at certain places and times in its history, its conflation with them must be resisted. Only by retelling and reclaiming 'lost' stories about multiple genders, sexes, identities, bodies and lives can God's own lack of annexability be emphasized. Even if individual intersexed or transgender people are happy to fit into an unremarkably binary system of gender – and there are plenty who are not – the significance of their existence is to break down the binary system's irrefutability. This does not mean transgender people or intersexed people are more culpable than any others if they choose to 'reinforce' a binary system of gender: they are caught up in it, just as everyone else is. Indeed, as intersexed and transgender people are statistically more likely to have dealt with violence or abuse because of their 'abnormal' sex-gender configurations, there might be a case for arguing that they have more reason, rather than less, for going along with a two-gender system if they can find comfort and safety within it.

In this sense, drawing on and devising queer theologies might be just as important and fruitful for people with variant sex and gender as for those with 'variant sexuality' (that is, those who are homosexual, bisexual, or something else other than heterosexual). However, at the same time, it is not somehow *more* inherently necessary or fruitful for them than it would be for anyone else. Queer theology resists partisan allegiances.

Queer theology: more than sex

There is another sense in which queer theology and interpretation might be said not to be synonymous with gay theology and interpretation. This is highlighted by the several scholars who have argued that queer theology and biblical criticism are 'about' more than just sex, and are therefore concerned with more than niceties of, or apologetics for, sexual orientation per se. We saw in the previous chapter the way in which Stuart's and Jantzen's reflections on queering death demonstrate Christianity's resistance to annexation by human ideology, and accentuate the Christian assertion that, with God, all things are possible. This profoundly showed that a hermeneutic informed by queer will question and reframe *all* ostensible absolutes and incontrovertibilities, not just those related to heteronormativity specifically. Another more-than-sexual concern of queer theology, the issue of race, ethnicity and colonialism, is explored in more detail in the following chapter. I consider others briefly here.

Ken Stone, in his 2005 exploration of food and sex in queer biblical interpretation, shows overtly that readers bring their own concerns and preoccupations to the Bible: many Christians today, he says, might read Genesis 1 and 2 as being very evidently about human gender relations, and may therefore consider them foundational on issues surrounding marriage and sexuality; but Christians at other points in history have understood these chapters' main thrust as being about food and eating practices, not gender or sex at all. In this kind of account, it is not that the opening chapters of Genesis are 'really' about food rather than sex, or indeed 'really' about sex rather than food, but that *they are simultaneously about both* (and, indeed, about any other concern which may be read into them). There are clear parallels here with reception theory, whereby the interpretation of the influence of a given text – its 'afterlives', as Yvonne Sherwood puts it (Sherwood 2000) – is shown to be as significant as the 'plain text' and its 'original meaning'. The contexts and concerns of a particular reader or group will inevitably colour what they find there (Stone 2005, pp. 24–5), and no single reading is the 'real' or only one:

> In its original context . . . the Yahwist creation account was arguably a story that dealt with several different matters understood to be of great importance, including mortality and immortality, agricultural production and the securing of food, and sexual reproduction. These sets of concerns are not distinct but interrelated. (Stone 2005, p. 43)

Stone's observation has wider import, for queer interpretation is usually not merely attempting to put a sexual 'overlay' on texts (even if queer biblical critics have been accused of trying to justify their own behaviours and lifestyles by making the text say things which it does not). Rather, it is showing that it is simply not possible to find a single monolithic 'meaning' of a given text, full stop. It is for this reason that, despite the fact that some queer people have found themselves unable to remain in a hostile Christian tradition, in fact their detractors also cannot claim the text for their own exclusive use, try as they might. It is never possible to get back to the 'original meaning' of a text; but *even if it were*, this would make the text the poorer, for the layers and subtleties of meaning arising in and through the hermeneutical glosses provided by different groups are its beauty. Matters of sex and sexuality *are* always already present in the text, exactly because they are also always already present in some form in the minds of the readers, just as matters of economics, class and power will be there too (even if they are not always adequately interrogated). The Bible is therefore 'for' and 'about' queer people just as much as it is 'for' and 'about' anyone else. Stone says,

> Confronted with the fact that the Bible is so often utilized, not only by those who tolerate or support gender inequality, but also by those who wish to restrict legitimate sexual pleasure to the context of monogamous heterosexual marriage, we should not conclude that our only alternative to taking up an 'oppositional relation to the norm' is to reject the Bible out of hand. (Stone 2005, p. 109)

I am less happy than Stone to go along with James Barr's image of the Bible as a 'battlefield' on which conflicting traditions 'war', since there is still an implication in this problematically violent metaphor that a single truth will win through and be made incontrovertible in the end and that casualties are inevitable; nonetheless, I am sympathetic to his position that it might be salient actively to seek out deviant texts and 'countertexts' such as the Song of Songs in order to proactively show a multiplicity of voices and positions as co-existing there.

Of course, there will continue to be some texts which are far more easily annexed by a particular group to impose a particular point of view. It is for this reason that re-examining texts 'about' sex by consciously and overtly reading them alongside concerns 'about' other matters such as food, ecology or economics may help the resisting reader to break through layers of oppressive and unyielding interpretation. For example, exploring the possibility that the Hebrew Bible's food laws, particularly in Leviticus, communicate a specific historically located Israelite concern for maintaining clear boundaries (rather than being necessarily applicable to every time and culture), may help a contemporary reader reflect on the prospect that the pronouncements on sex and gender are performing a similar function and may be similarly provisional. Christians today tend to be relatively happy to accept that norms about diet – about which animals (if any) should be eaten, about the manner of food preparation and so on – are culturally relative, even if they are less willing to say that biblical injunctions about gender roles and sexual activity are similarly contingent on cultural context. This could provide a way in to showing that, just as norms and beliefs about diet have shifted, so might sexual and gender norms, and that texts which are commonly used to characterize homosexual activity as fallen or sinful (for instance) are not inherently or unproblematically propounding this perspective but are also, in the ways they are interpreted, demonstrating the concerns brought to the texts by readers.[10] Reflection on an issue such as food, then, precisely because it is often considered *less* important or absolute than sex, might be a useful arena in which to demonstrate how queer and resisting reading occurs.

Conclusion

> Queer theology, though it usually begins with issues of sexuality, is not really 'about' sexuality in the way that gay and lesbian theology is about sexuality. Queer theology is actually about theology. In gay and lesbian theology sexuality interrogated theology; in queer theology, theology interrogates sexuality but from a different place than modern theology has traditionally done, the place of tradition. Queer theology denies the 'truth' of sexuality and hence declares that it is not stable enough to build a theology upon. (Stuart 2003, pp. 102–3)

Stuart's assertion chimes with Walters' earlier remarks, from a non-theological context, on the instability and inadequacy of sexuality alone as a grounding for theory (Walters 1996, p. 859). For Walters, this is because queer reflection on sexuality and sexual practice takes insufficient account of gender particularity; for Stuart, it is because gay and lesbian theologies have focused too specifically and exclusively on sexuality, to the exclusion of asking how queer theology might interrogate other aspects of the Christian tradition – and, in turn, be interrogated by them. Stuart therefore ends up being far more optimistic about the potential of queer theology than Walters was about queer theory several years before. This occurs because of Stuart's strong convictions about theology's *over-againstness* even in its immanence – which means that, although theology must always take account of real bodies, bodily experiences, sexualities and so on, it is also interested in investigating how these are in dialogue with what might figured as God's *transcendence* of human discourse. This is emphatically not to say that God is not intimately involved with human particularities and specificities; but, rather, that God is not limited to being what one human being experiences, or what one group proclaims God to be.

Does queer theology succeed at resisting exclusivity and ghettoization any more than gay and lesbian theologies did? To some extent, this remains to be seen. It is important to note, however, *both* that much queer theology has expressed a commitment to resisting more forms of prescriptive normativity than those concerned solely with sexuality, *and* that queer theology is not unproblematically a 'successor' to or 'replacement' for lesbian and gay theologies. While specifically lesbian and gay theologies continue to value the centrality of personal experience and political identity, queer theology has expressed more suspicion and hesitation about these categories, though never unambiguously or conclusively. This is related to its strong commitment to the deconstruction of gendered and sex identities – which has sometimes been figured as unhelpfully nihilistic, as we will see, but which Stuart asserts is a profoundly Christian phenomenon ('Gender and sexual identities . . . are deconstructed through baptismal incorporation to the body of Christ.' – Stuart 2003, p. 102).

Queer theologies point to the potential for all hegemony and all normativity to be resisted and, in so doing, help to disturb and break down the walls sometimes put up between 'opposite' categories. This strand within queer theologies is a prophetic one, showing that division and exclusion have no place in right relationship. Paradoxically, however, this does not mean that all particularity and specificity need be erased: for queer theologies to advocate amorphousness would indeed be problematic, as some of those who have held to their hard-won political identities have expressed. Nonetheless, by insisting that *all* identity and *all* normativity must be queried, queer theologies are deeply egalitarian and deeply apophatic. They do not allow any one ideology or identity to become paramount, but act as a way to interrogate unproblematized resignation to the power of imperfect structures and norms.

However, queer theologies have not yet found a way to negotiate a resistance to prescriptive identity which does not also seem to risk erasing special protection for those who have felt themselves to be excluded by 'mainstream' theologies. Queer theologies, then, are not synonymous with gay and lesbian theologies – but nor have they superseded them. For this reason, it is likely that there will continue to be a place for lesbian, gay, transgender, bisexual, feminist, womanist, subalternist and other liberationist theologies, at least while queer theology is deemed to be mostly an elite, intellectualist, privileged, theoretical discourse, removed from 'real life'. In some respects, queer theology finds it more difficult to 'sell' itself to those who have strongly valued specifically lesbian and gay theologies than it does to those who have sought to query other matrices of identity – such as class, 'race' and socio-economic status. (We will see in the following chapters the ways in which queer theology's ambiguity is repeated in the ways in which it interacts with issues like 'race'.) Importantly, however, queer's non-linear character and resistance to definition mean that it also need not figure itself as 'better' than identity-based politics and contextual theologies. Its difference from them allows it to act as a mirror for them, helping to show where their commitments remain life-giving and where they might have become stultifying. In return, the continued input into burgeoning queer theologies from those disciplines which have been around the block help to keep it also always questioned, also always curtailed in any tendency toward absolutism or ultimacy. Lesbian and gay theologies, and those who have produced and inhabited them over the years, continue to stand prophetically themselves as testimonies to God's good work in non-heterosexual lives and relationships.

Notes

1 It is notable that many contexts in which the acronym LGB (lesbian, gay, bisexual) would once have been used now feature longer acronyms, appended with T, for 'transgender', I for 'intersex' and Q for 'queer' (or, sometimes, interestingly, 'questioning') – even if, for many people, the T, I and even B are still largely 'invisible', subsumed to lesbian and gay concerns. Such lengthy acronyms may be unwieldy, but this unwieldiness is significant: it highlights the fact that Q-for-queer cannot be said unproblematically to encompass L, G, B, T or any other identity which may come along. It is interesting, though, that 'LGBTQ' (where the Q stands for queer rather than questioning) implies 'queer' is an identity to be ranked with and alongside other identities – whereas many commentators have suggested that queer should in fact be understood as a thoroughgoing rejection of narrowly identity-based politics.

2 Sadly, says Robert E. Goss, homophobia was also prevalent within the US Christian Right of the period, and AIDS was even explicitly figured as God's judgement on a sinful homosexual lifestyle, as by Jerry Falwell. Such discourse, says Goss, 'envisions a postgay world, where homosexuality is eradicated by God. AIDS becomes God's way to rid the world of homosexuality and restore the world to Christian compulsory heterosexuality' (Goss 1993, p. 24).

3 For example, Jeffreys asserts that 'transsexual surgery needs to be understood as a harmful cultural practice and a violation of human rights' and that 'sadomasochism is a practice that eroticizes the dominance and submission that are seen to result from male-dominant heterosexuality' (Jeffreys 2003, pp. 36–7). By caricaturing these phenomena and failing to engage with the complex motives and experiences of those involved with them, however, Jeffreys does not adequately consider the possible overlaps and areas of consonance with the lives of some lesbian women.

4 Jeffreys feels that Butler's work is 'unoriginal' (Jeffreys 2003, p. 39) and that Sedgwick's status as a heterosexual married woman sympathetic to gay men renders her patronizing and less-than-truly queer (Jeffreys 2003, pp. 40–1).

5 Suzanna Danuta Walters reflects at some length on her own ambivalence concerning queer theory in the academy and whether or not it can or should be taught only by people who are themselves lesbian or gay. Although it is right and good that heterosexuals teach about queer theory, she suggests, they should not necessarily *call* themselves queer just because they do so; their life experience and ability to speak into queerness is still very different from that of a non-heterosexual. Walters says, 'Queer . . . lets you off the identity hook the way that gender studies has vis-a-vis women's studies, while cashing in on the trendiness of postmodernism. What are the implications of a queer theory disassociated from a gay and lesbian identity? This is not easy to answer, and I do not want to be claiming a sort

of essentialist . . . idea that insists one must *be* something in order to teach it . . . But the thorny issues of authenticity, experience, and co-optation are not resolved by an assertion that no identity is real. Are we really to evacuate the centrality of experience for the vacuousness of positionality (positionality as indicating the always provisional and temporal nature of political location and action)? While compelling and suggestive, I fear that the concept of positionality tends toward a voluntarism that ignores the multiple, felt, structural determinations on people's everyday existence . . . The deconstruction of identity politics . . . can . . . become the vehicle for co-optation: the radical queer theorist as married heterosexual. It becomes a convenient way to avoid those questions of privilege.' (Walters 1996, pp. 840–1)

6 The initials BDSM variously stand for bondage, domination, sadism and masochism; bondage, discipline, submission and masochism; or other combinations thereof. It incorporates sexual practices and fetish behaviour with a common theme of the sensation of physical pain as sexually pleasurable. Participants usually act out established roles involving conscious inequity in terms of power and control. Participants are often dubbed tops and bottoms, or dom(inant)s and sub(missive)s. Importantly, informed adult consent and 'safe words' are strongly built into BDSM culture, in order to avoid situations where participants are dominated against their will or where they have withdrawn their consent but the other participants have not realized.

7 The characterization of queer as entailing participation in particular sexual practices is itself deeply problematic, whether it is applied to heterosexuals or non-heterosexuals, as Walters makes clear. Queer theory, she says, has tried to move beyond the gendered specificity embedded in 'lesbian' and 'gay' identity; however, this means too much importance is ascribed to sexual practice: 'Those acts themselves are conceived as separate from the genders of the actors who do them, paving the way for a construction of the queer person as someone who performs certain kinds of sexual practices or has certain sorts of desires, regardless of the gender of themselves or their various partners. What we have here is then a new sort of sexual essentialism. Now no longer "known" by some self-defined identity that encompasses sexual acts but perhaps moves beyond and through them, we are now known only by what we do sexually (and not at all by whom we do it with). Again, personal transgression or predilection has metamorphosed into political and theoretical action. Sexual hobbies do not a theory make' (Walters 1996, p. 859).

8 There has been much discussion about whether or not 'the homosexual' can really be said to exist in terms of the Bible, since it is a decidedly twentieth-century category and it may be anachronistic to project it onto the past. In other times and contexts the act of sex between men was not necessarily understood as 'homosexuality', or perceived to render a man 'a homosexual'. As Foucault holds, pinning

the birth of 'homosexuality' to the 1870s, 'Homosexuality appeared as one of the forms of sexuality when it was transposed from the practice of sodomy onto a kind of interior androgyny, a hermaphrodism of the soul. The sodomite had been a temporary aberration; the homosexual was now a species' (Foucault 1990, p. 43) (compare Stone 2006a, p. 207, Fausto-Sterling 2000, pp. 14–15). In particular, some authors argue that the concept of sodomy, now usually understood to mean anal sex, cannot in fact be assumed to be the specific phenomenon to which the biblical writers refer when they mention the 'sin of Sodom'. See, for example, Mark D. Jordan, who argues that 'Sodomy' to mean homosexual penetration is a 'medieval artifact', of which 'no trace' is found before the eleventh century's Peter Damian (Jordan 1997, p. 1). The Church Fathers seem to have understood 'sodomy' to be pride, lasciviousness, blasphemy or licentiousness, not homosexuality specifically. In common with some other contemporary authors, Jordan suggests that the real 'sin of Sodom' is perhaps inhospitality, or a broader sense of 'sexual irregularity', not simply homosexual congress. He says, 'There is no text of the Christian Bible that determines the reading of Sodom as a story about same-sex copulation. On the contrary, there is explicit scriptural evidence that the sin of the Sodomites was some combination of arrogance and ingratitude' (Jordan 1997, p. 32). See also Carden 2004, especially Chapters 5, 6 and 7: Carden argues that it was Christian austerity and suspicion of excess, coupled with *pre-existing* opposition to homosexuality, which eventually led to the present-day construction of sodomy and the assumption that this is what is outlawed in Genesis. Compare Ebrahim's analysis of the genealogy of the Lut story in Islam, whereby Muslim exegetes overplay the Qur'an's condemnation of homosexuality in later texts such as the *hadīth:* 'Rather than the Qur'ān having influenced the *hadīth,* the *hadīth* literature has managed to connect Lot and same-sex sexuality exclusively, thus influencing various interpretations of the Qur'ān' (Ebrahim 1997, p. 99).

9 As Judith Butler has noted, transgender has been figured not only as a crossing from one thing to another, but as 'not exactly a third gender, but a mode of passage between genders, an interstitial and transitional figure of gender that is not reducible to the normative insistence on one or two' (Butler 2004, p. 43). See also Kate Bornstein, *Gender Outlaw;* Bornstein understands her transgender as a patchwork (Bornstein 1994, p. 148), a third kind of gender rather than a crossing from masculinity to femininity.

10 This is a complex process; there are many readers who say something like, 'I'm not homophobic, and I don't *want* the Bible to be condemning homosexuality; but it clearly does, so what can I do?' This seems to demonstrate not a commitment to a particular socio-political perspective on the sex issue itself, but more a perspective on the nature of hermeneutics and what it is and is not legitimate to do with a text, particular a biblical one.

3

Is Queer Theology Inherently
White or Western?

White middle-class lesbians and gay men . . . have produced queer
theory and for the most part their theories make abstractions of us
colored queers . . . They occupy theorizing space, and though their
theories aim to enable and emancipate, they often disempower and
neo-colonize . . . Their theories limit the ways we think about being
queer. (Anzaldúa 1991, p. 251)

With the admittedly worthy goal of queer theory to allow abidingly
affluent white westerners to somehow theorize beyond themselves
– if not beyond their privileges – having at best a turgid relationship
with actual existing diversity, and the reluctance of individuals outside academia to embrace personal queer identities . . . queer theory
is in rather poor shape to deal with the current state of sexual politics.
(Abraham 2007, p. 4.2)

The dominant queer Christian community often imposes its own
codes of conduct upon people of colour and other minorities within
the community. (Cheng 2006a, p. 629)

Many critics have objected to queer theory's supposed Western or
Eurocentric bias, which, they suggest, 'makes it insensitive to the largely
identity-based politics of ethnic communities' (Jagose 1996, p. 99; see
also Smith 1996, p. 280). Judith Butler herself believed, early on, that
the language of queer had been utilized differently and perhaps less

effectively, in non-white communities (Butler 1993b, p. 20). But Eve Kosofsky Sedgwick observed that queer theory's dimensions were not just to do with gender or sexuality and were being used by individuals who recognized their 'race'[1] as queer, or who utilized queer 'to do a new kind of justice to the fractal intricacies of language, skin, migration, state' (Sedgwick 1993, p. 9; cited in Jagose 1996, p. 99). Queer's capacity to include categories of 'race' as well as sex and gender came to be regarded ambivalently: as Suzanna Danuta Walters warns, queer can be just as colour-blind[2] as lesbian and gay studies, negating raced specificity within a conception of queer in which whiteness is naturalized as normative (Walters 1996, pp. 842-3). Importantly, however, although civil rights for LGBT and queer people have often been portrayed analogously with civil rights for black African Americans in particular, for many writers there is still a sense either that minority racial concerns are marginalized and elided within queer discourse, or that it is inevitably not possible to give sufficient weight to multiplicities of raced experience when it is the category of sex/sexuality which is most central to, and characteristic of gathering around, a queer symbolic. As Hall notes,

> Coalitions among individuals whose only commonality is an experience of oppression based on sexual activity are always fragile ones, especially when gender, race and class diversity is obscured temporarily by a political agenda that concentrates on sexual identity alone. (Hall 2003, p. 42)

As we might expect, and as the quotation above from Patrick S. Cheng makes clear, concerns about whiteness, Westernism and colonialism are not limited to secular queer theory but have been (and continue to be) levelled at queer theologies too.

In this chapter I discuss the accusations made by Cheng, Tat-siong Benny Liew and others that Western queer theologians' over-emphasis on issues of sex and sexuality is hegemonic, and fails to engage adequately with questions of ethnicity and 'race'. I discuss accusations that queer theory has mainly been constructed by white gay males and explore the many reasons why this may be problematic. I ask whether

73

queer theology's history means that it can really only queer the *Western* body (as the subtitle of Gerard Loughlin's 2007 edited volume implies). Querying queer theory's 'whiteness' and questioning whether 'queer' is a term that can stand for or be used by people of various ethnic heritages is, as Damien W. Riggs notes, analogous to the project of highlighting the whiteness of feminism and interrogating the raced assumptions in the construction of the term, as took place in the 1970s and 1980s (Riggs 2006).

It will be important to bear in mind throughout this chapter the overlaps and differences between 'queer theology' and 'gay theology' or 'LGBT theology', as explored in the foregoing chapters. Identity-based theologies *may* be more prone to downplaying issues of ethnicity and 'race' if the sexual identity is considered fundamental or primary, whereas queer theologies often more consciously query categories of identity and may have more space for multiple, overlapping and even apparently contradictory matrices of identity. However, this does not mean that queer theology is automatically less problematic: in fact, its resistance to identity categories may itself lead to an unwitting exclusion of non-white people, since questions of ethnicity and 'race' may be dismissed as mere social construction – eliding the painful realities of being a person of colour who is marginalized within LGBT culture.[3]

Theoretical privilege: the question of access to queer theoretical discourse

> What is to keep queer from instantiating the same old exclusions of race and class? Why are so many of the purveyors of queerness white, male (or gay male identified) and economically privileged? (Walters 1996, p. 864)

Hall (2003, p. 89) and others have suggested that the disproportionately large number of white people in Europe and North America who have access to university education, academic and professional jobs, as well as the disproportionately high levels of men at professorial and senior management level, means that the kind of queer discourse being done at graduate level in universities (and thereby published, disseminated and recognized as characteristic of the field) is likely to be strikingly white and male. Queer theory is *theory*, which 'is accessible primarily to those with a university education and . . . references previous intellectual work which itself is class-inflected' (Hall 2003, p. 90). This does not mean it is condemned to be a solely cerebral field, or that its proponents will inevitably be disconnected from political and grass-roots activism, but it does set up a possible disconnect between the work lauded as 'academically' queer and that which is arguably more representative of the concerns and situations of a majority of queer-associated people. It is for this reason, among others, that some lesbians and black homosexual men in the USA have consciously dissociated themselves from the term 'queer', which they understand as 'characteristically white, male, and financially well-off' (Harper 1996, p. 205; cited Hall 2003, p. 92).

Such tensions are also at work within queer theology and queer biblical criticism. In his response to the essays in Ken Stone's edited collection *Queer Commentary and the Hebrew Bible*, Tat-siong Benny Liew says (addressing Stone),

> What you and other contributors to the volume continue to (dis)miss is how various texts elide nation and culture – and thus race and ethnicity – within sexuality and gender. You point out in your essay, after all, that Hosea frames its rhetoric about food and sex within a contest between the (male) fertility God of *Israelites* (Yhwh) and the (male) fertility God of *non-Israelites* (Baal). Likewise, [Lori] Rowlett states that part of the power dynamics within the sadomasochistic play of Samson and Delilah has to do with the fact that Delilah is a foreign woman . . . but she does not go on to scrutinize the implications of this statement . . . Why are these issues of race and ethnicity mentioned in passing rather than que(e)ried in pursuit? (Liew 2001, p. 186)

Liew also believes, for example, that Mona West's reading of AIDS in the USA has been diminished by her lack of engagement with racial and ethnic factors (Liew 2001, p. 189). In general, claims Liew, 'queer racial minorities are pretty much absent in [the] volume . . . Not only do they not write as contributors, they are not even written about' (Liew 2001, p. 189). It is salient to ask, with him, whether this is because of 'a color line within the queer community, a color line within the community of biblical scholars, a divide over sexuality within communities of color, or all of the above' (Liew 2001, p. 189). The claim that queer racial minorities are 'absent' echoes those made by theorists discussing 'racial' and ethnic tensions within queer theory more broadly (see for example Eng and Hom 1998; Ferguson 2003; Johnson and Henderson 2005; Gopinath 2005), but Liew suggests that it is of especial importance for queer theology and biblical criticism.

With its significant legacy of lesbian and gay history, and the ongoing assertion by many people that the queering of normative gender and sex should remain central to its project, it might seem odd to suggest that queer theological interpretation focuses *too much* on issues of sex and sexuality – yet this is exactly what Liew claims. For Liew, rather than 'supplementing' queer readings with those from other genres, 'queer theory should develop a multifocal reading that attends simultaneously to sexuality, gender, class as well as race and ethnicity' (Liew 2001, p. 188). This chimes with Barnard's analysis that in a profoundly race-driven culture[4] 'it is only white queers (and white people in general) who can have the luxury of not naming race, of not naming their own race' (Barnard 2004, pp. 15–16) – that is, whose queer identity can be 'about' sex and sexuality prior to or exclusive of being 'about' class, money, ethnicity or anything else.

Barnard criticizes people who suggest that the real essence of queer community must be an emphasis on sexuality (rather than race or class). Queer, he suggests, is 'especially amenable to an understanding of sexual identity as formatively shaped by . . . race, as opposed to an identity politics model that must premise its generation of subjects on the assumptions of commonalities between "queers" (as it also constructs monolithic communities marked by race, gender and so on)' (Barnard 1999, p. 200). Of course, it might be countered that Barnard's construction of queer is itself too prescriptive, and does not allow queerness to be truly open-ended or to continue to resist definition. While the lack of definition in queer theory might be understood as one of its main weaknesses – rendering it an empty referent, a victim of its own deconstructive bent – this is also one of its strengths, since it makes it much harder to colonize or wield as a weapon by those who purport to be 'right'.

In a more developed version of his argument, Barnard says,

> Queer theory and characterizations of queer theory have often (re)produced the kinds of racial normalizations and exclusions demarcated by queer community and political organizations . . . While the work of people of color is drawn from by queer theorists, it does not itself qualify as queer theory. Queer theory and queer theorists are constructed as white, while queer intellectuals of color are situated at an earlier – less sophisticated, more primitive? – moment that enabled but does not participate in queer theory. (Barnard 2004, pp. 5–6)

Barnard works hard to show that queer theory need not, in fact, be given over wholly to white ideology. In fact, he suggests, queer theory has 'theoretical possibilities' which can allow it to resist exclusionary racialization. For example, queer is good at subverting the assumption that one can tell someone's sex or sexuality just by looking at them, even if it has historically been less good at avoiding the trap of assuming that 'race' is universally evident to the observer (Barnard 2004, p. 9). The risk, in Barnard's analysis (as for Walters and others), is that queer will simply reproduce the racism of white lesbian and gay discourse, just under a trendy new name. The question is whether this is also the case within queer theology.

Along similar lines as Liew and Barnard, Kwok Pui-lan criticizes, from a postcolonial theological perspective, Goss' queer Christology in 2002's *Queering Christ: Beyond Jesus Acted Up*. She says that his vision 'is not inclusive enough for people of color', that he draws too exclusively on white European and North American sources, and that 'he ignores the fact that the sexuality of European and Euro-American men has been much shaped by the colonial impulse and cannot be read in the metropolitan center alone' (Kwok 2005, p. 141). In other words, the concerns of well-fed, well-educated Westerners, even if they face genuine danger and oppression because of their sexuality, will not be the same as those of people – even queer people – whose day-to-day subsistence is less secure, or whose agency and identity have been compromised by their status as those colonized by a foreign empire. Overall, she asserts, white queer theology does not adequately explore the intersections of race, religion and imperialism that have been instrumental in constructing homophobia. She also believes that Elizabeth Stuart's *Religion is a Queer Thing* (Stuart 1997a) is insufficiently candid about the fact that it draws mainly on white queer theologians despite having sited queer theology as having come after, and in some sense been informed by, black and womanist theologies. For Kwok, it is also problematic that Stuart and her contributors do not more explicitly interrogate their own British context with its legacy of colonialism. Kwok suggests that this may be because so many of the queer theologians examined are North American rather than British themselves, but the result is that 'the book gives the erroneous impression that the struggles of gay, lesbian, bisexual, and transgender people are transhistorical and everywhere the same' (Kwok 2005, p. 142).

Kwok is perceptive: there has thus far been insufficient reflection on the need to question specifically British colonialism and neo-colonialism in queer perspective (and, indeed, recent volumes such as Jagessar and Reddie's 2007 *Postcolonial Black British Theology* barely touch on the axis of sexuality). Racial and ethnic tensions have played out differently within Britain and its former colonies than in the melting-pot of the United States. In some respects, racism is less endemic in Britain, with less pronounced economic disparities between white and non-white groups. However, it is important to acknowledge that many of the ongoing tensions surrounding sex and race which are going on in the British churches are directly informed by Britain's colonial past. For example, notes Kwok, the tension within the Church of England and the other Churches of the Anglican Communion surrounding homosexuality is still coloured by nineteenth-century missionary attitudes to African and other indigenous cultures. If the sexual mores of the African Churches (and of some Christians of African and Caribbean descent now living in Britain) are now too conservative for much liberal British and North American taste, this is directly related to the manner in which Victorian British norms were imposed on Africa by missionaries (Kwok 2001, p. 64). In some cases, these attitudes have been assimilated to such an extent that black African Christians claim that homosexuality is a white Western phenomenon, something 'not African' – though the growing visibility of African-based LGBT groups since 2000 means that this argument is beginning to lose its force. However, the Church of England must now deal with the fact that resisting imperialism means giving up authority over non-Western sister communions in the area of sexual morality (for discussion of this and related issues, see Douglas and Kwok 2001). African bishops are making it clear that they will not kow-tow to the Church of England or to the Episcopal Church in the USA, and that to resist Western hegemonic modes of discourse means, as far as they are concerned, resisting liberal attitudes to homosexuality where these are understood as unilateral impositions by the Western churches, or as grounded more in Western hegemonic human rights discourses than in Christianity (Valentine et al 2010, p. 932). The Nigerian Archbishop Peter Akinola said in 2004 in response to the publication of the Windsor Report on the state of the unity of the Anglican Communion in light of the consecration of Bishop Gene Robinson and the blessing of same-sex marriages in Canada,

> A small, economically privileged group of people has sought to sub-vert the Christian faith and impose their new and false doctrine on the wider community of faithful believers . . . Why, throughout the document, is there such a marked contrast between the language used against those who are subverting the faith and that used against those of us, from the Global South, who are trying to bring the church back to the Bible? . . . Where are the words of 'deep regret' for the impact of [the Episcopal Church in the USA]'s actions upon the Global South and our missionary efforts? Where is the language of rebuke for those who are promoting sexual sins as holy and acceptable behaviour? The imbalance is bewildering. (Akinola 2004)

Benjamin Kwashi, the Archbishop of Jos in Nigeria, said in a 2008 BBC documentary about the run-up to the GAFCON (Global Anglican

Future) conference, 'From the mother Church of England, there is the assumption that . . . we can do anything and Africans will automatically come with us, or respect us. I think that is an insult' (Kwashi speaking in Read 2008). Kwashi said that the Western churches ignored the issues really pressing to African Christians, such as AIDS and infant mortality, and did not take their concerns seriously.

All this goes to say that queering theological norms must, as Kwok and the foregoing authors have acknowledged, be about more than bringing sex into the open. To recognize homosexual narratives as legitimate sites of talk about God is an important part of queer theology – but it must also go further, by continually querying hegemonies and defying the notion that resistance to heteronormativity is more central or ultimate than resistance to other kinds of oppression, including those imposed on the Global South by the Global North via systems of capitalist economics. Kwok Pui-lan and the Nigerian archbishops start from very different political, social and theological assumptions, not least in terms of the ways in which they respectively affirm and deny LGBT-identified people: Kwashi's figuring of sexualities equality as less pressing or central for African Christians than AIDS and infant mortality undermines the experiences of many non-heterosexual Christians in Africa, as well as disregarding the close relationship between sexual norms and the transmission of HIV. Nonetheless, the fact that Akinola and Kwashi can loudly and vehemently cite the same kinds of injuries that postcolonial theologians and biblical scholars like Kwok, R. S. Sugirtharajah, Fernando F. Segovia, Joerg Rieger, Mayra Rivera and others have so strikingly exposed over the past decades shows that the interactions between sex, colonialism and global economics are still far-reaching and devastating (see for example Sugirtharajah 2003; Keller, Nausner and Rivera 2004; Rieger 2007; Rivera 2007; Segovia and Sugirtharajah 2009). The ways in which some LGBT groups choose to align themselves with discourses of human rights and so on may be deemed to demonstrate alliance with distinctly Western – and, by association, possibly colonial – mores; for example, Valentine et al comment,

At Lambeth [2008], the LGCM weighted the importance of LGBT rights and the perceived needs of LGBT parishioners above issues of religion or belief by adopting a strategy of visibility. In doing so, it unintentionally reproduced an Anglo-American human rights perspective that its critics suggested ignored the sensitivities of theological arguments and colonial/racist histories within and outside the Anglican Communion. (Valentine et al 2010, pp. 939–40)

Althaus-Reid and Isherwood counter that theology has, so far, been *more* successful at recognizing the racism and class prejudice implicit in its history than it has been at recognizing the extent to which particular (hetero)sexual narratives, narratives of 'sexual domestication' (Althaus-Reid and Isherwood 2007, p. 305), exist at its heart and therefore make theology even more vulnerable in their excision. The question of whether either sexuality or race is elided in queer theological discourse is thus an unsettled and unsettling one. Nonetheless, queering implicates *all* normativity and therefore means that no mossy rock of privilege or historic incontrovertibility can be left unturned. The point stands, then, that these concerns must also continue to speak to one another, with neither sex, class, racial or economic privilege going unchallenged.

To steal a title: sex, race and God

Gay experience tends to get universalized as white, and a lot – probably most – of white gay people don't understand what it is to be African-American and gay. (Comstock 2001, p. 213)

The absence in *Queer Commentary and the Hebrew Bible* of – for example – attempts to explore 'how sexuality can be racialized or ethnicity can be sexualized' (Liew 2001, p. 188), even though the texts 'beg for such an examination' (Liew 2001, p. 189) means, for Liew, that queer biblical interpretation becomes less credible as a discourse. It risks having a one-way relationship with other disciplines,[5] failing to stand over against them and testify to their gaps and shortcomings – which it could do effectively if it took more account of the intersections between race and sex. So even if it is true that secular queer criticism is sometimes unprob-lematically white or Westernized, this does not necessarily render it incapable of dialogue with theology: in fact, theology could be part of what critiques and challenges its Western ethnocentrism or colonialism. Liew seems to be advocating for an integrated queer biblical scholarship which does not consider racial and ethnic issues simply as interesting add-ons to the 'real' queer concerns of sex and sexuality, but in which the multiplicities of raced experience are always already assumed to exist as complicating factors alongside other socio-corporeal particularities. (This is developed in his more recent work alongside a commitment to exploring the ways in which queer criticism might disrupt other kinds of dyadic relationships set out in the biblical narrative: parent/child, friend/ relation and slave/master among them – Liew 2009, pp. 269–70.)

Examples of such readings can be found in work by Irene Monroe, Patrick S. Cheng and others. Monroe discusses the centrality of the Exodus narrative in black African Americans' accounts of their own journey to freedom from slavery, but argues that this liberation narrative 'remains in both gender and sexual captivity' (Monroe 2000, p. 83). She suggests that it has purported to be liberating for *all* black people, but actually relies on a particular narrative about 'endangered black males' which takes insufficient account of the concerns of women, transgender people and homosexuals. Black people may have escaped subjugation by white masters (at least officially), but Monroe suggests that they have simply transferred their loyalty to a dualistic and proscriptive black church which divorces people from their own bodies and sexualities. Lesbians, gay men, transgender people and others who put their con-cerns about sex and gender oppression above what is presented as the more primary concern, black nationalism, may be considered traitors to the cause. She concludes, 'The liberation of black bodies and sexualities using the Exodus motif is as impossible as the liberation of black bodies under the domination of white male supremacy' (Monroe 2000, p. 85) – unless a new emancipatory reading can occur that will take full account of the complexities of gender, sexuality and class experience.

This account is more critical than constructive, and does not itself sketch out what such an emancipatory reading might look like; but her essay highlights the manner in which an over-emphasis on one aspect of oppression can fracture, rather than unite, the very people who are disempowered (Monroe 2000, p. 90). This is echoed by Liew in his exploration of the trope of nationalism in John's Gospel; he asserts, 'Jesus' new family or kinship is one that is neither heterosexually monogamous nor racially-ethnically "monotonous": it is, instead, a transnational or even transworld alliance that exceeds ... the very category of nation' (Liew 2009, p. 277). Transcending nation means transcending 'race' too: not in order to deny it, but in order to recognize that it does not tell the whole truth about a person and that it, too, can become a site of exclusive and destructive clinging to a static identity.

In a response to Monica A. Coleman's essay 'Must I Be Womanist?' (Coleman 2006), which criticizes womanism for its apparent disregard for non-heterosexual female identities, Monroe notes that, as a lesbian black Christian minister, 'I stand in the womanist religious scholarship camp similarly to the way I do in the Black Church – as a sister outsider. As a sister outsider, I am tangentially aligned to these communities with the nagging experience of marginalization, if not complete dispossession' (Monroe 2006, p. 108). Controversially, Monroe suggests that the reason why many womanist scholars have been slow to oppose heteronormativity is that 'their own deep-seated internalized heterosexist beliefs and practices make them black churchmen and theologians "in drag"':

> As 'drag kings,' they disassociate themselves from their female center – Eros and Spirit – to don, in token moments, their usually highly respected, visible, and vital positions within these heteropatriarchal institutions. And it starts with these patriarchal women in both the church and the academy maintaining the status quo by policing queer behaviours. (Monroe 2006, p. 111)

Although Monroe primarily blames Cheryl J. Sanders for womanism's exclusion of queer, she suggests that many queer womanist scholars are also culpable, for in not openly speaking from queer locations they are complicit with the silencing propensity of 'heteronormative universality'. This essay ends on a similarly bleak note, with Monroe noting that many black Christian women scholars have not only left black churches but 'also have abandoned our individual and collective hopes that womanist religious scholarship will lead the way' in combating theologically sanctioned homophobia (Monroe 2006, p. 113).

The kinds of tensions noted by Monroe and Liew are also picked up by Patrick S. Cheng, who, in his commentary on Galatians, notes,

> As a queer person of Asian descent . . . I not only read Galatians as critiquing those right-wing fundamentalist Christians who would impose their own legalistic codes of sexual conduct on us, but I also read Galatians as critiquing the ways in which the dominant queer Christian community often imposes its own codes of conduct upon people of colour and other minorities within the community. (Cheng 2006a, p. 629)

He says that non-white queer people of faith must deal with the racism of their churches, families and LGBT communities as well as the homophobia of society at large, adding another layer of exclusion and marginalization to what already comes simply by virtue of claiming a non-heterosexual identity. Both queer people and people of colour might be understood via the lens of *multiplicity*: they are multiply named (by themselves and others), multiply silenced, multiply oppressed and multiply fragmented (Cheng 2002, pp. 122–3). For example, Cheng says that Asian and Asian-American Christian theologians, themselves a small group, almost universally do not engage with matters of sexuality (though he notes exceptions in Kwok Pui-lan, Chung Hyun Kyung and Rita Nakashima Brock – Cheng 2002, p. 125). This means that queer Asian and Asian-American Christians are 'silenced' by falling between various stools: both queer theologians and Asian-American theologians may purport to speak for them, but in fact, nobody does so adequately.

Critique of the differencing and othering of non-white bodies is a relatively uncommon trope in queer scholarship across the board. Although, says Cheng, 'Those of us who are gay Asian men often search in vain for an affirmation of our penises in a world of "*white* men and *white* male beauty"' (Cheng 2006a: 629), non-white standards of appearance are not always unproblematically dismissed or pathologized; sometimes they may be exoticized (Cheng 2006b, p. 236). Similar issues are explored by Barnard, who notes that South African gay porn videos (made for the US market) often rely on a white actor-subject exoticizing the non-white partner. Sexual interest in black or Latin American men is portrayed in these movies as fetishistic, with a slavering and essentialist emphasis on 'huge black cocks': even where a black man appears in the 'dominant' role of anally penetrating a white man, this still occurs within a white-produced and white-directed movie as a product of white male fantasy and agency (Barnard 2004, pp. 37–40). Alan Han describes a similar situation in Australia, where queer Asian Australians are 'racialized' by queer white men who '[ascribe] them desirability according to the queer white male gaze' and thereby avoid having to face up to ways in which their own queerness and race is *un*racialized and considered the norm from which others differ (Han 2006). In this account, 'desire circulates as capital claimed by queer white men' (Han 2006). Structures of attraction between queer men of different races are considered remarkable enough that Asian men who desire white men are dubbed 'potato queens' and white men who desire Asian men are called 'rice queens'; tellingly, there is no such epithet for desire between two white men (Han 2006).[6] Han suggests that, by and large, queer desire *is* white desire: non-white queer men who go along with the norm of deeming only white men attractive perpetuate the notion of whiteness as capital within queer culture.

Outside-in: ethnicity and otherness

In short, queer people of colour are 'rarely seen for who [they] truly are' (Cheng 2006b, p. 236). They may experience a sense of 'metaphorical homelessness', and so 'experience exclusion from multiple communities' (Cheng 2006b, p. 235; Farajajé-Jones 1993, pp. 141–2). They must also, however, address the extent to which their *own* fear of being recognized as different exacerbates their fracturing as a community:

Many of us are ashamed of our identities and try to conform to the dominant culture by rejecting our ethnic and cultural heritage. In our desire to be accepted, we take on the language, food, dress, spirituality and customs of the dominant community to such a degree that we sometimes ignore or fail to reach out to our LGBT Asian brothers and sisters, even when we are in the same space such as a coffee shop, dance club, bar or church. (Cheng 2006a, p. 629)

So the problems arise *both* because of what Cheng perceives as the hegemony of whiteness within queer culture *and* because of non-white individuals' complex relationships to this dominant discourse. It is unsurprising that he also perceives an alienation of such individuals from their own bodies, since these are such evident signifiers and reminders of pathologized difference (Cheng 2006b, p. 236). He follows Kathy Rudy in reading Galatians' emphasis on freedom from legalism and outmoded patterns of identity as prophesying a Christian community where faith, rather than gender or sexual orientation, is primarily significant (Cheng 2006a, p. 626); this freedom might also extend to ethnic and 'race' identities, as in Galatians 3.28 where it is asserted that, in Christ, there is no longer Jew or Greek. To say that ethnicity entirely ceases to exist or matter might be deemed naïve and might be deemed actually to elide difference and diversity; the point here is that freedom to love also means freedom from the fear of rejection, and freedom to embrace the beauty and legitimacy of one's physical and cultural specificity. Cheng concludes, 'Galatians can speak powerfully to those of us who are of queer Asian descent, as well as other queer Christians of colour. Specifically, it frees us from the yoke of slavery to the implicit codes of conduct that are imposed by the dominant white queer community' (Cheng 2006a, p. 629).

One of Cheng's own survival strategies has been to query the dominant Christian tradition of his parents and American youth, and to seek out the Buddhist spirituality of his more distant ancestors. As someone who is himself 'rooted in the Christian tradition', he identifies this as 'a true recognition of the diversity of the Body of Christ' (Cheng 2006b, p. 236). Ironically, though, this kind of strategy could itself be figured as colonial or assimilationist, since it attempts to understand other faith traditions via a Christian metaphor, through a Christian 'lens', despite the fact that proponents of these faiths may not be happy to be used or integrated in this way. However, Cheng sees the reading of the Bible alongside texts, practices and traditions from the Eastern faiths as a strategy 'that would reflect our experiences as radical outsiders both in terms of our sexualities and our geographies' (Cheng 2002, p. 129).

Queer theology and biblical scholarship elsewhere might also provide means to querying dominant discourses of male beauty, for example. Stuart Macwilliam's recent literary analysis of ideologies of male beauty in the Hebrew Bible concludes that the beauty ascribed to Joseph, David and Absalom represents not the blunt, brawny power one might expect of mythic heroes, but something entirely more complex and vulnerable. Joseph's beauty is described in strikingly feminine terms – in fact, apart from the gendered pronouns, identically to that of his mother Rachel – and may thereby signify 'vulnerability and danger, just as female beauty often does' (Macwilliam 2009, p. 275). David is deemed beautiful in the eyes of God despite his lack of the muscular masculinity of his adversaries Saul and (more excessively, Macwilliam might say more 'camply') Goliath (Macwilliam 2009, p. 278). The beauty of David's son Absalom might be figured as marking him out for tragedy rather than villainy, since his heritage condemns him and he is left 'paying the price of his father's failings' (Macwilliam 2009, p. 285). What all this suggests is that divine endorsement of male beauty cannot be understood as unproblematically cohering with the dominant norms of a culture. Reading such subversions within a biblical text might provide empowerment and esteem to those whose physical appearance is considered less desirable or attractive within a given social group.

Identifying tensions: the black African American case

Black gays and lesbians are going to have to know that the struggle in their own Black community and in the gay community is going to be tough. Because the gay community is primarily white and the Black community is primarily heterosexual, how to be a part of both and each of those is hard, but you have to find a way of struggling as every oppressed group has to find. (Cone interviewed in Comstock 2001, p. 214)

In this next section I focus in more detail on one case, that of black African American Christians who also identify as queer, and the problems they face. These tensions may, in some respects, echo those undergone by queer people of other minority ethnicities in the USA, and of queer black Christians elsewhere. However, they cannot be unproblematically universalized. The experiences of queer African American Christians, queer Asian American Christians, queer African-Caribbean Christians in Britain and so on cannot be conflated. I focus on the black African American case here because it is relatively well-documented, but this is in no way to underplay the importance of existing and emerging work in these and other areas.

There are still relatively few black theologians who also identify openly as queer. Elias Farajajé-Jones was one of the first to do so. He acknowledged, however, that the word 'queer' may carry its own baggage, and in his 1993 essay therefore preferred to characterize his theology as 'in-the-life' – a practice continued by other queer black theologians like Irene Monroe (Monroe 2006, p. 108). This draws on the term's genealogy in African American culture as denoting inclusivity, liberation, broadness and struggle, 'especially for a people continually confronted with suffering and death' (Farajajé-Jones 1993, p. 140). Farajajé-Jones describes how surprised he was to discover, in the late 1970s, that queer black people were 'totally invisible to Black theologians' (Farajajé-Jones 1993, p. 145). At this time he had not heard anti-homosexual sermons preached in church: rather, homosexuality was never mentioned in church at all. But, he suggests, such silence is dangerous if it leads to homosexual people keeping their sexuality a secret: it will ultimately be destructive for the 'in-the-life' black church if closeted gay people enter into heterosexual marriages and have children who grow up seeing their parents fight, or if people with HIV/AIDS are not fully open with their partners about their statuses (Farajajé-Jones 1993, p. 146). Renée L. Hill adds that lesbian voices in womanist theology are similarly necessary, for it is in recognizing how lesbians have been 'disappeared' by womanists that black women can 'find the tools to re-examine and do away with . . . other negative images of Black women . . . In listening to the lesbian voice womanists, heterosexual and lesbian, can learn the importance of self-naming' (Hill 1993, p. 350). Far from being alien to black Christianity, then, for Farajajé-Jones, queer 'in-the-life' theologies are crucial to the continued growth of black churches. 'In-the-life' queer theology can actually help combat the 'Eurocentric interpretation of Christianity' which 'has spawned the homophobia/biphobia/AIDSphobia/sexism/ heterosexism that are quite literally killing us' (Farajajé-Jones 1993, p. 158).

Kelly Brown Douglas, building on work by Hill (1993), Toinette Eugene (1998) and Emilie Townes (1995), seeks to interrogate the lack of engagement with sexuality within much womanist discourse despite the dimension of sexuality within Alice Walker's womanist 'manifesto'.[7] Douglas comments,

> Our history of oppression as Blacks in America has impeded the Black church and community from appropriating the meaning of God's revelation on this matter, and it has also contributed to a slow response to HIV/AIDS – even as it has contributed to a void in womanist theological discourse when it comes to the complexity of Black sexuality. (Douglas 1999, p. 5)

For Douglas, black sexuality has been used as a pawn by white culture. The former has been exploited and manipulated by the latter, in the interests of maintaining white patriarchal hegemony (Douglas 1999, pp. 7, 12). Black people's internalization of this white hegemony leads to their becoming divorced from both their own sexuality and their capacity to critique norms of black sexual discourse (Douglas 1999, p. 68). Black homophobia comes about, in part, because of black people's overcompensation for the role of sexual predators in which they have been cast by white people. The figure of Jesus becomes important, since his body acts as a site of resistance. Black women can appeal to him as a figure of solidarity, and his body is a site of other forms of elided bodily experience – which might include homosexual experience, since, says Douglas, Jesus' life compels his followers to appreciate the sanctity of all human sexuality: sexuality is 'God's passion bursting forth from the human being as an insatiable desire to foster life in all aspects of one's living' (Douglas 1999, p. 120). However, Douglas is criticized by Alistair Kee, who feels her argument is 'circular':

> Douglas is . . . in the position of blaming heterosexism found in the Black church on the heterosexism found in the white community – that community which the Black church condemns for its homosexuality. Clear? . . . In some desperation Douglas ends her book with an appeal to the authority of the teaching of Jesus. But . . . this authority has been seriously undermined by womanist theologians. What did Jesus know of the experience of black women? (Kee 2006, p. 120)

In common with many 'womanist theologians', claims Kee, Douglas' work is not actually theology as such, since it does not engage with the (European) 'sources of Christian theology' (Kee 2006, p. 111) and relies too much on appeals to black women's biography. Note, however, that this is a distinctly historicist reading, and negates the matrix of ongoing revelation. Moreover, Douglas explicitly states that her argument begins 'not with formal "God-talk", but with the reality out of which God-talk . . . emerges. It starts by trying to understand the social-historical context that has shaped Black people's response to sexuality' (Douglas 1999, p. 6).

Gary David Comstock's 2001 series of interviews with twenty gay-affirming male and female African American ministers, several of whom call themselves queer, demonstrates that homophobia in the black churches is by no means universal. Indeed, he says, 'To conclude . . . that Black churches are more homophobic than white churches would be a mistake, even though some Black religious leaders do not hesitate to make that claim' (Comstock 2001, p. 1). Iconic black Christian leaders such as Jesse Jackson have spoken out on gay rights, and statistically, black Christians are only averagely conservative in terms of their attitude to same-sex marriage (Comstock 2001, p. 2).

Nonetheless, for E. Patrick Johnson, writing at the same time as Comstock, the black (African American) church in North America is particularly dualistic, drawing a strong distinction between body and soul and portraying physical sexual urges and desires as 'a symptom of the "sinsick" soul' (Johnson 2001, p. 88; Farajajé-Jones 1993, p. 152). Johnson reads the lifestyles of some black church members as analogously dualistic, since they party hard on Saturday nights but still manage to attend church classes on Sunday mornings (Johnson 2001, p. 89). Ironically, given the strikingly sensual character of much black church worship, any overt sexuality – but particularly homosexuality – is unwelcome in church. Johnson suggests that this is, in part, because the black church is a *place*, which he understands as 'a site scripted and narrativized in advance', rather than a *space* open to multiple, plural interpretations (Johnson 2001, p. 95). He suggests that the 'space' of the nightclub, where physical and spiritual experiences are allowed to intermingle, provides a more open and invitational environment in which black gay men may be 'out' in their sexuality even as they experience communion with those around them. After describing a night in a club where the DJ encouraged festal shouts of thanks to God for safety and mercy over the top of the music playing, he says,

> The 'sacred' place of the church where the rhetorical discourse of the service censures and confines the body is revisioned within the secular space of the nightclub so as to liberate the body . . . The space secularizes the whole notion of the 'shout' or 'holy dance'; in turn, a secularized body is offered in praise of God. (Johnson 2001, p. 105)

He reads this as a reframing of the motifs of black church worship in a secular nightclub space, thereby simultaneously reframing or reinterpreting what the black church preaches about body, soul, sexuality and spirituality, so that the 'utterly perverse club' becomes 'a space where the identities of African American, homosexual, and Christian no longer compete' (Johnson 2001, p. 106). In all this, significantly, there is a clear sense that such queer reframing could not possibly take place *within* the black church itself. The nightclub is the site of salvation, a new and superior spiritual home *beyond* that of the church. Ashon T. Crawley, in dialogue with Johnson's work, seeks to overcome this binary church-versus-club picture. He says,

> If the homophobic, guilt-ridden and self-hating rhetoric of the Black Church is carried in the bones and flesh of the churchgoers, are we somehow freed of theology that we believe once we exit the walls of the church; how is it that the church has become oppositional to the club? . . . The problem with positing that the church is *place* and the club is *space* is that it does not incorporate the church as part and parcel of everyday life but is somehow tangentially related, not integral to identity formation. (Crawley 2008, p. 215)

The dynamics of the nightclub, with its privileging of young, firm, muscle-bound, hyper-masculine bodies, repeat some of the exclusive patterns of church-sanctioned heteronormativity. It is thus naïve, believes Crawley, to present the club as an unambiguously liberating 'solution' to churches' shortcomings (Crawley 2008, p. 216).

Horace Griffin makes a similar point to Johnson, suggesting that black Christians in the USA have gone along with and internalized the white stereotype of black sexuality as dangerous, voracious and in need of salvation (Griffin 2006, p. 56; Douglas 1999, p. 11). One imperative to represent themselves as blamelessly sexually continent and moral, suggests Griffin, may have come from black individuals' rejection of their portrayal by white colonists and slave-owners as lustful, sexually predatory rapists (Griffin 2001, p. 116). This led to the overall devaluing and negation of an holistic embodied black sexuality, as well as more specific injustices such as 'insatiable' black women being held responsible and culpable for their rape by white men (Griffin 2006, p. 57). James H. Cone suggests that white attitudes have led to narrow black views on sexuality in a different way: like Kwok, he suspects that white colonial religion has deeply influenced black African American Christianity. Controversially, Cone suggests that, since it is only relatively recently that black and white Christians have been allowed to worship alongside one another in the United States, black Christians now tend to 'rush over

to the side of white conservatives, because their language is so familiar'
(Cone interviewed in Comstock 2001, p. 210). Cone says,

> Blacks don't have sophisticated theologians to tell them that every-
> thing that *looks* like truth is not *really* the truth. So, when they join the
> community of white conservatives, the only thing they watch out for
> is racism . . . Blacks can discern and are suspicious of racism, but not
> homophobia. We lack a tradition of critical theological inquiry and,
> as a result, don't know what questions to ask. (Cone interviewed in
> Comstock 2001, p. 210)

Since black people in US society are disproportionately likely to be poor
and to live in situations which render them vulnerable and powerless,
they may also be disproportionately attracted by brands of theology
and biblical interpretation which seem to offer them certainty (Cone
interviewed in Comstock 2001, p. 211). More positively, however, Cone
believes that this black tendency to fundamentalist conservatism is less
strong than the more prior black tradition of showing solidarity with
anyone who is oppressed, no matter what group they belong to, and will
not survive long-term.

Along similar lines as Cone, Griffin comments that, where a group of
black Christians fail to acknowledge homosexual desire among their own
number and figure themselves as necessarily heterosexual in opposition
to white lesbians and gays, neither party is made to face up to its prejudice: 'When there is a refusal to acknowledge African American lesbians
and gay men by both groups, white lesbians and gays are not challenged
to confront their racism and black heterosexuals are not forced to deal
with their homophobia' (Griffin 2001, p. 111). Griffin suggests that a significant reason why discussion of homosexuality is discouraged in black
churches stems from a suggestion that it is inappropriate and somehow
treasonous to air one's dirty laundry in public. In other words, drawing
attention to the 'wrongdoing' of a black person (where homosexuality
is considered sinful or degenerate) is seen as selling-out, as collusion
with those who stigmatize or belittle black people (Griffin 2001, p. 112;
Hill 1993, p. 346). It is ironic that, as Griffin notes, black Christians who

reject the biblical interpretation of non-white races as 'cursed to slavery' still tend to accept readings condemning homosexuality, although such injunctions could be understood as time-bound and culturally specific, just as those legitimizing slavery are (Griffin 2006, p. 65; 2001, pp. 113–4). It has been suggested that this is because 'expressing homophobia/biphobia to reaffirm their heterosexual privilege is often the only situation in which many Black Christians feel that they have any form of privilege at all' (Farajajé-Jones 1993, p. 141). E. L. Kornegay Jr concurs,

> In creating black homophobia as a means of silencing what we fear (either the loss of identity, feminization, the threat to black patriarchy, or the admittance of [black identity] being a product of whiteness), we have in fact re-enacted the silence of Ham and placed the yoke of grotesqueness firmly upon our own necks. We have come to sustain our own oppression by *becoming oppressive* as evidenced by our abandonment of multivocality (representing the many) for supravocality (representing the righteous few or the righteous one). (Kornegay 2004, p. 40)

There is also an element of unwillingness to accept certain liberal exegeses of Scripture if these are perceived as 'white' readings and perceived to go against solid, traditional 'black' readings (though, as Griffin notes, and as we saw above, much anti-homosexual feeling among black Africans can be traced to the attitudes brought by white Victorian missionaries – Griffin 2001, p. 114). Kelly Brown Douglas minces no words when she says,

> It is going to take more than 'traditional' (White) biblical scholarship to persuade many in the Black community that homosexuality is not condemned by scripture. This mistrust of White people's handling of the Bible runs too deep for Black people, who, as a result, find it hard to accept White renderings of biblical texts on any matter, including sexuality. (Douglas 1999, p. 192)

Douglas suggests that the 'homophobic understandings handed down in the Black oral/aural tradition' have 'served Black people well' (Douglas 1999, p. 192), so there is no particular incentive to move beyond them – especially if more liberal readings are perceived to be imposed by supercilious white scholars who believe conservative interpretations to be unenlightened and primitive. It is here that the legacy of white colonialism is still inescapably present, and it seems likely that only progressive biblical scholarship done by non-white people will break the deadlock.[8]

Some black lesbians and gay men may be unwilling to join churches of the denominations which are openly welcoming to queer people, such as the Metropolitan Community Church (MCC), because these denominations are also predominantly white, and they may feel they have nothing except their sexuality in common with the other members (Griffin 2006, p. 187). Gay-friendly black churches like Faith Temple, founded in 1982 by James Tinney, and Unity Fellowship Church, are still exceedingly rare (and Unity has been criticized by some for being too male-led – Comstock 2001, p. 70). The result, however, is mainstream black churches where lesbians and gays are tolerated at best – though they must 'stay in a place of inferiority' and be 'willing to play by the rules of listening to statements that homosexuality is sinful and immoral and gays are in need of change' (Griffin 2001, p. 117). It is telling that black female ministers have tended to be less willing to go along with opposition to homosexuals in church congregations, perhaps because they themselves are used to having Scripture wielded against them (Griffin 2001, p. 119).

Kornegay draws on the work of James Evans, who suggests that there are three key elements to understanding the role played by the Bible for black African Americans. These are multivocality, multidimensionality and interpretation (Kornegay 2004, p. 30; cf. Evans 1992, pp. 53–62). Kornegay suggests that the prevalence of homophobia in the black churches demonstrates that these three facets – which might all be recognized as somehow queer – are not, in fact, as present in the African American Christian tradition as they could be. In particular, Kornegay wishes to queer *what is not readily apparent* with regards to black homophobia in the black church and the community' (Kornegay 2004, p. 31). For example, like Griffin, he suggests that the very phenomenon of black homophobia arises for complex reasons including black oppression and the colonial legacy, which have led many black people to over-compensate for the stereotype of voracious sexuality imposed on them by white people. This results in an over-careful, over-conservative attachment to 'normal', continent sexuality, which is often understood to be necessarily heterosexual. However, Kornegay believes that such a strategy fails, because however hard black people may try, their sexuality will always be understood as 'other' and inferior to that of white people, *even if* it is heterosexual and continent. In short, he says,

> Our claims to be wholly identified still suffer from the delusional concepts offered within the idea of heteronormativity. Black hetero-normativity can never be achieved because the 'archetypal Other' is needed to maintain white hegemonic discourse and fuel its concepts of supremacy. Black homosexuality suffers the weight of this unresolved ontological argument of normality for it presupposes the accursed-ness of the 'archetypal Other' which blackness seeks to escape. Black homophobic discourse is created in defense of the perceived ability to proclaim any type of prototypical identity that might be considered righteous, normal, and beyond the constructed 'Other' of blackness. (Kornegay 2004, p. 34)

Black homophobia is therefore not so much to do with homosexuality itself as it is to do with a striving after normality and acceptance and an unwillingness to acknowledge the extent to which black Christian identity has been formed by white supremacist ideology (Kornegay 2004, p. 35). Utilizing queer theory, suggests Kornegay, might help to break down the binaries he claims are so beloved of the African-American church: gay/straight, male/female, sinner/saved and so on. In this way, black Christians might 'destabilize the colonial constructions of our imposed grotesqueness and be truly transformed' (Kornegay 2004, p. 34).

Rereading black history and the Bible queerly might involve strate-gies such as reframing the notion of the 'curse of Ham',[9] by noting that Noah is the one who curses and Canaan is the one who is cursed. It is not Ham's curse at all, but Ham is the one who is made the scapegoat for Noah's transgressions and for failing to conceal them from his brothers.

Kornegay's hint that Ham's transgression may have been a more overtly sexual one chimes with other interpreters' readings; however, I find his suggestion that the character of Ham 'repeats' the character of Eve, becoming 'feminized' through being blamed for Noah's error, less persuasive. It seems to me more likely that Noah curses Ham's son *not* because Ham is 'as a woman' to him, but because Ham himself has undermined Noah's own patriarchal masculinity, either by seeing him in an undignified state or by actually penetrating or otherwise assaulting him (as suggested in, for example, Nissinen 1998, pp. 52–3). If anything, it is *Ham* who renders *Noah* 'feminized'. Kornegay's characterization of the perpetuation of black homophobia as 'sexual/cultural autism' (Kornegay 2004, p. 39) is unhelpful, and ironically risks caricaturing and 'othering' yet another group (that is, those with autistic spectrum disorders)[10] even as Kornegay purports to value a multiplicity of perspectives and interpretations. It is also not clear whether Kornegay fully appreciates that the extent to which queer rejects identity might make it too difficult for black Christians for whom this identity has been central, and who may reject Kornegay's reading that black identity has often been nothing but a reaction to whiteness (Kornegay 2004, p. 44). Letting go of the empowerment attached to black identity may be a step too far, even if Kornegay insists that such clinging to identity is actually what perpetuates both black homophobia and black oppression, and that concern for those Jesus identifies as 'the least' should extend to those marginalized by black people because of their sexuality as well as those marginalized by white people because of their skin colour (Kornegay 2004, p. 45).

Ian Barnard (1999, 2004) attempts to formulate a model of 'queer race', which he understands as 'the ways in which particular racializations are and can be queer, the ways in which queerness is variously racialized and can be racialized differently, a queer race theory, and the enigmatic intersections of these possibilities where race itself becomes/is queer' (Barnard 2004, p. 18). As we saw above, Barnard claims that, in the United States at least, any politics based in gender or sexuality will be 'white-centered', since 'only white people in this society can afford to see their race as unmarked, as an irrelevant or subordinate category of analysis' (Barnard 2004, p. 4). Whichever identity is understood as the basis for community, 'it will, in turn, create and enforce marginalizing prioritizations and exclusions' (Barnard 2004, p. 4). Even if this analysis is too pessimistic, we see this tension played out time and again in the stories of those who recount the difficulty of being recognized (or even recognizing oneself) as simultaneously queer and Christian, queer and black, black and lesbian, and so on. In particular, suggests Barnard, 'Race and sexuality are not two separate axes of identity that cross and overlay in particular subject positions, but rather, ways to circumscribe systems of meaning and understanding that formatively and inherently define each other' (Barnard 1999, p. 200).

In the black British context, little work has been done thus far on interrogating the attitudes toward homosexuality of black Christians. However, in a 1996 essay on the figure of Christ as transformative of black sexuality (rejecting the notion of black bodies as sexually libidinous or excessive), Robert Beckford notes,

The bifocal and multidimensional trajectory of a black sexual Christ (of black socio-political sexual wholeness) means that as well as confronting racist hegemony of black sexual representations we have to confront the role we, as black men, play in the reproduction of less than human representations of black male, female and gay sexuality. We are compelled to engage with black gay men and women in order to gain a greater understanding of how the black messiah sides with those who risk life and limb by asserting their full humanity. (Beckford 1996, p. 20)

Caroline Redfearn, an MCC minister is, at the time of writing, engaged in research into inclusivity and black religious experience in Britain. Redfearn suggests that a suspicion of homosexuality among Christians of Caribbean heritage in Britain may stem from associations between penetration and enslavement, and an unwillingness by black British Christians to repeat what they understand as practices of subjugation. Rape on plantations and slave ships was, she notes, commonly used as a subjugatory tactic by white slave-masters (Redfearn 2007, pp. 116–7). Redfearn's argument is made less persuasive by the fact that, as she admits, 'Current research has not unearthed any accounts of forced rape or consensual sodomy between White slave masters and Black slaves' (Redfearn 2007, pp. 119). However, she suggests that the rape of black slaves may have been omitted from official records because it was not considered significant.

Christology: a site of mediation?

The overlapping of axes of identity has been identified as important in the queer race discussion by Barnard, and it echoes the overlaps with other aspects of identity which we have seen elsewhere. It is exactly here that Christology might come to the fore for Christians, as Douglas' work begins to show: although there are plenty of examples of the ways in which portrayals of Christ's somehow universal body have been exclusionary (particularly when it has been understood as an inherently male, Caucasian, able and implicitly heterosexual-celibate body), there is also a sense in which Christ's symbolic taking-on of all humanity in all its difference means that it is not possible to think of any particular body as superior or prior. Indeed, although it might be significant to remind ourselves that Christ's historic situation as a Jewish man in first-century Palestine makes it overwhelmingly likely that he was ethnically non-white, it is also the case that the very distance and uncertainty surrounding the appearance of Christ's physical body has its own ideological worth. It is simply not possible to say for sure what Jesus looked like, and to do so would tell us no more about his capacity to stand as cipher and exemplar for every person who has ever lived and ever will. It is for this reason that attempts to reconstruct the 'real face of Jesus' (as, for example, by the makers of the 2001 BBC series 'Son of God') are ultimately red herrings. It is important to recognize Christ's historic non-whiteness inasmuch as it is proof positive that whiteness is not synonymous with perfect, legitimate bodiliness; but beyond that, Christ's skin colour is only as significant and as insignificant as his assumed maleness. As Thomas Bohache notes, even for the early black liberation theologian James H. Cone, 'the question is not "*Was* Jesus black?" but "Why *couldn't* Jesus be black?"' (Bohache 2008, p. 70). Christ 'is who he was' historically (Bohache 2008, p. 70; Cone 1989, p. 119) – that is, not black in the same way that African American persons are black – but, since he identifies with poor and marginalized people, he also 'is who he is', and can be figured metaphorically as black wherever black people are poor and marginalized (Cone 1997, pp. 110, 112–3, 125). Cone comments that Christ is 'black' not because black people need to feel psychologically endorsed by him, but because it is where people are poor and despised that Christ enters the human world.

Patrick S. Cheng attempts to construct a queer Christology which is grounded particularly in his identity as an Asian Pacific American. Although Asian, Asian Pacific American and queer Christologies are all useful to an extent, Cheng feels that 'none of these contemporary christologies is adequate because each represents only a *portion* of the QAPA [Queer Asian Pacific American] experience' (Cheng 2001, p. 12). Asian Christologies speak particularly to ethnic suffering, Asian Pacific American theologies to the strengths of ethnic community, and queer Christologies to marginal sexuality, but each tends to exclude the others. Cheng appeals to the story in John's Gospel about the cruci-fied Christ instructing John and Mary to recognize each other as a new family, saying,

> For me, this story is at the core of a QAPA christology because it reveals to us the Jesus Christ who, in the midst of suffering, brings together ethnic community and marginalized sexuality . . . First, the theme of *suffering* is present in the physical, psychological, and emo-tional pain of Jesus in being nailed to the cross. Second, the theme of *ethnic community* is present in Mary, who – as Jesus' mother – repre-sents the biological and cultural roots of Jesus of Nazareth. Third, the theme of *marginalized sexuality* is present in the Beloved Disciple, who is described by the Fourth Evangelist as the one 'whom Jesus loved' . . . Thus, at the moment of his greatest suffering, Jesus cre-ates a new 'family' that is a hybrid of both his ethnic identity and his marginalized sexuality. (Cheng 2001, p. 19)

In Christ, therefore, neither sexual nor racial identity is primal any longer, and the crucified Christ represents God's ability (and humans' ability in God) to work beyond suffering and oppression, coming to a radical place of restored relationship (Cheng 2001, p. 21). Cheng describes his first encounter with other Queer Asian Pacific Americans as an extremely positive one, since he did not have to hide or apologize for any aspect of his identity. However natural such preference for like-ness might be, though, it suggests that queer theology does not always go far enough to problematize the reasons why we cling to identity in this way at all.

For Bohache, Liew, Cheng and others, the 'queerness' of non-white Christologies is actually analogous with the 'queerness' of specifically 'sexual', that is non-heteronormative, Christologies. Importantly, Bohache notes the objections of black women scholars (including Douglas) that black Christology has sometimes focused too exclusively on questions of race to the omission of questions of gender, class and sexuality (Bohache 2008, p. 74; see also Douglas 1994 and Douglas 1999). Concomitantly, however, black womanists have themselves not always addressed economic justice and heterosexism (Bohache 2008, p. 137; Douglas 1994, pp. 101ff; Hill 1993, p. 346). Similarly, Mary Daly criticizes Cone himself for having produced a black God and Christ who are 'merely the same patriarchs after a pigmentation operation – their behavior unaltered' (Daly 1986, p. 25), since – she believes – Cone has not sufficiently critiqued extra-racial dimensions of oppression, includ-ing sexual and gendered ones. We therefore see the same spirals of tensions echoed here as in other areas: is it possible for more than one identity to be simultaneously 'primary', or to be simultaneously valued and endorsed by a group? Are 'black, Christian, woman' three separate (and competing) facets, or is 'black Christian woman' a single identity around which community and political activity may coalesce? Is 'queer black Christian woman' even a concept that can be entertained? (Com-pare, for example, Khan 2010 for similar questions concerning matrices of queer Muslim identity.) Like 'sexual' queer Christology, non-white Christologies may hold as paramount the hermeneutic of suspicion, not taking on wholesale the assumptions or teachings about Christ evident in white Western culture, but interrogating them in the present and his-torical context of a particular society or ethnic group. As Bohache notes,

CONTROVERSIES IN QUEER THEOLOGY

the postcolonialist work of scholars like R. S. Sugirtharajah has been important in reminding us 'that the true context of Asian Christology is Christ's importation by colonists from outside Asian culture . . . These bearers of Christ were in many cases opposed to Asian culture' (Bohache 2008, pp. 76–7; see also for example Sugirtharajah 2003, Kwok 2005, Chung 1990).

For Tat-siong Benny Liew, Jesus' body (especially in the Gospel of John) is a site of multiple intermingling and crossings-over of identity. He says,

> Jesus' cross-dressing body in John is a truly porous and polysemic site/sight in which a collection or a range of gender meanings converge, collude, collide, and compete with each other . . . John's cross-dressing Jesus shows that a so-called 'core' is but a(n significant) effect of bodily acts . . . What this effects is not a premature celebration of freedom that one can be anything that one wants to be but a call to analyze and perhaps even challenge the discursive and material forces that discipline one's acts, practices, and identities. (Liew 2009, p. 260)

As a result, Christ can stand as a place of co-valence in which sexual and 'raced' identity are not exclusive of one another, but rather are mutually informing and mutually challenging. Liew hints that such non-fixity of identity, such crossing of matrices of race, sexuality, class and so on, may come more easily to non-white queer people. He suggests, after Linda Schlossberg, that coming out as queer may be more of a white concern because white people are so used to being 'unmarked' and 'invisible' – the 'white neutral' which considers only those of other ethnicities to be 'coloured' – that anything which alters this is considered a huge shift of identity. By contrast, people of colour are well used to the way in which their perceived race can lead to their exclusion from privileged social sites: the visibility of queer sexuality is perhaps therefore less of a shock to them, and they may be more comfortable existing as 'wily' queers rather than explicitly 'out' ones (Liew 2009, p. 267).

Likewise, the queer-indecent Christology of Marcella Althaus-Reid melds sexual, ethnic, postcolonial and economic concerns in its suspicious treatment of the religion brought by the *conquistadors* to Latin America. For Althaus-Reid, Christ as understood through the lens of S/M and leather fetishism is a 'bottom', a suffering servant who does not exploit his power (Althaus-Reid 2000, p. 160). This is deeply ambiguous, especially since Christianity has a problematic history of reinscribing submission and quietism as goods onto those of its children who are already cowed and disadvantaged. It may be for this reason that Althaus-Reid does not make more of the figure of Christ, preferring to focus instead on the numerous queer Mariologies expressed in the folk religion of Latin America (which may be less problematic than the sanitized, asexualized images of Mary sanctioned by the Roman Catholic authorities – 2000, pp. 39–40, 57). Even so, Christ is not an obsolete figure in terms of narratives of queer race; she notes,

> On a positive note, our theological dealings with Jesus are queer, of an indecent nature, precisely because Jesus' gender performance is blurred with a sexuality which depends on a subtle divinity consciousness (his own, and that projected onto him by friends, family, enemies and admirers) and on location. These locations are not the historical ones, but the narrative ones. (Althaus-Reid 2000, p. 114)

In other words, Jesus exists precisely to be a blank sheet onto which we can write, project and reinscribe our longings and fears. The narrative locations in which Christ comes to find himself are multiple. This does not undermine but rather expands his historic specificity. The ultimate palimpsest, Jesus gives up and gives over the authorship of his signification into the hands of others. A queer understanding of Jesus makes clear that colonial authority is to be resisted, since the latter elides multiplicities of stories. Rather, difference and diversity are written and overwritten here, the parchment becoming denser and darker as spiralling narratives feed off and subvert one another.

It is for this reason that postcolonial theologies might prove to be a particularly useful tool for weaving a creative and mutually enhancing tapestry where sex is the warp and race the weft. Thus far, postcolonial theologies have been more directly influential on non-white theologians – many of whom have experienced European colonialism either at first hand or via the experiences of parents and grandparents, and who continue to expose the enslaving effect that capitalist economics has on the Global South – than on non-heterosexual ones. (For a useful overview of some innovative developments in postcolonial theology, see Keller, Nausner and Rivera 2004; for foundational texts in postcolonial theology and biblical interpretation see Chung 1990, Kwok 2005 and Sugirtharajah 2003; and, for a creative and stimulating postcolonial reinterpretation of the doctrine of divine transcendence, see Rivera 2007.) Rivera and others pick up on Gloria Anzaldúa's assertion that the 'borderlands' between different cultures and ruling norms always consist in racial, sexual and spiritual liminalities (Rivera 2004, p. 187; cf. Anzaldúa 1991, p. 25).

Conclusion

We can see, then, that questions of sex and questions of race are always inextricably related. Queer theologies that do not recognize this are naïve. The 'Western body' in the subtitle of Loughlin's 2007 book refers, it seems to me, to the Western *Church* – in distinction from the Eastern Orthodox tradition – and the influences of and on Roman Catholic and Anglican theologies in particular. To 'rethink the Western body' should not be assumed to mean that predominantly white, predominantly wealthy bodies are the only ones on whom queer theological thinking can come to bear. Rather, the point is that the theologies of the Western Churches continue to build and shape *Western* human bodies – that is, those whose contexts and cultures have been shaped in large part by Western Christianity, and which, in turn, build and constitute this particular portion of the Body of Christ. 'Western' human bodies have not been similarly influenced by the Eastern Orthodox tradition: the Orthodox Churches might engage in their own queer theologizing, though this has not yet occurred to my knowledge. It is therefore something of a red herring to suppose that 'Western' Christianity, including its queer theologies, can have no conversation with (or will be inherently repressive of) those whose origins are in countries which have not had Christianity as a major or dominant historical religious tradition, or which experienced Christianity first of all as a religion of empire. The 'West' in this context contrasts not with the 'East' of the Middle East or East Asia, but the 'East' of the Eurasian Orthodox Churches.[11]

Queer theology is not inherently white and Western – that is, it is not condemned to be white and Western, nor to exclude non-white cultures – but it must recognize that its genealogy in Western lesbian, gay and feminist theologies (and, most significantly, in Western Christianity) may prejudice it in this direction. It is therefore also possible that there will always be people who do not feel able to place themselves under its umbrella because of uncomfortable associations with elements of its history. But the fact that sexually and racially marginalized people may use similar language and imagery in figuring their experiences – that of wilderness, diaspora or exile, or discovering their 'somebodiness' (Bohache 2008, p. 135), for example – does not mean that they would unproblematically recognize one another as allies or some kind of queer cohort. Queer theology is therefore neither unproblematically in thrall to the West nor unproblematically a programme of liberation from Western modes of discourse. Just as postcolonial theologies help to refigure the past and present not just for former colonies but also for their former metropolises (since *both* colonizer and colonized must consider what it means to exist 'after colonialism', that is in a world which has colonialism as part of its history), so queer theologies help refigure dichotomies of privilege, class and social background.

Nonetheless, it seems likely that for the conversation between race and queer to progress productively, it will necessitate the kind of community work described by Renée L. Hill, whereby no one facet of oppression should be deemed to 'trump' another kind. Hill says,

> If someone really wants to connect as a gay man or a lesbian to the broader lesbian and gay community, you have to be concerned about racism and classism, and folks aren't doing that very well. They have not been able to do a simultaneous struggle working on different oppressions and identities. That's why we always have oppression,

because people can't root it out and see its multiple roots. (Hill interviewed in Comstock 2001, p. 196)

For example, Hill says that it is not good enough for her to claim oppression as a black lesbian without also interrogating the ways in which her middle-class status renders her privileged.

In short, it seems likely that ongoing dialogue between queer theology and ethnicity/race will be deeply pragmatic, simultaneously querying regulatory categories of identity *and* acknowledging that exposing the 'unreality' of race may be a luxury afforded mainly to those who are not oppressed and struggling under its all-too-real reaches. Gloria Anzaldúa warned two decades ago,

Queer is used as a false unifying umbrella which all 'queers' of all races, ethnicities and classes are shoved under. At times we need this umbrella to solidify our ranks against outsiders. But even when we seek shelter under it we must not forget that it homogenizes, erases our differences. (Anzaldúa 1991, p. 250)

To this end, it may be useful to be mindful of *pragmatic* categories: Judith Butler's 'provisional unities' come to mind, as does Serene Jones' 'strategic essentialism'. Butler suggests that gatherings around particular identities should emerge organically and temporarily in response to the course of events, rather than '[setting] up an exclusionary norm of solidarity at the level of identity that rules out the possibility of a set of actions which disrupt the very borders of identity concepts' (Butler 1990, p. 15). Thus it might be legitimate, and important, to identify as a queer black Christian in order to highlight the special problems and exclusions faced by queer people and by black people, even as one seeks to undermine the efficacy or permanence of identity-based politics. Jones uses the language of strategic essentialism, noting that it can be read as a 'pragmatically compelling' third way between gender essentialism (which seems to repeat unhelpful stereotypes) and gender constructivism (which sometimes seems divorced from real situations and political identities). She says,

This in-between position applauds constructivist critiques of gender but feels nervous about giving up universals (or essences) altogether. While its proponents respect the hard questions posed by the debate, they believe that the divide between essentialists and constructivists fails to capture the complexity of daily experience. (Jones 2000, p. 44)

The strategic essentialist feminist is interested in praxis, in the outworkings in real women's lives of questions about women's emancipation. Strategic essentialism acknowledges that this web of gender, sex, class, race and so on is really the way things are, and is the setting in which real people do their theology and play out their lives – but without following this to the conclusion that this is the *only* way for things to be, that there is no alternative. Could this kind of third way be useful for queer theologians who are also mindful of the fact that issues of race and class continue to be real felt concerns by people who are negotiating less privileged positions? Perhaps; but for Jones, strategic essentialism involves making strong normative judgements (Jones 2000, p. 45), since rejecting old paradigms and ideas about the nature of women necessitates adopting new ones. This may render a strategic-essentialist schema too prescriptive to be embraced by content-shy queer theorists (and Ellen T. Armour, for one, is unconvinced that it could work as Jones proposes).[12] However, Jones concludes by saying that 'strategic essentials are constructed anew for each generation of activists and new terrain of struggle' (Jones 2000, pp. 47-8). For this reason, even the new normativities (those demanding equality and justice rather than perpetuating tired hierarchies) are repeatedly called into question rather than being allowed to stand as 'self-evident' or incontrovertible. Jones believes that feminist theology, and in fact theology in general, is inherently about wanting to make normative claims: that all people are loved by God; that embodiment is good; that violence and injustice 'fundamentally contradict God's will for humanity in creation' (Jones 2000, p. 51). I have not come across a single queer theologian who would want to contradict these statements – so it seems that a Jones-type strategic essentialism, holding embodied realities at the centre even as it seeks to question and resist social norms that reinscribe violence and oppression, might be a productive language for queer theologians to explore.

Randy Miller says,

> Perhaps the distinctive witness that African American lesbians and gay men of faith have to offer is simply that such living is possible . . . Maybe the gift we have to give is our unique perspective as those who, of necessity, live within the context of at least two experiences of oppression and still make it to freedom. (Miller 1997, p. 235)

This 'twoness' is picked up in discussions of hybridity. In a 2010 essay on models of sin and grace for LGBT people, Patrick S. Cheng suggests that a particularly useful image for negotiating matrices of sexuality and 'race' can be found in the notion of the hybrid Christ. Christ's 'hybridity' arises from his simultaneous existence as divine and human (as affirmed in the Athanasian Creed), and means for Cheng that 'singularity' is a very dubious good indeed. He says,

> Sin – what opposes the Hybrid Christ – is singularity or the failure to recognize the reality of existing in multiple worlds. For example, sin is failing to recognize the complex reality of multiple identities within a single person, which in turn silences many experiences of those individuals who exist at the intersections of race, gender, sexual orientation, age, and other categories. As postcolonial theorists have pointed out, this kind of singularity (for example, defining the 'gay' community solely in terms of sexual orientation and not taking race into account) results in the creation of a number of 'others' who are never fully part of the larger community and thus feel like perpetual outsiders. (Cheng 2010a, pp. 114–5)

Hybridity in postcolonial thought is most often grounded in the concept as developed by Homi K. Bhabha (1994), who argues that colonizer and colonized cannot be unproblematically polarized. In fact, both colonizer and colonized are changed in their encounter, within a liminal or third space between their positionalities. Hybridization, for Bhabha, involves *negotiation,* both in the sense of parleying and bargaining among those from differing conceptual sites (one of whom may be ostensibly more powerful than the other), and in the sense of discursivity which takes place *between* two places and has to navigate these uncharted waters:

> Hybridity is the revaluation of the assumption of colonial identity through the repetition of discriminatory identity effects. It displays the necessary deformation and displacement of all sites of discrimination and domination. It unsettles the mimetic or narcissistic demands of colonial power but reimplicates its identifications in strategies of subversion that turn the gaze of the discriminated back upon the eye of power. For the colonial hybrid is the articulation of the ambivalent space where the rite of power is enacted on the site of desire, making its objects at once disciplinary and disseminatory. (Bhabha 1994, p. 112)

Of course, the concept of hybridity within postcolonial discourse raises its own problems, since, notes Richard A. Horsley, in some accounts it 'fails to distinguish the different ways in which colonial power affected peoples in different contexts according to various factors such as class, gender and race' (Horsley 2003, p. 306). Citing Aijaz Ahmad, Horsley says, 'Hybridity appears as a postmodernist "carnivalesque collapse and play of identities," possible mainly for "the migrant intellectual" who "thus disperses with a sense of place, of belonging, of some stable commitment to one's class or gender or nation"' (Horsley 2003, p. 306; cf. Ahmad 1995, pp. 13–14). Justly or not, this criticism has been levelled at Bhabha in particular. Hybridity may also fail adequately to interrogate the more sinister aspects of the ostensibly multiculturalist transnational corporations who also appeal to it as a good (Horsley 2003, p. 307). Moreover, notes Laura E. Donaldson, the advocating of 'mixedness' as a good in the postcolonial context often benefits colonizers more than those colonized, with the colonized peoples eventually becoming lost in the mainstream into which they have become subsumed (biologically, culturally or otherwise). Mixedness and hybridity therefore risk assimilationism, with the conquered genealogies, stories and treasures becoming lost (Donaldson 2006, p. 164).

Nonetheless, hybridity also has built into it an awareness of colonial authority and the powers of naming and representation (Kwok 2005, p. 170). It thereby has the potential to continue to query and resist the either/or characterization of races and cultures that sometimes underlies both imperialist colonization and its rejection. Since it always remains aware of the inequities of power and culture coming to the table, post-colonial hybridity in fact allows for a more sophisticated rejection of *both* binary difference *and* its unproblematized opposite, amorphous assimilationism. Kwok appeals to Rita Nakashima Brock's concept of 'interstitial integrity' (Brock 1997) to speak of the fruitful space between difference and assimilation. Tracy Sayuki Tiemeyer comments that this interstitial integrity allows for 'complex, multifaceted identities and communities of struggle and salvation . . . The interstitial self . . . is the self of the strong and connective spaces between worlds. Interstitial integrity is not mere survival: it is a flourishing within these dis/junctures of worlds' (Tiemeyer 2006, p. 230). In this sense, as I have already hinted, we might trace close affinities between postcolonial theology and queer theology, especially given Sharon A. Bong's observation that 'theologizing in a "post-colonial" context . . . involves "strange encounters"' (Bong 2006, p. 498).

Indeed, for Cheng, if singularity is sin for queer people, then hybridity is grace, since it is a Hybrid Christ in whom Christians participate. Importantly, hybridity is not a magic bullet: it carries its own problems, as we have seen; and, moreover, notes Cheng, 'Jesus Christ is "in-both" worlds . . . and yet he is also "in-between" both worlds . . . Although this can be a painful experience, metaphorically speaking, Jesus has no place to lay down his head' (Cheng 2010a, p. 114). Those who negotiate dual or multiple identities may therefore find themselves existing in a kind of limbo where *no* one identity 'fits'. This difficulty and placelessness cannot easily be resolved; however, Cheng's suggestion that hybridity and placelessness themselves are divine qualities may be, for some queer Christians, a source of some comfort and hope.

Notes

1 Many scholars believe that race is an arbitrary category which is based more in social assignment of significance to certain characteristics than to actual differences in biology: 'There are no generic races precisely because "race" is a metaphor, a social construct, a human invention whose criteria for differentiation are neither universal nor fixed but have always been used to manage difference' (Gibel Mevorach 2007, pp. 239–40);

> The concept of race does not hold up as a scientifically viable way of grouping human beings. It does not identify a cluster of genes at the biological level that could serve to sever human beings into neatly separable groups. It does not help identify discrete packages of color and morphology that could separate groups. It is muddled and asymmetrical in its groupings of individuals by ancestry. (Warnke 2001, p. 126)

For example, people may be considered 'black' on the basis that they possess a certain kind of hair or nose, but this categorization works only because these types of hair and nose have already been designated 'black'. The use of inverted commas around 'race' is designed to highlight and problematize its use as a term.

2 This phrase is commonly used to refer to people who claim not to notice someone's race or the colour of their skin, often carrying a negative sense (that is implying that the person in question is naïve, or insufficiently aware of matrices of racial identity). Critics of 'colour-blind' politics and legislation suggest that it is a way to avoid engaging with real and ongoing matrices of exclusion and inequality linked to ethnicity. For more on this argument, see Bonilla-Silva 2006; Ansell 2006; and Simpson 2008. 'Colour-blind' also, of course, refers literally to those who are unable to distinguish between certain colours, commonly red and green. For this reason, using 'colour-blind' in a metaphorical sense might be considered as problematic as using other disabilities as metaphors for absence or lack. I utilize it here because it is ubiquitous in the critical literature.

3 I am grateful to Patrick Cheng for a conversation in which he helped me to clarify my thinking on this issue.

4 Barnard is originally from South Africa and much of his work draws on this setting with its specific history of apartheid, but he lives and works in the USA and interrogates the areas of accord and dissent between how queer theory is understood and disseminated in these and other 'Western' countries.

5 Liew says that, although queer theologians and biblical scholars may draw heavily on secular queer theory, such borrowing seldom if ever happens the other way: 'We use queer theory to cultivate our sensibilities and then apply what is applicable to challenge "conventional" readings of Scripture, yet we seldom challenge any conceptual emphasis that we find in a prevailing theory . . . As biblical

scholars, we must not only read the Bible with the help of queer theory, but we must also use our reading of the Bible to interrogate, or even transform queer theory' (Liew 2001, p. 185).

6 However, Cheng states that the term 'sticky rice' is used to refer to queer Asian Pacific Americans who desire others of the same heritage (Cheng 2001, p. 9).

7 In this account, being womanist is linked to being 'womanish' as a young girl – that is, wanting to know and speak about things that are beyond one's supposed developmental stage. It has connotations of precociousness and rebellion. Walker appeals to 'the black folk expression of mothers to female children, "You acting womanish," i.e. like a woman ... usually referring to outrageous, audacious, courageous, or *willful* behavior. Wanting to know more and in greater depth than is considered "good" for one.' Importantly, although this aspect is often elided, Walker also notes that a womanist 'loves other women sexually and/ or nonsexually. Appreciates and prefers women's culture ... [and] sometimes loves individual men, sexually and/or nonsexually ... Committed to survival and wholeness of entire people, male and female' (Walker 1983, pp. xi–xii).

8 As Deryn Guest explains, the situation is complicated by the fact that 'entrenched conservative views may be the result of white influence rather than an indigenous Black perspective ... Blacks who were separated from white evangelicals did not develop such a literal mode of scriptural interpretation' (Guest 2005, p. 193; see also Comstock 2001, pp. 208–11).

9 This refers to the story in Genesis 9.20–7 where Ham 'uncovers the nakedness' of his father Noah after the latter has become drunk, and tells Shem and Japheth about it. When Noah finds out what has happened, he curses Ham's son Canaan and says thereafter that he will be a servant to his brothers. Historically, many interpreters have asserted that this explains and/or justifies the subjugation of 'Hamitic' black people to white rulers, since black people (in some accounts, those descended from people of North African origin; in others, anyone with black African heritage) are said to be descended from Ham and Canaan. See, for example, Origen's sixteenth homily on Genesis: 'For the Egyptians are prone to a degenerate life and quickly sink to every slavery of the vices. Look at the origin of the race and you will discover that their father Cham [that is, Ham], who had laughed at his father's nakedness, deserved a judgment of this kind, that his son Chanaan [Canaan] should be a servant to his brothers, in which case the condition of bondage would prove the wickedness of his conduct. Not without merit, therefore, does the discolored posterity imitate the ignobility of the race' (Origen in Heine 1982, p. 215). For an overview of historical Jewish, Christian and Muslim texts about the curse of Ham, see Goldenberg 2003.

10 For a recent and deeply moving theological account of profound learning disabilities and of the challenges of living with a family member who has severe autism, see Gillibrand 2010.

11 I am well aware that this distinction is in itself problematic and to some extent arbitrary, particularly since some of the early texts commonly read as somehow proto-queer date from an era before the eleventh-century Great Schism between Rome and Constantinople.

12 Reviewing Jones' book, Armour says, 'It is not clear to me that strategic essences are either as permanent or as malleable as they would need to be to work as Jones envisions. Insofar as a strategic essence is flexible, what grants it the onto-logical status that Jones argues it needs to ground normative claims? What will prevent a strategic essence from becoming frozen in some particular evolutionary stage?' (Armour 2003, p. 214)

4

Is the Bible Queer?

Why bother with the Bible at all? . . . The Bible is the creation of the early church, a church whose patriarchal assumptions we no longer share. It can therefore have little authority for us. (Stuart 1997a, p. 45)

The Christian tradition is often figured as inherently anti-queer. In considering the accuracy of this picture, however, we might just as pertinently ask whether the discourse of queer theory is inherently anti-Christian. As Mark D. Jordan notes from the North American context, 'The ubiquity of religious discourse about sexuality makes its relative absence in queer theory all the more puzzling' (Jordan 2007a, p. 564). Jordan's own suggestion is that secular queer theory *cannot* fully engage with religion, because to do so would be to concede that religion seems to have a certain unstoppable power to direct and construct particular notions of sex and gender – even when individuals may have rejected the authority of the Bible, clergy or other religious leaders over their lives and choices. Acknowledging religion's undeniable power, suggests Jordan, 'might show that [queer] theory was so much revolutionary fantasy'; entering into dialogue with religious discourses might lead to a loss of agency for secular queer theorists, since the former might once again 'reinscribe a religious power to make and manage desire' (Jordan 2007a, p. 564), which those who have historically been oppressed by Christianity have only recently managed to escape.

But this dichotomous positioning of queerness and religion might not represent the full complexity of the tale. Indeed, much of the queer theology and biblical criticism done over the last two decades has sought to uncover traces of queerness *within* the Christian tradition – in its art, its doctrine of God, the early foundational texts of the Church Fathers, and particularly in the Bible itself. I turn to some of the former themes in Chapter 5, but the remainder of this chapter is given over to consideration of the Bible.

Queer traces

There is much debate, among queer scholars and others, about the extent to which biblical texts themselves are to be understood as promoting a particular heteronormative ideal, and the extent to which this sense has been read back into the Bible by its overwhelmingly heteronormative interpreters down the centuries. Arguments about the real meaning of terms like *arsenokoites* and *malakos* (in 1 Corinthians 6.9–10 – and often translated as 'homosexuals' and 'sodomites') have been mainstays of dialogue ever since the early days of gay theology, and I will not rehearse them here: interested readers would do well to seek out Helminiak 1994, Vasey 1995, Nissinen 1998 and (especially) Martin 2006 for examples of the genre. Such readings might be summed up as coming to one of three broad conclusions:

1   The Bible does not really condemn what we now understand as homosexual activity, especially loving and committed homosexual relationships. Words like *arsenokoites* and *malakos* are notoriously difficult to translate. Passages which appear, in English, to condemn homosexuality, are actually condemning other more specific acts, such as anal rape, cultic prostitution, or male–male sex between men who are heterosexual rather than homosexual.

2   The Bible *does* condemn what we now understand as homosexual activity. However, this condemnation was contingent on the time and culture in which the texts were produced. Utilizing the Bible creatively in the present day will mean working out what to make of these texts, perhaps concluding that, like clothing and dietary laws, what was binding on sexual behaviour in ancient Israel or the first-century Mediterranean is not binding now. The Bible is still a normative text

for us today, but the bigger imperative of love and justice throughout the Bible should be our guiding principle, not a few scattered texts about homosexual activity.

3 The Bible *does* condemn what we now understand as homosexual activity. However, it is an ancient, remote text and should in no way be considered normative for us today, so there is no need to explain away the 'clobber passages' or 'texts of terror',[1] which are simply abhorrent.

More broadly, however, queer readings of both the Bible itself and of its historical interpretations abound, some writers claiming that there are queer streams evident in the Bible all along which can be rediscovered or reclaimed, and others suggesting that queer resistance to the dangerous legacy of the Bible is necessary.

The assumption that the Bible itself contains queer traces underlies, for example, the 1997 collection edited by Robert E. Goss and Amy Adams Squire Strongheart, *Our Families, Our Values: Snapshots of Queer Kinship*. Several of the essays in this volume appeal to queer encouragement in the Bible: for instance, in the book of Ruth, with the eponymous character's declaration to Naomi that 'Your people shall be my people, and your God my God' (Ruth 1.16),[2] and immense loyalty to her as another woman (West 1997); and, perhaps more surprisingly, in the Epistle to the Romans, which Hanks asserts is fundamentally about liberation and authentic freedom and shows Paul greeting a large number of 'unusual' households not headed by a married man (Hanks 1997, pp. 139, 142–3). Some of the essays in the collection overtly appeal to queer 'ancestors', or specific affirmation in the texts (for example Kolakowski 1997, p. 47, with her suggestion that the New Testament is not only neutral but actively positive about eunuchs, whom she identifies as the forebears of today's transgender people). More recently, Eugene F. Rogers has noted that even Paul of Tarsus might be understood as promoting certain queer principles, as when he diminishes the importance of biological procreation by setting it in a context of resurrection (Rogers 2009, p. 30). Even if Paul's own motivation is to promote celibacy rather than same-sex sexual activity, the querying of the absolutist heterosexual model creates a space for further queer interpretation which cannot be said to be entirely alien to Scripture. In short, says Rogers,

> If male and female mark extremes of bodily variation, all of which Christ orients to himself; if Israel and the Church are both communities in potential to the Kingdom of God; if in Christ 'there is no longer Jew or Greek, there is no longer slave or free, there is no longer male and female,' then Paul allows God – for short periods! – to queer religion, gender and class (where 'queer' means to query the significance of social roles). (Rogers 2009, p. 31)

Rogers shows that reading queerness into Paul is possible *despite* many conservative Christians' propensity to appeal to Paul to sanction opposition to homosexual activity – while not erasing the fact that Paul is by no means queer-all-the-time, and that this is itself ambiguous.

Many of the same conservative Christians who read Paul as unequivocally opposed to homosexuality (as, for example, in Rom. 1.26–7) would balk at the idea that the Bible could be seen to tolerate, let alone endorse, more broadly 'queer' lifestyles and identities. However, to claim the biblical texts as unproblematically endorsing contemporary heteronormative 'family values' is just as thorny, if not more so. One cannot assume, for example, that one 'knows' what a given text is about: to contemporary readers, the first chapters of Genesis may be very evidently 'about' human sexual differentiation and (for some readers) gender complementarity and heterosexual normativity. However, as Ken Stone notes, historically such texts were sometimes used – as by Tertullian, Jerome and John Chrysostom – to promote celibacy and asceticism, rather than marriage and reproduction (Stone 2008, p. 22; Stone 2005, pp. 29–31). Moreover, as we saw in Chapter 2, these chapters have also been used to pronounce on quite other areas: food, appetite, eating and fasting – yet 'many modern readers . . . fail to see in the text any significance for our contemporary attitudes toward food, which so concerned many ancient Christian readers' (Stone 2008, p. 22; see also Stone 2005, pp. 23–45). In fact, drawing on Butlerian analysis, Stone suggests that the biblical foundations often appealed to in underpinning a particular heteronormative narrative of the human realm are profoundly incoherent, and that any 'continuity' a modern reader might try to trace with biblical notions of sex, household, marriage and family is dubious at best and 'actually not at all clear' (Stone 2006b, pp. 60, 65).

Jane Shaw, too, shows that institutions and norms often pronounced 'traditional' (and contrasted with those of their 'liberal' or 'revisionist' detractors) are often strikingly modern ones. She demonstrates that seeing Christian endorsement of marriage (as opposed to dedicated singleness or virginity, monastic or otherwise) in the Bible has moved in and out of vogue during Christianity's history. For its first thousand years, based on the Bible, Christianity promoted celibacy over marriage (Shaw 2007, p. 219). Shaw argues that it was the Protestant Reformation, and with it the dissolution of many nunneries, which left a landscape in which it was far more difficult for a woman to gain legitimacy and social stability if she chose to remain a confirmed virgin rather than entering into marriage, which (in light of Luther's *Commentary on 1 Corinthians 7* in particular) came to be considered an equally if not more holy state than celibacy. Luther interpreted Paul as saying that chastity, and therefore virgin singleness, was the gift of only a very few, and that marriage is a gift of God as much as it is a pragmatic necessity for the ardent who would otherwise burn with passion. Marriage therefore came to be seen as the normal state: all-female monastic communities in post-Reformation Britain were deemed dangerously Papist, even though during the medieval era, remaining unmarried had been considered the more holy vocation (Shaw 2007, p. 217).[3] Indeed, Luther believed nuns were 'showing off' their peculiar gift of chastity, relying vainly on their own work of purity rather than trusting in God for their salvation, and that these women were thereby more like 'brides of the devil' than brides of Christ (Shaw 2007, p. 220; Luther 1973, p. 16–17). Similar attitudes led to the legalization of clerical marriage in 1549 and the legitimization of the children of such marriages from 1552 onward.[4] Crucially, then, the 'family values' and exhortation of heterosexual marriage, which many conservative Christians today seem to see so unambiguously endorsed in Scripture, were in fact read back into it only *after* marriage had become socially and theologically popular. Socio-theological norms affected the 'self-evident' sense read out of the biblical texts, just as they do now, but in a somewhat different direction.

Shaw notes that another major shift occurred in light of the new science of sex and gender which arose in the eighteenth century, wherein women's physical and emotional *difference* from men was emphasized. This provided further fuel for the argument, growing popular at the time, that males and females had very distinct social roles. This, too, was theologized during the Evangelical Revival of the late eighteenth and early nineteenth centuries: essential biological difference was figured as complementarity, with a hierarchical theological anthropology coming to emphasize, in particular, the biblical texts about male headship and submissive female wifehood, such as Ephesians 5.22–4, Colossians 3.18–19, Titus 2.3–5, and the creation of woman as man's 'helpmeet' in Genesis 2.20–5 (Shaw 2007, pp. 224–5). However, the somewhat ahistorical bent in some present-day evangelical circles means that the mutability and recentness of such doctrines are elided. Shaw says,

> Ideas about sexual difference and complementarity that our ancestors would have barely recognized 300 years ago, let alone 3,000 years ago, are regularly mapped back onto the Hebrew Scriptures, especially the creation stories in Genesis 2 . . . Genesis 2 is taken as the blueprint for sexual difference and therefore for heterosexuality. The position . . . is described by its proponents as 'traditionalist' and is pitched over and against views which are often more attentive to the nuances and history of the Christian Scriptures and tradition but which are misleadingly called 'revisionist'. (Shaw 2007, p. 226)

But as Shaw points out, there is not a single unbroken line stretching back to Genesis which can be read unproblematically and without any reference to the social and historical norms of a given era. Reading the text critically means reading it in light of real bodies in their real contexts – which means, she concludes, that 'the so-called revisionists take the tradition far more seriously than the so-called traditionalists' (Shaw 2007, p. 227).

All this is to say that queer readings are not simply postmodern overlays on ancient texts. Even if queer theory itself is a distinctly recent and postmodern discourse, queer theology and biblical criticism reach back to proto-queer and proto-resisting streams which are as old as the texts themselves.

Queer ancestors

Indeed, Gerard Loughlin argues that 'same-sex affections and affiliations . . ., non-heterosexual structures, unexpected affinities' (Loughlin 2008, p. 146) are, once one begins to look, 'oddly central' to the Christian tradition that has latterly marginalized them. Indeed, some scholars have consciously sought queer precedent or even queer 'ancestors' in the biblical texts. Nancy Wilson (Wilson 1995, pp. 148–64) explicitly argues that figures such as the businesswoman and head-of-household Lydia in Acts 16, and the centurion with a deep affection for his ill slave in Matthew 8 and Luke 7, are lesbian or gay, saying, 'I believe that it is essential for gay men, lesbians, and bisexuals to take back the Bible. If we are not included among the stories and characters of the Bible, then it cannot be our book' (Wilson 1995, p. 164). For Wilson, queer stories always have been present in the Bible, but have been erased by commentators who 'vilify' homosexual people and desexualize the close same-sex friendships attested in Scripture. Heterosexual people have, however, been more than happy to use Ruth's words of commitment to Naomi in their own marriage services; Wilson protests, 'Heterosexuals have ripped off our love stories for too long! . . . *You can't steal them!*' (Wilson 1995, p. 156). This reclaiming of queer ancestors/trancestors (see below) has proven important for Wilson and others, with its assertion that homosexual people have existed at all points and times in history. However, Koch (2001) among others has suggested that it is a highly precarious strategy, as I will discuss later.

Queer ancestry might be sought in strategies, tropes, images and narrative strands, not just individual characters. Indeed, recognizing that some of the biblical figures may represent mythic or composite personifications rather than single historical individuals renders their 'queernesses' even more telling, since these are likely to betray something of a group's self-understanding or self-projection, and (given the process of redaction that the biblical texts have undergone) must either have been consciously repeated and reproduced, or have slipped under the radar of a more socially conservative editorial process. This in itself is fascinating, and means that queer readings are never only anachronistic projections of present concerns onto ancient texts (though they are, of course, always that to an extent). Queer readings are also ways in which to fan tiny, barely smouldering embers of imagery, representative of almost inconceivably distant expressions of the human condition and the nature of the divine, into small fires strong enough to warm those who have found Christianity a chilly place of late. Seeking queer precedent does not only involve claiming that Ruth and Naomi, Lazarus or the eunuchs are proto-queers (as in for example Alpert 1994; West 1997; Duncan 2000 and Perkins 2000), but also the kind of exploration undertaken by Ken Stone, whereby a term in current parlance ('homosexual') is read in parallel with a biblical term ('Canaanite') in order to demonstrate that both have often been assumed to have a single or stable referent, but both also turn out to be less distinct and less 'other' than their 'heterosexual' and 'Israelite' detractors might wish (Stone 2004). In fact, Stone concludes,

'The homosexual' is actually not outside heterosexual identity at all, but rather is always already inside heterosexual identity as a kind of necessary support for the illusion that such an identity is coherent and secure. The homosexual is thereby positioned with respect to the heterosexual in something resembling the way that the Canaanite was positioned with respect to the Israelite. (Stone 2004, p. 129)

Such readings show that while it might be deemed anachronistic to seek post-homosexual queer *individuals* in the biblical texts (since 'homosexuality', 'heterosexuality' and 'queer' as we know them do indeed make sense only in modern terms), ambiguous and subversive *qualities* can certainly be found therein and might be appealed to as ancestral, if not foundational, to today's queer interpreters. Moreover, readings like this demonstrate that, even if queer interpretation has been particularly linked to and invested in questions of sex, gender and sexuality, many queer readers wish to emphasize a broader conviction about the ways in which subversive, resisting and counter-cultural strands are 'always already inside' the biblical texts and the Jewish and Christian traditions.

A queer biblical theology might, in fact, come to rejoice in the plurality and creativity of multiple interpretations and a lack of any finality in expression (Stone 2008, p. 24). This does not, of course, mean that some texts will not be found to be much more 'friendly' to queer interpreters than others. There may be an argument for agreeing, with Stone, that certain texts 'should not be read by all readers in all situations' (Stone 2005, p. 148); that they are literally bad for some readers' health (as I discuss below). Of course, there is also always a risk that this kind of self-imposed censorship leads to a watering-down of the Bible's inherent difficulty and discomfiture: an acquaintance of mine actually excised the Song of Songs from his Bible with scissors because he felt, as a young single Christian man, that its erotic bent was 'unhelpful' to his continued celibacy. It is questionable whether this is quite what Jesus meant when he advocated cutting off what causes you to sin.[5] However, Stone acknowledges,

> An approach to biblical interpretation which recognizes the potentially dangerous effects of reading certain texts in certain situations – because, for example, those texts incorporate patriarchal assumptions – need not proceed by distinguishing, in a simplistic and totalizing way, 'good' texts from 'bad' texts. What one needs is not a firm list of universalized hermeneutical rules, or a firm list of acceptable and prohibited texts, considered equally valid for everyone, everywhere. (Stone 2005, p. 147)

Rather, suggests Stone, the reader must interrogate the texts to take account of 'the rhetorical situations in which they were written, and their histories of effects' (Stone 2005, p. 147) and assess these in light of one's own context and what one is aiming to accomplish through reading: we might say, what one is asking the Bible to *be*.

Stone suggests that strategies such as simply constructing a list of places where the Bible discusses homosexuality, and setting out to say what these texts 'really' mean, are limited. However, even a book such as Martti Nissinen's *Homoeroticism in the Biblical World* (Nissinen 1998), which situates the texts in their historical context, may be problematic. Although Nissinen both examines texts in historical perspective and draws on present-day debates (Stone 2001c, p. 109), Stone notes an interesting tension here. Nissinen is well aware of a disjunction between modern definitions of homosexuality and heterosexuality and the ways in which certain behaviours would have been understood in the ancient world (Stone 2001c, p. 111). He thus bolsters the group of scholars who assert that knowing what the Bible may or may not say about homosexuality is not necessarily of much use in constructing a normative ethic of homosexuality today – since, Nissinen states, the very act of bringing together a group of brief and diverse biblical references and saying that they are 'about' a thing called 'homosexuality' is imposing a modern, and possibly heteronormative agenda on them (Stone 2001c, p. 113). However, ironically, says Stone, Nissinen himself might actually reinscribe a kind of heteronormativity in his approach:

> After all, the very question, 'What does the Bible say about homosexuality?', is structured in such a fashion that 'homosexuality' remains an object of discourse, whether we are speaking about the discourse inscribed within the Bible itself or the discourse of biblical interpretation . . . Such a gesture frequently betrays a tendency to privilege speech *about* and visions *of* homoeroticism. (Stone 2001c, p. 114)

In other words, even someone like Nissinen is still speaking about homosexuality with the assumption that it is a discrete 'thing' to be spoken about. This may in itself set up homosexuality as more of a cohesive phenomenon than the biblical 'texts of terror' themselves (stretching across many hundreds of years, from Genesis to Jude) actually render it.

Moreover, Stone claims that Nissinen fails to problematize *hetero*sexuality, assuming that it has basically had a stable and continuous character since the biblical texts were written even if homosexuality has not (Stone 2001c, p. 114). This is important, for Stone's conclusion is that queer biblical criticism must undermine the self-evident nature of *both* heterosexuality *and* homosexuality, as well as their dichotomization (Stone 2001c, p. 115). Furthermore, by having as its goal the furthering of 'more queer ways of life' (Stone 2001c, p. 116), queer commentary will also problematize the assumption that 'good' or 'legitimate' biblical interpretation must always and only be historical-critical. Rather, such analysis is only one possible mode, and queer critics might reinvent biblical criticism, 'constructing novel ways of interacting with biblical and other religious texts from a whole range of queer reading locations' (Stone 2001c, p. 118).

Queer 'precedent' in the Bible might, then, be found not only in texts about sex or eunuchs or gender roles (although these have proven important for some readers), but also in the *strategies* recorded. For example, Stone persuasively shows that Jesus' hermeneutical strategy in the Sermon on the Mount might be figured as queer. In one particular passage, Matthew 5.38–42, Stone argues that Jesus 'moves beyond the reference to tradition and makes a point that, so far as I can see, no conventional response to the "plain sense" of Scripture would easily have reached . . . he shows little interest in the meaning that the Torah text might have had for its original author or audience, and little interest in translating the supposed original meaning into his own context' (Stone 2007, p. 159). Rather, Jesus is doing something that might well be figured as queer, shifting his audience's attention from what has been spoken and heard in the past to what needs to be spoken and heard now. 'You have heard . . . But I have said . . .' is a trope which exceeds this specific instance and could be shown to be the nub of Jesus' broader mission. Gerard Loughlin concurs that 'queer theology is a call to return to a more fully realized anticipation of the Kingdom, which is not a return to the previous or the same, but to the new and the future' (Loughlin 2008, p. 150). This is not to disregard Jantzen's reminder that the intervening troublesome period of salvation history cannot be expunged or disregarded in favour of returning to a 'purer', less 'distorted' golden era; rather, Loughlin and others recognize that the timeframe of the Kingdom is profoundly beyond and discontinuous with the timeframe of human experience *even though* it is also profoundly related to it. Thus we can truly speak of 'getting back to' a given point – in terms of tuning in to a certain strand of the tradition – without naïvely supposing that we can excise everything in between that has proven recalcitrant or unjust.

Further queer readings

The 2006 volume *The Queer Bible Commentary* represents an extraordinary achievement: it is a collection of 44 essays[6] by 30 contributors, all of whom write their commentary from the perspective of queer theology and/or biblical criticism. However, the authors also have multiple ethnic and national backgrounds, ages, genders and denominational allegiances. Several are Jewish. As might be expected, many of the pieces have an especial concern for the liberationist, sexual and (especially) proto-homosexual traces in the texts, and for non-heteronormative strands of assertion about gender (both human and divine) and family. But they go deeper than that. Many of the essays are driven by a desire to query the very notions of inclusion, exclusion, community and what it means to be a people whose identity relies on shutting out or cutting off those who do not belong. While most of the essays follow the conventions of biblical commentary, albeit without close attention paid to every single verse or to close questions of the date and place of composition (and this might, in itself, be considered a queer strategy, rejecting the manner in which 'modernist-thinking historicist scholars sought to categorize, compartmentalize and legitimize potentially subversive writings' – Hornsby 2006b, p. 412),[7] some, like Jennifer L. Koosed's reading of Ecclesiastes/Qohelet, consciously play with the norms and boundaries of academic and biblical-critical writing. Koosed intersperses her reflections on the queerness of Qohelet with autobiographical interjections (like her story of how a teenage friend's parents encouraged Koosed's relationship with their son in order to 'reform' him of his homosexuality) and direct questions to the reader in a different typeface from the main text: 'What do you see when you look into the book?'; 'What have you assumed about me?' (Koosed 2006, pp. 342, 343). She also sets up instances where Qohelet addresses *her* directly, interacting with her responses to a drag show (Koosed 2006, pp. 344–5). In this way, Koosed plays with the reader, noting, 'Above all, I experience a perverse pleasure, gaiety if you will, in writing in ways a biblical scholar is not supposed to write' (Koosed 2006, pp. 343). It becomes clear that Koosed's departure from the mores of commentary is conscious and invokes the queerness she finds in Qohelet itself:

> My commentary does not pretend to be comprehensive, and my six readings are not all necessarily consistent with one another. But who is singular within themselves, transparent to the world around them, simply and straight-forwardly read? (Koosed 2006, p. 355)

Timothy R. Koch's commentary on Isaiah in the same collection points to another important aspect of queering a biblical text: namely, imagining oneself, as reader, as a character or actor in the text, but in an unexpected way. Koch begins with Isaiah 6.5–8, and suggests that rather than placing themselves as the 'man of unclean lips' (which is, as he notes, a role in which queer people may often find themselves cast by others), queer readers might imagine the story from the point of view of the seraph who touches the burning, purifying coal to the prophet's lips. He explains, 'This is the seraphic task of those of us engaged with in biblical studies on behalf of the LGBT community: to choose the right coal for the right situation' (Koch 2006, p. 371). For Koch, this is part of a strategy of empowerment and agency for disempowered readers. Importantly, this kind of strategy is not quite the same as that criticized by Koch in Wilson and others – that is, identifying 'queer ancestors' in the text. Rather, it is a conscious over-writing of the 'text itself' or 'text-as-it-is', precisely in order to subvert or make different its perspective. This has striking similarities with work done from the standpoint of physical disability by John M. Hull (2003), Hannah Lewis (2007) and others. Hull's work from blindness, in particular, demonstrates that scriptural attitudes to disability are ambiguous and can be read very differently if the 'impaired perspective' is held to be the text's vantage-point, rather than something external or peripheral to it. Hull does not assume in every case that the author or editor of a given text was 'really' blind rather than sighted; rather, he shows that if the *reader* no longer assumes a sighted location, then the 'obvious' or 'given' meaning of a text may no longer be self-evident or incontrovertible. A sighted reader might take Jesus' warning that the narrow gate is the harder and (thus) more valuable route at face value, but for a blind person a narrow gate is much easier and safer to navigate than a wide one, since the walls can be touched at all times in order to gauge exactly where one is in relation to them.

In a reprise of his 2001 metaphor of 'cruising' the Scriptures (discussed below), Koch makes clear in his 2006 essay that the engagement of a queer reader with biblical texts is likely to be pragmatic and highly selective; and that this is crucial to conserving their energy. Using the metaphor of mining, Koch suggests that those who mine for a given mineral are not particularly interested in the detritus and debris they will also, of necessity, encounter: 'I am not . . . required to drop my search for coal in order to deal with blue sandy shale! If someone else wishes to mine shale, then so be it' (Koch 2006, p. 372). Koch believes that, by stopping to deal with every shard of non-pertinent 'rock', queer interpreters are allowing their 'mining' efforts to be subsumed into the agendas of others who want them to apologize for or face up to, for example, texts of terror like Leviticus 20 or Romans 1. But Koch believes that queer people can never 'win' that game, as they will always be accused of misinterpreting the texts. Better, then, for queer reader to 'clear away and/or blast through others' agendas that get in the way' (Koch 2006, p. 372), and continue to seek their own coal.

While this is a neat metaphor, albeit with somewhat violent and environmentally destructive connotations of which Koch is already aware (Koch 2006, p. 372), its main weakness is that it allows queer interpretation to remain a specialist – and therefore ghettoized – interest, rather than something deeply transformative of all biblical reading. If queer readers can 'blast' through other people's agendas, this fails to resist the methodology of the opposing readings which have similarly 'blasted' queer people for so long. This seems to risk the same kind of 'pissing contest' which Koch rejected in 2001.[8] If it is the case that 'your (and our) aspirations, your needs and your questions are the best maps to guide your (and our) excavations' (Koch 2006, p. 376), it is difficult to see how the text could stand over against human interpretations, or how interpretations could be ranked as variously less or more ethical and justifiable. While Koch seems to advocate a privileging of queer readings among queer people, he does not suggest that queer readings should also be privileged over those done by non-queer detractors among the non-queer detractors themselves. It is as if he is saying, 'Your reading might be right for you, but our reading is right for us.' While this might be understood as profoundly queer in terms of its non-normativity and its refusal to impose one particular ethical standard, it is also frustratingly parochial – seeming to restrict queer concerns only to queer people – and defeatist in its assumption that non-queer detractors' minds can never be changed. It is especially odd given that Koch is quite happy to identify as 'lies' assertions like the one that homosexual people pose more of a sexual threat to children than heterosexuals do (Koch 2006, p. 377). He is not shy of certainty here, nor in the vision of justice and a challenge to the status quo that he identifies as the content of the 'Fourth Isaiah' which queer people may be being called to create (Koch 2006, p. 384).

Like the contributors to *The Queer Bible Commentary*, the authors in Goss and West's 2000 edited collection *Take Back the Word* seek not only to pull out certain ancestors and proto-queer or queer-friendly characters from the Bible, but to reframe the whole way the Bible is read. This, the editors say, is 'a strategy that outs the queer community by articulating the community's lived experience in and beyond the closet as well as its particular concerns when encountering and appropriating the biblical text' (Goss and West 2000, p. 4). So while finding queer ancestors might be of comfort or empowerment for queer people, a radical reframing of the *whole* Bible will go further in developing this community's self-understanding and the ways in which it relates to the Bible as a collection of texts. This might include what Virginia Ramey Mollenkott identifies as a strategy of reading from 'low and outside', utilizing wily or subversive kinds of knowledge and behaviour because they lack sanctioned access to 'real' authority as hegemonically granted. In this way, low-and-outsider perspectives will require readers to become 'tricksters', who may to choose to work craftily from inside contexts which would evict them if they were more overt (Mollenkott 2000, pp. 14–16). However, other authors in the same collection strongly reject the notion that it is best to be circumspect about their sexuality or gender for the sake of pragmatism, believing that the time has long since come to stand up and be counted (for example West 2000; Alpert 2000). Benjamin Perkins is especially vocal in his assertion that coming out is a necessary step for queer people, albeit one made safer by taking place within a loving and supportive community (Perkins 2000). Mollenkott, by contrast, does not believe that coming out is either necessary or possible for everyone, suggesting rather that queer communities should sustain both 'closeted' and 'out' members, 'supporting people in the often painful and messy realities of their lives' (Mollenkott 2000, p. 18). Either way, for queer readers to move from understanding the Bible as death-bringing to understanding it as life-giving will necessitate readings that resist the notion that some readers are more legitimate or more worthy 'owners' of these texts than others (Goss and West 2000, pp. 5–6).

Many of the readings in these two collections are grounded in devotional contexts, even if their authors would describe themselves as biblical critics as well as, or instead of, theologians. But one of the most stimulating discrete readings in existence is that by Stephen D. Moore, who explores the queerness of the Song of Songs, and of the allegorical commentaries written on it by Origen, Bernard of Clairvaux, Denis the Carthusian, St. John of the Cross and others, without feeding it back into any particular confessional situation (although the influence of his childhood in Roman Catholic Ireland is apparent). I discuss Moore's reading in more detail in order to show that queer reading is often ambiguous, shifting and multivocal. Moore's reading of the Song of Songs and its interpretations demonstrates that queering is always ambivalent, always itself implicated, and that it never occurs as a one-way trajectory. Queering a text requires it 'to be opened up through entering into dialogue and dialectic with the life of the reader' (Abraham 2007, p. 4.5). This might be understood as making a text vulnerable to misappropriation and misinterpretation even as it also interrogates and constructs its reader – but part of what queer analysis is doing is drawing attention to the fact that exactly these risks have *already* been run (and sometimes concretized) in the text's 'safer' prehistory of 'solid' hermeneutical elucidation. Queer reading means a suspicion of *prima facie* truths, and a constant reversal of assumption and certainty. As Moore shows, it is no safer to assume that reading a text queerly means resisting allegory as it is to resist literalism wholesale.

By the nineteenth century, says Moore, carnal readings of the Song of Songs had all but superseded allegorical ones: it came to be read as a staunchly heterosexual poem of morality in marriage (Moore 2001, p. 79). 'Reclaiming' the Song of Songs' potency as an erotic song between a man and a woman might appear more 'liberated' than insisting that it is actually a poem about God's love for the Church; however, this in turn might repeat socio-theological conservatisms. Moore argues that part of the 'genderbending' evident in Origen's, Bernard's and John of the Cross's commentaries (where it is the *Bridegroom* who has breasts) may 'have proceeded smoothly from the Song's own propensity to blur gender boundaries' (Moore 2001, p. 41). The queerness of the Song thus exists not only in its literalist, non-allegorical sexual interpretations, which bring sexuality to the fore in a way that may be considered queer through their refusal to elide or bowdlerize sexual attraction and carnality from a sacred text, but also exactly in and through the ostensibly *non*-sexual allegorical interpretations. What is even more interesting in Moore's reading is his perceptive and persuasive observation that, while queering the Bible might often be about refusing to 'write out' the sexual motifs and implications within it, it might also be just as queer – or more so – to refuse such literalistic, face-value readings. Allegory reveals, even as on the surface it hides; self-conscious rejections of the 'concealing' nature of allegory do not point unproblematically to candid ingenuousness, but rather raise questions about why it might be so important for a reader, interpreter or culture to be *seen to be* frank and forthright. Moore's debt to Derrida is particularly clear here. Moore notes,

> The literal readings [of the Song of Songs] purport to reveal what the allegorical readings sought to conceal. The allegorical readings can themselves be read as discourses of sexual repression. But it is as

discourses of sexual *expression* – and of 'deviant' sexual expression, at that – that I shall be reading them … That which must under no circumstances be mentioned in the allegorical readings – the fact that the Song is suffused with erotic desire, that its cheeks are flushed with it, its pages moist with it – everywhere comes to expression in these readings. (Moore 2001, pp. 22–3)

As in Derrida, hiding something might merely draw more attention to it; as in Foucault's *The History of Sexuality*, protesting too much might point to the revelation of what is hidden and proclaiming just how free and liberated one is in contrast to one's recent forebears might say a lot more about one's own cultural context and its attitude to sexuality than it does about theirs.[9] As Moore insists,

Allegorizing [the Song] only had the effect of turning it into something yet more unthinkable: not just the torrid expression of a sizzling sexual relationship between a horny young woman and her hunky young man … but the expression of an erotic relationship between two *male* lovers instead … The austere expositor's attempt to evade the perilous embrace of the Song's female lover through allegory plunges him instead into the arms of another lover, a *male* lover, no less – God or Christ. (Moore 2001, pp. 27–8)

Where God is understood as symbolically male, and where the reader (historically, usually a monk, priest or other educated man) is also male, the reader is placed into one of two positions: *either* taking on the 'female' role of obedience and submission to a male husband-God, *or* maintaining a confirmed 'masculinity' in which case the God-human encounter is a homosocial (and symbolically homosexual) one. Where the Bridegroom (that is, God) is read as feminine – and Moore notes that, at least in Origen, the Bridegroom possesses breasts and 'slits' but no penis-like organ (Moore 2001, p. 44) – the male reader is implicated *either* in queering the hierarchy where human is subordinate to God, *or* in questioning the subordination of human females to human males (since the 'milk' of the Bridegroom's 'breasts' nourishes and instructs). In each of these four cases – none of which is necessarily mutually exclusive – the really interesting question is why this imagery is so appealing and what it says about the collective psyche of those who promote it.

Moore's own assumptions are, of course, also inescapably written into his own text and his interpretations of other interpretations of the Song of Songs. For example, he might be accused of somewhat masculine preoccupations: even as he attempts to queer heteronormative readings of the Song, and even as he highlights homoerotic imagery, he might also be suspected of unwittingly quashing a female voice. The Song of Songs is one of the only biblical texts where feminine voices (those of the Bride and Bridesmaids) carry the narrative at length; but, by asserting that the Song's female protagonist is essentially a fantasy object onto which male interpretative desires are projected (Moore 2001, p. 53) – that is, by assuming that all this woman has to say is what men have made her say – Moore may ironically strip her even further of agency. His reading follows that of those, like Clines and Polaski, who have figured the Song of Songs as pornographic, who have read the woman as constructed in order to be stared at, ever-available, and unable to escape a male gaze (Moore 2001, p. 225; see also Clines 1995, pp. 102–5; Polaski 1997, pp. 76–7; and compare discussions of paintings representing the apocryphal story of Susanna and the Elders – see for example Bal 2005a; Garrard 1982; Pollock 1999; Salomon 1991); but could it not be that the reason the woman does not resist being looked upon is simply that she is enjoying it, that she is pleased with her own body's beauty and its capacity to feel and arouse desire? Despite being one of the most daring, incisive and imaginative readings of the Song of Songs extant, Moore's text highlights a peril of male homoerotic interpretation: that it may further push women from view and go along with eroding their agency. For Moore, the upshot of the Song of Songs is that 'woman . . . is symbolically annihilated in the very gesture through which she is idealized' (Moore 2001, p. 54), because – in his account – cloistered male interpreters could not cope with the existence and three-dimensionality of real women. It would be ironic indeed if, in reclaiming the queer homosexual undercurrents of the Song and its readings, the real experiences of women enjoying their own sexual agency were similarly written out.[10]

As Moore also makes clear, queering a text always entails queering its readers. Queer readings might seek to resist polarized gender imagery whereby men must be hard, macho actor-gods and women soft, meek, submissive vessels. But to resist such epithets is not merely to reverse them: Moore comments, 'We might begin by asking what logic dictates that a submissive male be characterized as "feminine" or "feminized" in the first place. To so characterize the submissive male is to code the erotic exchange in terms that are ineluctably "hetero"' (Moore 2001, p. 170). As James B. Nelson has argued, the fullness of masculine sexuality and identity goes far beyond 'bigness' or 'hardness', and the erect penis is not synecdoche for them or, indeed, for rape and violence. Heterosexual intercourse might be understood not as a penis penetrating a vagina (a male-proactive and, perhaps, implicitly violent event), but as a vagina embracing, swallowing or enveloping a penis (which undoubtedly figures the female anatomy as less passive, but which may or may not also be interpreted as similarly violent; there may be a Gnostic hint of vast, dark caverns at play, as well as of the mythic *vagina dentata*). For Nelson, not only are men *capable* of having a soft penis as well as a turgid phallus, but in fact the penis is soft far more than it is hard. However, this is still a uniquely *masculine* experience: it is a masculine softness, of male-related anatomy, not a feminine one (Nelson 1992, p. 100). Assuming a 'hard' woman is masculine and a 'soft' man is feminine is itself heteronormative, pointing to an inability to see beyond these binary categories (a problem continually debated in the rhetoric of tops and bottoms, butches and femmes: does the repetition of a 'dominant–submissive' dynamic in homosexual pairings indeed mean that male–female relationships are more prior or 'natural' than homosexual ones, or is it simply that we lack the imagination to read power systems in anything other than gendered terms?).

This brief conversation with Moore's reading of the Song of Songs and its interpretations is salutary for understanding how queer reading takes place. If the Bible and its elucidations are indeed historical and shifting, then good hermeneutics is never a case of getting back to the 'real', 'original' Bible to measure all the various interpretations against it. In particular, Ibrahim Abraham notes, following Ricœur, that the 'correct' understanding of a text is not guaranteed by attempts to apprehend the author's original situation (Abraham 2007, p. 4.5; Ricœur 1976: 76). Indeed, Jantzen warns (from the perspective of feminist philosophy of religion) that such would be of limited use given everything that has happened in the time between:

> One of the chief obstacles to claiming Christianity as liberatory for women is the fact that, even if one argues . . . that Jesus and the early Christian community were much more egalitarian than they have often been presented, and that this was suppressed by the developing church, this egalitarianism cannot be appropriated in the late twentieth century as though the intervening centuries of patriarchal Christendom had never occurred. (Jantzen 1996, p. 96)

Queer scriptural criticism, therefore, also cannot entail a complete rejection of the structure and history of a text – especially for one like Abraham who asserts that 'it should not be so easy to escape the binds of scriptural structure, without dealing with the dangerous texts that have been – and still are – used to exclude and oppress' (Abraham 2007, p. 4.6). Christianity is about *all* the events of the last two thousand years, including those we would rather had not happened – not just about the lives and teachings of Jesus, Paul and the Apostles.

Dangerous texts?

> I find myself much less optimistic about the ultimate success of creative strategies of reading for disarming the Bible's potential for 'clobbering' . . . marginalized or oppressed groups. As lesbians, gay men, bisexual, transgendered and seeking people, do we really want to 'take back the word'? And if we do, what 'word' is it that we want to 'take back'? (Tolbert 2000, p. vii)

As I noted above, some of the early work by gay and lesbian interpreters of the Bible focused on the kind of textual criticism which aimed to show that the texts of terror so often used to outlaw homosexuality may have been mistranslated or misinterpreted. In other words, the suggestion was that the texts did not *really* say what they had been assumed to say, and were therefore not inherently oppressive for queer people. However, subsequent scholars have countered that it is simply not possible to explain away all the horror of these texts, and that relating to the Bible even as queer readers must involve mourning, challenging or railing against them, rather than simply parsing them out of existence.

In her Foreword to the 2000 collection *Take Back the Word* (Goss and West 2000), Mary Ann Tolbert suggests that the history of the Bible has been doubly harassing for queer people, due to both 'the text itself and its authorized readers' (Tolbert 2000, p. vii). Its status as having been used to promote and protect social mores, however, should prompt not just queer readers but *all* thoughtful Christian readers to feel deeply ambivalent about the Bible (Tolbert 2000, p. viii). However dearly Christians may hold some passages or verses, this is not enough to outweigh the 'textual harassment' that has been used over the centuries to subjugate and exclude non-Christian, non-white and non-heterosexual people. Queer readings may simply be dismissed by detractors as biased and subjective, even if this is only as true of queer-friendly readings as of any others (Tolbert 2000, p. x). Nonetheless, the Bible can be empowering and generative for queer people. 'Of course, the Bible itself does not kill people', says Tolbert; 'groups of readers of the Bible do that in its name' (Tolbert 2000, p. ix). Even so, this power should not be underestimated:

> No matter how creatively and joyously queer readers of the Bible reclaim some of its texts by destabilizing them, playing with them, laughing at them, allegorizing them, tricking them . . . as long as there are groups of Bible readers who fear, hate, or want to make invisible lesbians, gays, bisexuals, transgendered or sexually seeking people, a barrage of killing interpretations will continue to be aimed at queer communities in public and church debates. (Tolbert 2000, p. ix)

For this reason, the Bible is always likely to remain dangerous for queer people in some respects, precisely because its open-endedness means that it will always be used oppressively by certain interpreters even if sympathetic strands also exist within it.

Of course, some queer biblical critics have consciously and overtly held that the biblical writers were *not* sympathetic to a queer project, and have acknowledged the texts' complicity with anti-queer rhetoric and ideology. Michael Carden, in his short but excellent commentary on Genesis, aims very overtly to make clear the acute *foreignness* of the text. This is done, in part, to remind Christians that Genesis was a Jewish text before it was a Christian one, and is therefore 'not Christian property' (Carden 2006, p. 25).[11] But Genesis/Bereshit's strangeness for present-day Christians is not only a religious one; Carden stresses, 'It is not my intent either to depatriarchalize or to homosexualize Genesis. Genesis comes from an ancient and alien culture and if there are aspects of that culture that shock and dismay today then so be it' (Carden 2006, p. 25). The worlds that shaped Genesis had specific standards for appropriate sexual and social behaviour, and to retrospectively read certain behaviours as heterosexual, homosexual and so on would be anachronistic (Carden 2006, p. 24). The Bible simply *is* ancient, and alien, and strange – which is (as befits the Word of God) a double-edged sword, for it means that neither present-day queers nor their detractors can claim it, own it, or colonize it to the exclusion of everyone else. This is particularly important to note when it comes to Genesis, since it is a book so often appealed to as being foundational on questions of sex, gender and theological anthropology (and so often used to reinforce conservative gender norms and heterosexuality). Carden believes, however, that despite its ancientness and otherness there are still some elements of Genesis that are notably more 'queer' (or 'queerable') than others, as in the reading that not only the first humans, but perhaps also Abraham and Sarah, somehow transcend binary gender and patriarchy (Carden 2006, p. 33; see also Gross 1999). Carden's reminder that the biblical texts are foreign and grounded in another time and place is an important counter-balance to interpretations which too easily annexe the Bible for the bulwarking of modern concerns, queer or otherwise.

Such annexation is also rebuffed by Koch, who warns against the attempts of individuals such as Nancy Wilson 'to "out" a number of biblical characters in order to document our (queer) tribe's presence in the pages of Scripture' (Koch 2001, pp. 14–15). Koch believes that there is a risk that such 'reclaiming' of the Bible to show that queer people are already a part of its story – as Wilson seeks to do – 'begins to sound a good deal like saying that, if we search the pages of Scripture, there is a glass slipper that will fit *our* feet, too, and that we, *too*, will get to return to the Ball, for we, *too*, have the right to be there!' (Koch 2001, p. 15). The problem, says Koch, is that, just as Cinderella's older, uglier sisters had to mutilate themselves to make the slipper fit (one cutting off her big toe and the other her heel, in the decidedly dark and not-suitable-for-children Grimm Brothers incarnation of the tale), so too might present-day queer people have to 'squeeze' themselves in unacceptable ways in order to make themselves fit into the story that Wilson and others say the Bible is telling about them. Koch, for example, rejects the notion that he, a gay man, should see a biblical eunuch as a queer ancestor, saying:

> While Wilson does a compelling job of expanding the definition of eunuch to refer to a larger group of people than those who were physically castrated . . ., I nevertheless am quite alarmed by any invitation to see that I 'belong' by virtue of stories and reference to people whose lives were sexually and socially circumscribed. (Koch 2001, p. 15)

This is an important objection, though it is not necessarily inevitable that such an objection should lead (as it does for Koch) to an assertion that the biblical texts cannot be normative for queer persons' lives or ethics at all. Koch believes that queer people should rely instead on their own internal erotic power and instinct. He suggests that rather than taking on the Bible wholesale, they should 'cruise' the Scriptures, pursuing what speaks to their own desires and taking responsibility for the consequences – without seeking 'institutional validation, an external set of directives for life ethics, [or] some "proof" that we, too, can own a piece of the Rock' (Koch 2001, p. 16). In Scripture as in life, he suggests, queer readers are likely to encounter some friends, some enemies, and many more casual acquaintances whose existence does not particularly affect them one way or the other. In his own reading, Koch picks out not the 'obvious' or well-established 'queer-friendly' figures like Ruth and Naomi, David and Jonathan and the eunuchs, but rather several small tableaux or apparently passing details of lesser-known stories. He owns that other readers may be unconvinced by his analyses of these stories, but says that this is not important: 'The point here is that an approach that we *each* base on our own erotic knowledge allows us *all* to pursue that which catches our eye, which calls to us, which holds out at least the hope of connection and transformation' (Koch 2001, p. 21). Goss concurs,

> Outing . . . grants to the Bible too much power to authenticate our lives as queers . . . If we come to the text with the purpose of finding validation for our erotic lives, then we limit our encounters with the text of scripture because we place authority entirely in the text as a parent. (Goss 2002, p. 214)

In fact, says Goss, queers must come to view the Bible as an equal, not a superior authority, and must read it through the lens of what their own contexts, experiences and orientations add to it, having *already* 'recognize[d] the blessing of their sexualities before they engage the biblical text' (Goss 2002, p. 214).

This chimes with Andrew K. T. Yip's observation that 'queering texts means personalizing and individualizing the interpretation of texts, by adopting a hermeneutic lens based on the authority of self' (Yip 2005, p. 56). For Yip, queer people tend to have come to consider religious authorities' pronouncements on matters of scriptural interpretation concerning sexuality less significant than their own personal convictions. This does not mean rejecting the texts wholesale; rather, queer people 'wrestle the authentic interpretive authority from religious authority structures and relocate it to their self – their own reflection, evaluation and experience' (Yip 2005, p. 56). Although this has always taken place to some extent, Yip believes that current social processes of de-traditionalization and individualization are accelerating it (Yip 2005, pp. 59–60).

There might be some elements of Scripture, then, which come to be deemed simply unhealthy or oppressive for queer people, either because of the text itself or because of how it is commonly interpreted (although Yip's concept of counter-rejection might be said to mitigate this). Discussing the texts often wheeled out in arguments against homosexual activity, Stuart says simply, 'The first task of a queer biblical hermeneutic is to deconstruct these texts of terror' (Stuart 1997a, p. 43). This is important because, while queer readers might be very aware of how their own socio-political background and setting have influenced the way they read biblical texts (exactly because, perhaps, they have had a strong incentive not to have to take apparently oppressive texts at face value), many mainstream scholars have failed to see how their *own* context (and that of the translators who have mediated the texts for them) likewise affects their 'interpretive grid' (Stuart 1997a, p. 42). Indeed, Stuart identifies a hypocrisy in Christians who wish to take anti-homosexual Scriptures as peculiarly normative when they no longer accept the entirety of the social system in which they were written – and are happy, for example, to shave their beards, eat shellfish, wear mixed-fibre clothing and so on (Stuart 1997a, p. 43). Deconstructing the texts of terror might mean reinterpreting them; it might also mean accepting that although some passages *are* unreservedly oppressive, there is also a strong stream within the Bible of solidarity with marginalized people. More expedient might be to focus on what Stuart identifies as a constant theme of sexual subversion and flouting of law throughout the Bible. It is grasping hold of this that might prove truly liberating, rather than engaging in an unwinnable game of whose reading of the texts of terror is the 'best' (Koch 2001, pp. 11–13). Indeed, claims Stuart, 'The fact that most books on homosexuality, whether by straight or by queer people, begin with the "texts of terror" demonstrates how brainwashed we all are by heterosexist readings of the Bible' (Stuart 1997a, p. 44). Queer biblical interpretation has its sights set higher than just grasping back a few isolated passages about 'sodomy'.

Queer reading, in fact, in some accounts, necessitates a reworking of entire hermeneutical and critical systems: like Butler, some queer theologians insist that it is not enough to employ the Master's grammatical tools to tear down the house, and that whole modes of textual discourse should be resisted and treated with suspicion. Jaime Ronaldo Balboa contends that Comstock, Mollenkott and Goss in particular are, in fact, just as 'logocentric' as the conservative theologians whose biblical interpretations they oppose. Balboa comments that Comstock et al seem to believe that the oppression of LGBT people by other Christians would cease 'if they [i.e. the detractors] only understood the Bible the "right way"' (Balboa 2003, p. 96). However, this actually undermines what Balboa understands as a truly queer project, namely celebrating difference and diversity in reading. Each side, when it claims to have reached a more infallible or true reading, is being logocentric. This is a failure, he suggests, to recognize the *deferred* nature of the Bible's meaning: in fact, no original or final truth is open to any one reading group in the present age, but is context-dependent. This clearly Derridean reading[12] has affinities with Koch's suggestion that conservative and liberal wrangling for the 'truth' of 'what the Bible *really* says about homosexuality' (as in Helminiak 1994) are nothing but a 'pissing contest' (Koch 2001, p. 12). Rather, each side should acknowledge that they *produce*, rather than *uncover*, the 'truths' of Scripture (Balboa 2003, p. 131). Balboa's warning against simply turning oppressive, violent readings around on those whose interpretations one dislikes is a salient one. The questions he poses have no easy answers:

> Logocentric heterosexism continues its onslaught against queer folks and must be answered. But how do we respond to such rhetorics and acts of oppression without simply turning the mechanisms of theoretical violence against another population? How do we do so without committing the same acts of epistemic self-privileging? (Balboa 2003, p. 116)

Mary Ann Tolbert suggests that the history of biblical 'textual harassment' is such that queer interpreters must not risk simply imposing a new normativity. As such, she says,

If lesbians, gay men, bisexuals, transgendered and seeking people are to take back this word for themselves, they must take it back in a new way, a way that attempts to obviate its potential for harm while engaging its message of liberation and love. For me that new way entails first and foremost the firm rejection of any normative authority or doctrinal priority given to readings of the Bible. (Tolbert 2000, p. xi)

This does not mean, she says, that biblical texts should not be considered revelatory of God, or pivotal to the Christian faith. However, she suggests, it should not be seen as the last and final word on God and on humankind's relation to God, but simply one source among many.

Conclusion

The word 'queer' empowers diversity because of its imprecise and hard-to-pin-down meaning ... To 'queer' a scripture is to render it unusual and non-normative, to shake it up and see how it might be reconfigured. (Bohache 2006, p. 493)

Quite apart from the queering of individual texts, fascinating as these are, queering the Bible is about a more profound and devastating project of hermeneutical resistance to hegemony. Marcella Althaus-Reid recognizes this when she uncovers the ways in which the Jesus portrayed in Scripture has often been annexed by, and domesticated into, an interpretative narrative which both colludes with and is reinforced by heterosexual-capitalist ideology:

Reading Christ should not become a conclusive task. Revelation is not compatible with the closure produced by authoritative (and authoritarian) readings of the scripture. What we are looking for is a permanent displacement of references, a quicksand scenario as the alternative for a reading of the different of God in Jesus, beyond the ideological configuration of heterosexuality. (Althaus-Reid 2006c, p. 519)

This radical appeal to a deeply postmodern and postcolonial account of the God revealed in the Bible is not, however, necessarily post-*Christian*. Rather, Althaus-Reid seeks to assert that the God of the Bible was queer all along, even if this God's queerness has been hidden or locked away by those whose authority and power would be threatened if the doors of these closets were flung wide. As Kwok Pui-lan notes, what queer criticism does so effectively is to uncover, so that 'the sexual body of Jesus is not off-limits anymore' (Kwok 2010, p. 123).

The project of queering a biblical text is simultaneously, and always, about queering the reader. Not only does the process ask about the motivations and contexts of authors and other interpreters, but it also leads the reader to interrogate his or her own former readings, analysing where they come from and in what assumptions they are rooted. It is therefore always deeply intertextual. Furthermore, Ken Stone (2001b) makes clear that, although it is all but impossible to get back to what a text 'originally' meant, queer analysis will sometimes enable a peeling-away of present-day overlays of heterosexuality and other assumptions which may have obscured elements of the text's historical locatedness (Stone 2001b, p. 24).

Queer biblical criticism, says Stone, calls into question the assumption that there are certain issues – sexual or otherwise – which can be 'safely cordoned off from biblical interpretation' (Stone 2001b, p. 29). The trope of queerness in biblical interpretation, he says, 'continues to call to mind unorthodox combinations and transgressive juxtapositions of things normally kept apart' (Stone 2001b, p. 31). The tearing-down of this barrier might be disturbing for some readers; but just as the death of Christ which profoundly changes the epistemic distance between God and humanity coincides with the curtain in the Temple being torn in two from top to bottom, so the tearing of outmoded binary tropes also changes what God and human beings can do and be for one another. As a result, queer readings of the Bible also cannot be understood as a single, monolithic group in distinction from other, non-queer readings. Collections of queer biblical interpretation or queer commentary may be more heterogeneous (Stone 2001b, p. 32) than collections of feminist, liberationist or postcolonial interpretation. However, they may simply show up the fact that even ostensibly similar groups of readings are actually *all* different and distinct from one another. One understanding of queer reading is that it is reading done by queer readers, often assumed to be lesbian, gay, bisexual or transgender readers. But Stone notes that queer readers are not actually so discrete or categorizable, and cannot be simplistically demarcated from non-queer readers (Stone 2001b, p. 32).

It is for this reason that it is not possible to say whether the Bible is queer or anti-queer, since the texts in question cannot be understood in distinction from the way its readers and interpreters understand and disseminate it. Experiments in queer reading such as *The Queer Bible Commentary* (2006) demonstrate that even texts of terror can be read queerly if this is what the reader seeks to do. Importantly, this does not render queer biblical interpretation arbitrary and worthless: rather, it makes clear that queering the Bible is not distinct from the life of the text in the lives of its readers. The Bible is not a thing-in-itself, but a thing-as-interpreted. Those who would assert that they have access to the 'original' meaning of a biblical text, whether or not it happens to be 'friendly' to queer people, have failed to understand the profoundly unsettling nature of postmodern hermeneutics and the light it sheds on other discourses. Koch has shown that a 'pissing contest' of conflicting and ever-more-prior understandings of the Bible (Koch 2001) misses the point. Rather, as David Tabb Stewart remarks, a creative and honest queer strategy would be to write-in, rather than 'uncover', queer strands: 'I could dispense with the text as a "recalcitrant witness", and all my work to out-Foucault Foucault . . . excavating the history of sexual thought in the Bible, and simply jump directly to constructing queers in the text' (Stewart 2006, p. 102). Indeed, characters in literature, be they persons or tropes, have lives of their own: reading queerness back into them, even if their author or authors did not explicitly intend it, is part of their real 'afterlife' beyond the reach of the author's authority.

Notes

1 The term 'texts of terror' was used by Phyllis Trible in the early 1980s to refer to biblical texts which told stories with women as victims, like those of Hagar and Tamar. Believing that women were still oppressed and silenced by much patriarchal religious rhetoric, Trible commented, 'Ancient tales of terror speak all too frighteningly of the present' (Trible 1984, p. xiii). The phrase has also been used to refer to texts where God appears to sanction violence and genocide. By association, it has come to refer to texts considered particularly 'dangerous' for non-heterosexual people because they are often used to argue that homosexuality is sinful or abhorrent (see for example Stuart 1997a, p. 43).

2 Here and throughout, direct biblical quotations are taken from the New Revised Standard Version.

3 Interestingly, a recent study by Marta Trzebiatowska has traced strong parallels between the 'coming-out' narratives of lesbian women, and those of nuns, in Poland. In both cases, the women concerned faced opposition from their families, because they were failing to live out a 'traditional' or 'ideal' pattern of heterosexual femininity. See Trzebiatowska 2009.

4 Shaw notes, however, that this legislation was repealed under Mary I in 1553; and the situation was ambiguous under Elizabeth I, who allowed rather than endorsed marriage for clergy. Far from being universally accepted at this time, married priests were regarded with suspicion and cynicism (Shaw 2007, p. 221). Old attitudes about the second-best status of marriage would not die easily, so there came a huge surge of polemical literature idealizing marriage and the family (Shaw 2007, p. 222).

5 That said, Origen asserts in his *Prologue to the Commentary on the Song of Songs* that, although anyone who can listen chastely and with pure ears will come to no harm from reading the Song, this may not be the case for those who are not yet ready for its 'solid food'. Thus Origen warns, 'I give warning and advice to everyone who is not yet free of the vexations of flesh and blood and who has not withdrawn from the desire for corporeal nature that he completely abstain from reading this book [that is the Song] and what is said about it. Indeed, they say that the Hebrews observe the rule that unless some one has attained a perfect and mature age, he is not even permitted to hold the book in his hands' (Origen 1979, p. 218). (I am grateful to Morwenna Ludlow for drawing this passage to my attention.) However, the same limits are placed on three other passages: the Genesis creation account, and two portions of Ezekiel dealing with cherubim and the Temple. Origen's translator Rowan Greer comments that these passages were not even permitted for ordinary reading by rabbis because they were the basis of mystical speculation (1979, p. 218); it is therefore not necessarily the Song's *sexual* element which is unsuitable for immature ears. Thus Moore's assertion that

in Origen 'the Song is implicitly assigned the stock role of the female temptress, potentially a Potiphar's wife lying in wait to entice and entrap the spiritually immature (male) reader' (Moore 2001, p. 46) is somewhat reductionistic and, ironically, allows Origen only a singular meaning and motivation.

6 Not every biblical book has its own essay: some, like the Pastoral Epistles, the Books of Ezra-Nehemiah, and the books of the twelve Minor Prophets (as in the Jewish tradition), are grouped together.

7 Ironically, perhaps, Hornsby does go on to give a close overview of other scholars' work on the dating, authorship and likely location of Ezekiel's composition. She justifies this with the assertion that 'such an exercise is requisite for acceptance into an academic work, and, without those credentials, queer scholarship may never make it past the front door' (Hornsby 2006b, p. 412). It is interesting to contrast this with assertions by Althaus-Reid and others (as in Chapter 6 below) that for queer theological scholarship to become fully accepted in the academy would be for it to lose its oppositional edge.

8 Koch (2001) identifies three hermeneutical strategies which he says gay people employ in biblical interpretation, but which are all inadequate for various reasons. These are the 'pissing contest' (Koch 2001, p. 12) (whereby pro- and anti-gay interpreters fight to define what the biblical texts about homosexuality *really* mean); 'Jesus is my trump card' (Koch 2001, p. 13) (whereby the existence of Jesus' love is used unproblematically to discard any troubling texts – which seems very appealing, except that, for Koch, the monolithic nature of Christianity is still problematic); and 'I can fit the glass slipper, too!' (Koch 2001, p. 14) (whereby queers are identified as having 'been there all along' in Scripture, in characters such as the eunuchs).

9 Foucault argues that contemporary culture often portrays recent, and especially Victorian, history as having been repressed about sex. Even in the twentieth century, this 'repressive hypothesis' figures sex as having been made unspeakable and taboo, and personal liberation as inhering in ever more free and frank talk about sexuality. However, Foucault suggests that the repressive hypothesis is actually illusory, and that in fact there has been plenty of talk about sex since the eighteenth century as well as before. The repressive hypothesis, as a matter of fact, draws more attention to discussion of sex even as it claims it has not been happening. The really interesting question, therefore, implies Foucault, is why we are so keen to pretend that we are not allowed to discuss sex, that doing so is forbidden, and that we are being terribly rebellious if we 'break free'.

10 For further reflection on the Song of Songs as a feminist text, see Trible 1973, pp. 42–7, where the Bride is shown to initiate lovemaking and to exercise symbolic power in naming her partner and mutuality in sharing work; Ostriker 2000, where the Song is understood as a biblical countertext offering 'an extraordinarily egalitarian image of mutual love and desire' (Ostriker 2000, p. 37); and

Brenner 2000, where female voices in the Song are understood as more confident and self-assured than male ones and where the possibility of female composition is acknowledged (Brenner 2000, p. 163). Exum shares Moore's suspicion that the Song is not in fact a woman's text, that the 'women' who speak are products of male fantasy; but, by her rhetoric about other feminist scholars having been 'taken in' by positive women's readings of the Song (Exum 2000, pp. 25, 27), her belief that any woman who views the text positively is nothing but a silly romantic at heart, and her insistence that any woman who enjoys describing her appearance sexually has internalized a male gaze (Exum 2000, p. 33), she reinforces mono-lithic models of interpretation, readership and healthy female sexuality. Indeed, Exum herself comments in a later text that 'Even if it were the case that the poem subtly encourages women to adopt a male way of looking at themselves, it does not follow that real readers have to read it that way' (Exum 2005, pp. 82-3).

11 It is significant, for instance, that unlike almost all the other contributions to *The Queer Bible Commentary* (with the exception of Jennifer L. Koosed writing on Ecclesiastes/Qohelet), Carden's piece is also named in Hebrew, 'Genesis/Bereshit'. Moreover, he discusses the book in sections equating to the weekly portions read in synagogues.

12 Derrida's notion of *différance* carries a sense of both deferment and differ-entiation: words, as signs, can only ever be partial, because they always defer to other words, other signs, never finally arriving at the thing signified. 'The word *différance* ... is suspended between differing and deferring' (Moore 1994, p. 21); ostensibly repeated words both *differ* from themselves (because the meaning communicated on two separate occasions is never identical) and *defer* a fixity of meaning (because the 'final' or 'ultimate' meaning can never be reached, since all concepts are mediated by more words).

5

Is the Christian Theological Tradition Queer?

> Here is an institution whose culturally venerable assessment of same-sex desire is (perhaps now more than ever) predominantly censorious, yet one which has also sought to stimulate devotion by the display made of a male body iconicized *in extremis* – a nearly naked man offered up to our gazes ('Ecce homo'). (Rambuss 1998, p. 11)

As we have seen, much queer theology and interpretation has centred on reclaiming or rediscovering queernesses hidden in or erased from both the Bible and its historical readings. In Chapter 4 I showed that this has sometimes involved reflecting on biblical characters and tropes which might be understood as sexually, socially or otherwise subversive. In this chapter, I consider other strands within the Christian tradition, which might be figured as queer, and ask whether these are enough to outweigh the often overwhelming associations of Christianity with heteronormativity, sexual repression and univocity. I start by considering queer interpretations of God, before turning to discussion of artistic representations of Christ, the writings of the Church Fathers and other historical figures and traits and behaviours which might be understood as both distinctly queer and distinctly Christian.

Queer God[1]

> The Queer God is the God who went into exile with God's people
> and remained there in exile with them. (Althaus-Reid 2004a, p. 146)

To what extent might God be considered queer and to what extent
might queer hermeneutical strategies be considered to be grounded in
the character of the divine? This has been explored in detail by Marcella
Althaus-Reid and Lisa Isherwood, among others. In *The Queer God*
(2003), Althaus-Reid's notion of an economically and politically subversive deity is fleshed out. She holds that a truly queer God, who prefers
the needs of the poor and marginal, has been displaced by mainstream
theological heterosexual metanarratives of desire, lack and power. It is
only in overcoming such ideologies that human beings can see more
clearly the nature of God's solidarity with excluded persons. The first
step for a queer theology must therefore be 'the indecenting of the production of God and Jesus' (Althaus-Reid 2000, p. 96): there is nothing
'natural', she suggests, about the concretized linking of theology with
colonial, capitalist structures of power and legitimacy, which play out in
ecclesiastical and social structures of authority and 'decentness', but it is
all too easy for those wishing to grasp or maintain ideological dominance
economically to appeal to the controlling power of religion too. Althaus-
Reid's invitations to reflect on God as faggot and whore, as a deity both
pornographic and suicidal, are disturbing and effective because such
images are so far removed from the God of so-called traditional family
values enforced and reproduced by mainstream theologies.

For Althaus-Reid, as for Thomas Bohache and Carter Heyward (as
I discuss below), God is incarnate in every human life, present in communities of struggle and resistance. Christian emphasis on God's radical
fleshliness is hardly new; but figuring God as an orgy, an omnisexual
deity (Althaus-Reid 2003, p. 53), who refuses to stand over against the
human bodies and stories of God-seekers, is still profoundly disquiet-
ing. Theology in search of a queer God (theology 'after' a queer God
– that is, *post* this God's refusal to be colonized) is always an economic
project, because the limitations of neo-liberal capitalism are the limita-

tions of cerebral individualism and monoculture (both agricultural and aesthetic). Queer stands against 'idealism and the theological commercial values of profiting by not identifying multiplicity' (Althaus-Reid 2003, p. 110). This necessitates a willingness to travel 'off the path', seeking God in unfamiliar places, in order to resist theological imperialism (Althaus-Reid 2003, pp. 31–2); it also entails acknowledging the 'shadow-side' of God (Althaus-Reid 2003, p. 16). Unless God is allowed to 'come out' of the closets of human construction, argues Althaus-Reid, God's otherness will always be negated (Althaus-Reid 2003, p. 37). What is disturbed by queering God is not solid theological truth, but a heteronormative distortion of theology. Recognizing the veritable strangeness of God requires a willingness, also, to question assumptions about the structure and nature of culture and social interactions, particularly those grounded in norms or truths often considered unquestionable or incontrovertible. There are parallels with this aspect of Althaus-Reid's thought in work by Jeremy Carrette, who asserts that 'Christianity and sexuality are anchored in the same religious symbolic of dualism and monotheism. This epistemological framework, however, is broken in queer theory, which results in, and indeed demands . . . the death of the imperialistic regime of theology' (Carrette 2004, pp. 217–18). Indeed, Carrette suggests that it is crucial that queer's capacity to blur the normative should be deeply disruptive of religion's very space within Western thought (Carrette 2004, p. 220).

Influenced by Carter Heyward, the queerness of God in Althaus-Reid's work sometimes seems to border on the post-Christian – though, as we saw above, this is not how Althaus-Reid herself understood it. In this account, not only has God has not stopped creating, but God has not stopped *being created* – by, in and through humans' responses to, and interactions with, one another's bodily experience. Althaus-Reid says, 'The concept of participation in the Trinity means that the Queer strangers can now . . . talk of God from hidden experiences and distrusted knowledge' (Althaus-Reid 2003, pp. 74–5). This is 'true kenosis . . . where God does not grant Godself privileges and thus discovers the meaning of incarnation' (Althaus-Reid 2003, p. 75). This processive model of a God who is still coming into being via human activity is not

entirely orthodox: this God actually needs humanity in order to continue existing, since (says Heyward), 'Without our crying, our yearning,
our raging, there is no God. For in the beginning is the relation, and in
the relation is the power that creates the world through us, and with
us, and by us, you and I, you and we, and none of us alone' (Heyward
1982, p. 172). The boundaries between redeemer and redeemed are
therefore blurred (Althaus-Reid 2003, p. 138): perhaps the queerest
thing of all about this queer God is the indivisibility from the non-divine
realm. After Heyward, Althaus-Reid seems to be saying that God simply
cannot exist independently of human relationship and human action:
certainly 'God cannot be Queered unless theologians have the courage
to come out from their . . . closets' (Althaus-Reid 2000, p. 88). Queer,
transgressive human lives and stories contribute to the queer God's continued coming-into-being, and God and humanity mutually constitute
one another much more overtly even than in theologies which recognize
that humans might be co-creators and co-redeemers with God (as in the
work of Philip J. Hefner – see for example Hefner 1998). The instability and recalcitrance of Althaus-Reid's queer God induce continuous
journeying for those who walk with this deity.[2] This is not mere 'engagement with Christian categories', as Kwok Pui-lan figures Althaus-Reid's
work (Kwok 2005, p. 148), but rather a moving kind of Christian atheism
which rejects the false deities wrought in hegemonic bluster.

The lack of a strong Christ figure in Heyward's own theology, as in
that of Gary David Comstock and J. Michael Clark, brings them in for
strong criticism by Rollan McCleary. McCleary claims, 'All three of
these theologians share probably the lowest image and most dismissive treatment of Christ that a specifically Christian theology has ever
offered . . . There is nothing in Comstock's queer version of Christianity
which no neo-pagan could endorse' (McCleary 2004, p. 97). Figuring
these theologians as 'dismissive' of Christ, McCleary suspects they have
fuelled opposition to homosexuality from the US Christian Right simply
by being not recognizably Christian. However, McCleary's somewhat
alarmist warning that 'non-Americans are likely to find Comstock impossible' (McCleary 2004, p. 97) is unfounded, and his narrow view of what
Christian orthodoxy might look like (despite his own interest in explor-

ing mystical and esoteric spiritual expressions) means that he caricatures Heyward and others as merely 'cavalier' with the Bible (McCleary 2004, p. 98) rather than recognizing the extent to which they are creatively resistant with their hermeneutics.

It is true that Heyward, Clark, Comstock and Althaus-Reid go further than most in reframing and indecenting Christian orthodoxy in pursuit of a radically queer and relational God. We saw above that Althaus-Reid is especially aware of the extent to which Christ as a figure has been used to reinscribe systems of heterosexual normativity, and that this may have made her reluctant to appeal to Christ as openly or as unreservedly as someone like Bohache does. Nonetheless, other theologians also identify God's queerness, some more sympathetic than others to finding traces of this in the Christian tradition. Gerard Loughlin says, 'God's being is indubitable but radically unknowable, and any theology that forgets this is undeniably straight, not queer . . . God in Godself is an identity without an essence' (Loughlin 2007b, p. 10). Part of queerness is, perhaps, to be unpindownable, to be apophatic; Tina Beattie quotes Ephrem the Syriac's assertion that it is important that Mary the mother of Christ embodies the paradox of simultaneous virginity and maternity, for 'if Your mother is incomprehensible, who is capable of [comprehending] you?' (Ephrem 1989, p. 131; Beattie 2007, p. 293). B. K. Hipsher argues for what she calls a '*trans*-God' – not merely a transgender God, since even transgender imagery can solidify and exclude, but a God who is *trans*gressive of *all* human imagery and can be understood only apophatically (Hipsher 2009, p. 99; see also Cornwall 2009b).

Laurel C. Schneider concurs that queer readings of Scripture might achieve something more fundamental than rediscovering a queer ancestry in the human beings represented there, and might actually queer the divine. She says,

If we can plausibly reread the story of Sodom . . . as Yhwh's rescue of the queers and a burning of the bashers [Carden 2001], then we are reading a contemporary subject position funded by a very strong desire into the text perhaps more than we are reading some kind of mythic truth *out* of it. But the difference between these two positions may also be less relevant than the fruit such a reading can yield for our contemporary thoughts about a divine being whose founding tales could include such a deed. (Schneider 2001, p. 215)

Eugene F. Rogers, too, notes that God as portrayed in Scripture some-times seems to act in queer ways, as when the God of Israel in expanding the history of salvation to non-Jews behaves 'promiscuously', acting 'against nature' in showing solidarity with the Gentiles who, unbe-knownst to Paul, would become far more numerous as Christians than Jews would – and yet, who, in so doing, 'does not supersede or replace but queers himself' (sic) (Rogers 2009, p. 26).

Even if such imagery sometimes seems to risk rendering God a human-like figure to the exclusion of being a divine one, this in itself is important, for it never allows us to forget that conceptions of God and conceptions of legitimate human activity and behaviour are mutually constituting. We may not always recognize it, but our beliefs about what God should do and be are coloured by our prior experiences and beliefs about what humans should do and be. Someone like Stephen D. Moore may seem to render God too human and to focus too much on particu-lar aspects of human sexual experience, when he suggests that the book of Romans is a narrative of queered super- and subordination in which God is 'penetrated' and 'entered'. Moore unapologetically starts from the ways in which altered discourses of human sexual activity might alter perceptions of God:

Any expansion of the domain of the permissible in human sexual relations would ... result in a corresponding transformation of human-divine relations. What transformed relations might we then envision between the three central characters in Paul's epochal pas-sion play – between God and Jesus, Jesus and Paul, God and Paul? What else but those in which Paul would not only open himself utterly to Jesus, but Jesus, reciprocally, would open himself utterly to Paul. Most significantly of all, however, God would open himself to each of them in turn. The Bottomless Top, the conceptual pivot of Paul's entire theosexual system, would become a top with a bottom.

God would get a bottom of his own. And what might he not be ready for then? Sexual activity that would offer only the most precarious of toeholds to hierarchy, and thus would constitute a divine warrant for radically egalitarian forms of social behaviour? (Moore 2001, p. 171)

Crucially, however, he acknowledges that these altered understandings of God might then *further* affect the kinds of human sexual experience which can be deemed to show and tell something of the divine–human story. The implication is, therefore, that a similar process has already occurred before, several stages back, and that the heteronormative patriarchal story of God with which we are so familiar was not the 'real' or 'original' one but simply the product of an earlier narrative. This, of course, does not mean that our understanding of God is on an ever-forward trajectory becoming 'smaller and clearer as the years go by'; as Larkin's poem implies,[3] such is not entirely truthful, and elides the unspannable distance between what is and what has been. Indeed, we must be careful not to caricature the historical Christian tradition as a place bereft of flashes of resistance and counter-testimony.

In the spirit of recognizing and celebrating such flashes, I now turn to consideration of 'queer precedent' elsewhere in the Christian tradition, starting with possible 'queernesses' as identified in devotional art.

Tradition I: queer art

It is not possible here to engage with the full breadth of Christian representational art and the ways in which it might be considered to queer existing binary tropes of male/female, homosexual/heterosexual, human/ divine, dead/resurrected, and so on. I seek mainly to comment on just one kind of art, namely images of Christ produced for devotional purposes or consciously citing devotional tropes such as *pietàs* and depictions of Christ crucified or resurrected. Recent books by Kittredge Cherry (2007) and others identify a queer strand in some such Christian devotional art, including but not limited to Christa pieces (which I discuss below) and images of Christ which overtly portray him as homosexual or as an object of homosexual devotion.

These include recent images such as Elisabeth Ohlson Wallin's photograph *Sermon on the Mount*, modelled by gay men, depicting a white-robed, long-haired Christ atop a rock, arms outstretched, with men in leather bondage gear clinging to him and gazing up at him. This photograph is part of the artist's 1998 twelve-picture sequence *Ecce Homo*, another of which, *Jesu Dop (Baptism of Christ)* shows a very naked (and shaven) Christ partly submerged on the steps of a swimming pool or public bath, at the moment of his baptism by John the Baptist. The John figure holds one hand in blessing above Jesus' head, and with the other lightly touches his hip. Christ's penis is clearly visible above the white cloth he holds, and a white dove sits on his shoulder. Ohlsson Wallin's *Krucifix (Crucifix)* piece shows a white-sheeted vista from above, on which is laid out a sleeping or dead dark-skinned male, arms extended. Interestingly, although the man is naked, his genitals are concealed. But rather than a sterile loincloth of the kind criticized by Mark D. Jordan (below), this Christ's modesty is protected by the bent leg of another, white-skinned man who embraces him. The folds in the sheet around these two figures form the shape of a heart. Like ethnically non-white images of Christ, when used in mainly white settings, sexually queer images of Christ crucified may be problematic if used by non-queer people, since they may tend to equate queerness with suffering and abjection or to fetishize it. However, they also go a long way to ensuring that the soteriological functions of the Christ-body are not solely or uniquely pinned to bodies read as white, heterosexual and so on and help to expose the way in which the suffering of even a straight white Christ has been fetishized in its unchosen inscription onto other kinds of bodies.

Another well-known contemporary artist who has painted figures interpreted as queer Christs is the Franciscan Robert Lentz, whose 1996 icon of Saint Perpetua and Saint Felicity is the cover illustration for *The Queer Bible Commentary* (2006). Lentz's *Christ the Bridegroom* icon (1986) depicts an enthroned Christ being embraced by a young male figure, John. It was commissioned by Henri Nouwen for use during his personal devotions; Nouwen, who was quietly gay (and celibate), had requested an image symbolizing the offering of his love and sexuality to Christ, and Lentz commented that Nouwen 'used it to come to grips with his own homosexuality' (quoted in Cherry 2007, p. 49). Michael Ford comments that, for Nouwen, 'the icon became a means of grounding in the Incarnation his own struggle' (Ford 2002, p. 141).

Nonetheless, the *lack* of queerness in much artistic representation of Christ is criticized by Mark D. Jordan (2007b). Jordan claims that in Catholic sculpture and painting, Jesus can never be shown naked on the cross, and that, even where the figure is clothed in a loincloth, there is unlikely to be anything genital underneath (Jordan 2007b, pp. 283–4). Jordan understands these smooth, Action Man or GI Joe-like (though without moving eyes operated by a switch in the back of the head) representations of Christ to be evidence that Christians are ashamed of their own sexuality and therefore cannot acknowledge that of Christ. Artists and theologians, claims Jordan, have wanted to retain the centrality of Christ's masculine *gender* without ever fully engaging his male *sex* (Jordan 2007b, pp. 285, 287).

It is telling that Jordan does not appeal to specific works of art. This is odd, since he knows of Leo Steinberg's *The Sexuality of Christ in Renaissance Art and in Modern Oblivion*, which, particularly in its 1996 second edition, demonstrates an undeniable accent on the genitals of Christ in the Catholic art of the Renaissance. Although Jordan's emphasis is Christ crucified, it would also have been interesting to know how he would read the queerness of the many paintings showing Christ as a naked baby holding, pointing to or otherwise framing his own genitals[4] or even having them fondled by others – as by his grandmother, Saint Anne, in Hans Baldung Grien's 1511 woodcut *Holy Family* and in Giuseppe Cesare (the Cavaliere d'Arpino)'s 1593 painting *Madonna and Child with St John, St Anne and the Magdalen* (Steinberg 1996, pp. 8–11, 118). The oddness of this act can be read in various ways, but despite Philippe Ariès' assertion that it simply echoes a practice of admiring a male baby's genitals which was prevalent in the past (Steinberg 1996, p. 8; Ariès 1962, p. 103), Steinberg insists,

There are many things babies do . . . which no artist, however deeply committed to realism, ever thought of imputing to the Christ Child . . .

When a Renaissance artist quickens an Infancy scene with naturalistic detail, he is not recording this or that observation, but revealing in the thing observed a newfound compatibility with his subject. This rule must apply as well to the palpation of the Child's privy parts. The question is not whether such practice was common, but how, whether common or not, it serves to set Mary's son apart from the run of the sons of Eve. (Steinberg 1996, p. 10)

Steinberg's own conclusion is that such representations emphasize Christ's simultaneous humanity and divinity: his genitals may betray his status as a definitely human baby, but his upper body often does things of which no ordinary human baby would be capable – or which poignantly foreshadow his adult life and death. What is significant about Catholic Renaissance paintings of Christ as an infant is that they no longer, as in earlier pictures, have to 'prove' his divinity (Steinberg 1996, pp. 10–11): rather, the pictures of the period lay emphasis on his humanity. Fondling a baby's genitals might, then, *both* reflect broader practice *and* set Jesus apart as uniquely human–divine (Steinberg 1996, p. 13): this at once-ness, even if Steinberg does not characterize it as such – though Jordan might have done – is profoundly queer. Steinberg expounds,

This supreme feat of God, superior even to the primordial act of Creation, is perpetually manifest in the Incarnation, that is to say, here and now in this armful of babyflesh. The wonder of it, and its constant reaffirmation – this mystery is the stuff of Renaissance art: the humana-tion[5] of God; the more 'superwonderful' (St Bonaventure's word) the more tangible you can make it. (Steinberg 1996, p. 12)

Moreover, the emphasis on the baby's genitals is not unproblematically asexual: it has a 'select sexual accent', says Steinberg (1996, p. 14), citing images such as Francesco Botticini's *Madonna and Child with Angels* (c. 1490), where distinctly feminine-looking angels scatter flower-petals over the baby's genitalia. Incarnation, in fact, cannot *but* be sexual, for 'it is by procreation that the [human] race, though consigned to death individually, endures collectively to fulfil the redemptive plan . . . Thus understood, the evidence of Christ's sexual member serves as the pledge of God's humanation' (Steinberg 1996, p. 15): this too is queer. Alexander Sturgis remarks of the child's pose in the Campin *The Virgin and Child in an Interior* – with Jesus grasping the face of his mother Mary – that it mirrors that 'associated with adult lovers' (Sturgis 2000, p. 56).

More explicitly, Steinberg discusses at length the erect nature of the penis in several representations of both the infant and the adult Christ[6] (Steinberg 1996, pp. 76–90; 298–325) – the first passage representing the most controversial and contested aspect of the argument in the original 1983 edition of the book. I have some sympathy with those critics who found these infancy images ambiguous in terms of the erections. However, Steinberg's reading of the adult erections in the 'Man of Sorrows' pictures is more persuasive, particularly his conclusion that, since Augustine understood involuntary erections to be the result of the Fall, Christ's sinless erections here can only be voluntary and willed. This might provide the basis for a fascinating meditation of how since all are 'in Christ', all might share in the nature of the body of Christ 'in whom no law of body wages against law of mind' (Steinberg 1996, p. 324).

Steinberg's analysis, then, seems to belie Jordan's assertion that Catholic artists and sculptors have never had Christ's penis and testes in mind as they worked, have never meditated reverently on incarnation as the genitals are wrought even if they are subsequently to be covered (Jordan 2007b, p. 284). Indeed, claims Steinberg, 'only they, the painters and sculptors, kept all of Christ's body in their mind's eye. And some among them embraced even his sex in their thought' (Steinberg 1996, p. 17). This continues into paintings and sculptures of the adult Christ, centring on those representing the time around his death. Even if nakedness generally was linked to sex which was linked to sin, this was not enough to prevent the depiction of a nakedness *immune* from sin, as by Michelangelo in the 1514 *Risen Christ* (Steinberg 1996, pp. 19–22): Christ's upper body is turned toward the cross he carries, but his lower parts squarely face the viewer, with proportionate testes and penis in full view surrounded by only a smattering of hair. Many of the later copies made by other artists did conceal the genital region; however, says Steinberg,

If Michelangelo denuded his Risen Christ, he must have sensed a rightness in his decision more compelling than inhibitions of modesty; must have seen that a loincloth would convict these genitalia of being 'pudenda', thereby denying the very work of redemption which promised to free human nature from its Adamic contagion of shame. (Steinberg 1996, p. 21)

This, then, is not to dismiss Jordan's entire argument, since Christ's nudity is possible *despite* nudity in general still having shameful connotations: it does not quite match up to Jordan's appeal for crucifixes where the penis 'would be neither exaggerated nor minimized, fetishized neither as a commodity to be chased nor as a disgrace to be repudiated' (Jordan 2007b, p. 284). Moreover, even Steinberg owns that nude representations of Christ polarize to the beginning and end of his life, to infancy and circumcision scenes and to death and resurrection ones, with no naked Jesus in between (Steinberg 1996, p. 18). Images of the *ostentatio genitalium*, the holding or cupping of his genitals by the dead Christ even where they are otherwise concealed by clothing, point back to their parallel images of the dandled baby, coming full circle and perfecting his redemptive task (Steinberg 1996, p. 102). Examples of entirely naked, genital-baring flagellations, crucifixions and *piètas* also survive (see for example Michelangelo's unfinished *Rondanini Pièta* [1564], Hans Burgkmair's 1515 woodcut *Christ on the Cross,* and the Master of St Mark's 1355–60 *Crucifixion* panels; for discussion of the latter two and others see Steinberg 1996, pp. 135–9), even if loinclothed versions are more ubiquitous:[7] Jordan is simply wrong to suppose they do not exist in Catholic art.

But the fact they *do* exist in art might help rather than hinder Jordan and others in asking why reflection on Christ's genitals – even Christ's erections – is not more evident in mainstream Catholic theology: evidence, as Steinberg has it, of art where theology fails (Steinberg 1996, p. 323). And why *is* it that Christ's erections must be ascribed to rational will rather than to profoundly ordinary human arousal? Is it because, as Althaus-Reid suspects, Jesus has been 'dressed theologically as a heterosexually oriented (celibate) man. Jesus with erased genitalia; Jesus minus erotic body' (Althaus-Reid 2000, p. 114)? And there might also be questions to be asked about what makes the infant Jesus touching his genitals so offensive that the image has been mutilated on at least one occasion (Steinberg 1996, p. 279); if the Christian-artistic tradition has contained such oddness it has certainly not done so unequivocally. Indeed, Steinberg says, 'The record suggests that it is perhaps not so much their genital emphasis as their escape from destruction that now makes these works seem more exceptional than they once were' (Steinberg 1996, p. 261). Importantly, however, the queerness of the Christian tradition should not *continue* to be excised by those who would see only its expurgatory inclination: Jordan might, if he tried, find it queerer than he has supposed, particularly since (as Loughlin and Rambuss both note), Steinberg himself does not really go into the male homoerotic and anti-procreative potential of images of the naked, bare-penised, perhaps even erect adult Christ in the prime of his ministry (Loughlin 2007c, p. 126; Rambuss 1998, pp. 44–5, 63, 138).[8]

The majority of a certain kind of art produced during a certain period of time was designed to be devotional – to hang as altarpiece in public church or private chapel – which means that it can also be read as telling us something of the artists', and their patrons', cosmologies. There is also a wealth of other written texts – poetry, diaries, collections of sermons – to which we cannot hope to do justice here. But authors such as Richard Rambuss have attempted to show that these various texts 'afford us a plethora of affectively charged sites for tracing the complex overlappings and relays between religious devotion and erotic desire' (Rambuss 1998, p. 2), in ways that are sometimes distinctly queer if queer means (at least in part) an acknowledgement that eroticism – the stuff of how and why bodies respond sexually – is not to be divorced from the sacred. Christianity possesses its own 'contradictory, closeted libidinalities' (Rambuss 1998, p. 11). It is significant that attempts to 'queer' Christian iconography often occur from *outside* the church, for example, in subversive cartoons disseminated at Gay Pride marches – the critics' assumptions, presumably, being that such subversion would never take place from within the Christian fold. Indeed, Rambuss comments that it sometimes takes an outsider to show up what is already there:

At issue in these . . . contemporary homodevotional expressions . . .
is, I would argue, not just a perverse desire to pervert the sacred . . .
Rather, it is more a sense of how perverse the sacred is to begin with,
of how the sacred body *as such* – even the sacred body of Jesus, that
body whose eroticism is not serviceable to marriage, procreation,
domesticity – already glistens with the sheen of the transgressive,
holding forth both devotional and erotic possibilities of contraven-
tion and excess. (Rambuss 1998, p. 68)

But I wonder whether this is slightly naïve, not doing justice to the
equivocal relationship between Christianity and queerness expressed
by Stuart, Webster and others. To suggest, even implicitly, that Christians do not know any better, that they are incapable of critiquing and
reframing aspects of their own institution, and that it takes others to do
the 'naughty' work of showing up Jesus' queerness, is condescending
and somewhat polarizing.

Of course, the kind of queerness Rambuss identifies in text and art is
still problematic. For example, it is strikingly male, and this is necessary:
even if female sexual devotion or symbolic 'betrothal' to a male God is
disruptive of certain binaries (human/divine, carnal/spiritual, married/
virginal[9] and so on), it often serves to reinscribe conventional heterosexual ones. Moreover, Rambuss' analysis risks anachronism, assuming
that the sensual, lush imagery employed by poets like Donne and Her-
bert is always somehow sexual in the way we would now understand
it, which Bynum and others (though Rambuss is unconvinced by her
argument) have sought to show is not the case (see for example Bynum
1992, 1995). Finally, Rambuss somewhat misses the truly queerest questions: for example, why it is that *even* a religion so clearly concerned
with incarnation and with overturning expectations along certain axes so
readily falls prey to anti-corporeality and trite convention along others.

Bynum takes up the second of these three points, with her detailed
study of the ways in which Christ's body – particularly his crucified body
– is figured as 'feminine' in the art of the late-medieval period. Bynum's
readings appeal to paintings where Jesus is shown lactating from his
breasts, gushing milk from the wound in his side, mirroring his lactating

mother, or otherwise represented as providing 'food' (often grapes or wheat to echo the wine and bread of the Eucharist):[10]

> There are . . . medieval paintings that assimilate Christ to Mary. Over and over again in the fourteenth and fifteenth centuries we find representations of Christ as the one who feeds and bleeds. Squirting blood from wounds often placed high in the side, Christ fills cups for his followers just as Mary feeds her baby. Christ's body, like woman's, is depicted as food. In two very different fifteenth-century paintings, for example, Christ's wound is treated almost as if it were a nipple and produces in one case the wafer, in another case the blood of the eucharist. (Bynum 1986, p. 427)

Bynum notes the strong links made by scientists and others at this time between blood and milk, pointing to the widespread belief in the middle ages that all bodily fluids were either blood or other manifestations of blood. Breast milk, for example, was blood converted in form for the purpose of feeding children. Thus, she holds, all bleeding, but especially that from women's bodies, was tied up with nurturing and cleansing as well as (often) pollution. She says, 'Many medieval assumptions linked woman and flesh and the body of God. Not only was Christ enfleshed with flesh from a woman; his own flesh did womanly things: it bled, it bled food, and it gave birth' (Bynum 1986, p. 423). Christ's body was associated with the Church, which provided succour for those who sought refuge in it. Unlike Steinberg, Bynum suggests that the artists of the Middle Ages might be seeking to show forth *not* Christ's maleness but his femininity, to emphasize the Church's nourishing power.

But for Bynum, what is most intriguing – and what might be of most interest to queer theologians – is that all this is *not* 'sexual'; that is, that breasts and genitals can figure cosmically and semiologically without having to be unequivocally linked with their most obvious functions. What to a modern reader looks like orgasm or arousal might simply be just what it is presented as, religious ecstasy (for sometimes a cigar is just a cigar). In this anti-utilitarian account, genitalia are more than what a genitocentric culture understands them to be. As such, the entirety of personhood and identity does not reside in these parts (which is one of Bynum's major criticisms of Steinberg for situating the infant Christ's humanity so squarely in his penis). It may simply be, says Bynum, that 'there is a modern tendency to find sex more interesting than feeding, suffering or salvation' (Bynum 1986, p. 413). This in itself helps to provide another riposte to those who are overly abjectionist, who understand queer to be always and inherently a matter of alienation and suppression: crucially, Bynum's analysis seems to hint that 'queer sex' can only be written out of Christian history once it has first been written into Christian iconography. So to read the 'complex, polysemic' art of the Christian past in only one way (that is, a sexual way) is to limit not only what it can tell us about the period in which it was produced, but also what it can tell us about ourselves here and now. Bynum suggests, 'Rather than mapping back onto medieval paintings modern dichotomies, we might find in medieval art and literature some suggestion of a symbolic richness our own lives and rituals seem to lack' (Bynum 1986, p. 438).

Kwok Pui-lan brings another important dimension to considerations of the sexuality of Christ, reminding us that this should never take place without simultaneously analysing his 'racial', cultural and social context; Kwok suspects that 'the imaginations of white scholars . . . tends to isolate sexuality' (including Jesus' sexuality) from these dimensions (Kwok 2010, p. 123). Constructions of the sexuality of Jesus, whether in art or in written texts, have always been influenced by complex background discourses about the way artists and scholars understand their own, and Jesus', race – especially where Jesus is figured as founder of a new Christian faith whose adherents are racially and religiously superior to Jews (Kwok 2010, p. 128–30). It is for this reason, suggests Kwok from a postcolonial perspective, that in both art and written text, Jesus' sexuality has sometimes been 'hidden':

> The taboo of Jesus' sexuality in the nineteenth-century quest of the historical Jesus served not only to discipline individual sexual behavior, but also to maintain racial boundaries and cultural imperialism to facilitate the expansion of Europe. Jesus' sexed body provided a provocative site for the inscription and projection of powerful myths

about sexuality, race, gender, and colonial desire . . . In contrast to the sexualized natives and the lower classes, Jesus was seen as exemplifying bourgeois ideals: controlling his passions, managing his desires, and sublimating his bodily needs. (Kwok 2010, p. 132)

Among Kittredge Cherry (2007)'s collected queer depictions of Christ are those where the Christ-figure is female, like Janet McKenzie's crucifixion painting *Christ Mother,* and Sandra Yagi's 2003 *Crucifixion* (showing a woman in loincloth hanging on a cross as, below her, three men who seem to represent religious leaders empty out her handbag to see if it contains anything of worth). I have written elsewhere (Cornwall 2008b) of the phenomenon of the Christa, a painting, photograph or sculpture depicting a female figure crucified in place of Christ. Even if they have tended to end up in art galleries and museums, at least some of these pieces, such as James M. Murphy's *Christine on the Cross* (a woman with splayed legs nailed to an inverted cross), were originally created to be viewed in churches and used devotionally. Murphy's sculpture, created as part of his own Easter meditation, was initially displayed in the chapel at Union Theological Seminary in New York, in 1984 (Clague 2005a, p. 92). Edwina Sandys' *Christa,* created in 1974 and exhibited in the Episcopal Cathedral of St John the Divine in New York in Holy Week 1984 (Clague 2005a, pp. 84–5), was removed after eleven days due to protests (Clague 2005b, p. 49). Julie Clague notes that its location in a site of worship rather than an art gallery 'politicized people's reactions to the sculpture and gave rise to widespread comment' (Clague 2005a, p. 85). Other pieces have specifically repudiated aspects of institutional religion: Jens Galschiot's *In the Name of God,* a copper sculpture of a crucified pregnant teenager, was first set up outside the Church of Our Lady in Copenhagen (the main cathedral in Denmark), on World AIDS Day 2006, and was designed to comment on the impact of Roman Catholic and fundamentalist Christian opposition to contraception and comprehensive sex education (www.aidoh.dk/?categoryID=187). Despite criticisms that Christa pieces might tend to further objectify or victimize women, they have also been figured (as in Bohache 2008) as sites of queer amplification of Christ's solidarity with all who are poor or marginalized. Their associations with specifically female bodily experience (Margaret Argyle's *Bosnian Christa* is a textile panel depicting a female figure crucified within a dark red velvet vulva, and was designed as 'a personal Lenten reflection on the plight of the women who were raped and forcibly impregnated in the former Yugoslavia in 1993' – Clague 2005c, p. 41) might be read as a profoundly queer concern for particularities of carnality which neither erase nor make abstract the associations between gender, sex and violence. Recent work by Nicola Slee seeks to problematize the ubiquity of *crucified* women in Christa imagery, which might itself reinscribe suffering and abjection. Where, she asks, is the *risen* Christa? (Slee, 2011).

There have also been deliberately queer readings of broader Christian iconography, particularly representations of Mary the mother of Christ. Mario Ribas (Ribas 2006) holds that religious images are extremely influential in disseminating particular (predominantly heterosexual) paradigms, especially where the majority of the people who see and are encouraged to use them are both devout and illiterate. Throughout Latin America, icons and statues of saints are to be found in the midst of ordinary life, in bars and brothels as well as in churches. However, asserts Ribas, icons of Mary are often used to emphasize to ordinary women how *unlike* the virginal ideal woman they themselves are. Alternative representations of Mary and Jesus (perhaps showing their genitals,[11] or depicting Mary as something other than young, light-skinned and beautiful), might highlight their carnality and prompt viewers to face their own, messy, imperfect bodily specificities rather than assuming that these are not appropriate or legitimate sites of theological reflection.

Tradition II: queer history

As we have begun to see, scholars have sometimes sought queer ancestors or a queer genealogy not only within the Bible itself and in conceptions of God, but also elsewhere in the tradition, as for example in the writings of the mystics and in certain of the Church Fathers. It has been countered that it is just as anachronistic to call such figures unproblematically 'queer' as to call them 'homosexual', since these concepts did not exist at the time and have been projected backwards onto them: Martín Hugo Córdova Quero argues, 'To queer the past is not to transplant *gays, lesbians, bisexuals* or *transsexuals* into the past, but to *disrupt* monolithic discourses that oppress historical periods' (Córdova Quero 2004, p. 28).

It is perhaps less problematic, then, to identify not explicitly queer, but critical, counter-cultural or non-mainstream elements in the Christian tradition – which might, perhaps, come to be called 'queer with caveats'. Indeed, Virginia Burrus appeals to a 'counterspeech' lodged in the texts of the Fathers themselves (Burrus 2007, p. 148). Perhaps the most popular Father to have been claimed as queer is the Cappadocian, Gregory of Nyssa. Burrus herself formulates an account of Gregory as 'Queer Father' – not, she says, in an attempt to make Patristics 'naughtier' or more politically correct, but rather as part of a project of theological healing, uncovering the lack of finality and therefore lack of supremacy in aspects of the tradition that have been used abusively (Burrus 2007, p. 148). Moreover, queering ancient texts – by which Burrus means 'to designate (literary) practices of eroticism that actively resist and/or put into question the very category of the "normal," the "conventional," or the "natural" in a context in which resistance intensifies, critiques, and partly subverts the violence of both *domus* and *dominus*' (Burrus 2001, p. 449) – also brings about a re-consideration of the ways in which ancient and contemporary readings interact and stand in historical connection (Burrus 2001, p. 450).

Burrus claims that commentators such as John Milbank and Sarah Coakley have been 'alarmed' at the queerness they uncover in Gregory of Nyssa: Milbank, she says, seems to reject any suggestion of weakness in Gregory 'lest it spread like a sickness' (Burrus 2007, p. 159), whereas in actual fact Gregory's engagement with the weakness of subjectivity is a fascinating anticipation of present-day awareness of the vulnerability of the subject. Coakley, says Burrus, 'finds it necessary to deliver a stern admonishment', claiming that it would be wrong to read Gregory as promoting formerly outlawed sexual pleasures (Burrus 2007, p. 162).[12]

It is significant, though, that many of these commentators are playful, tongue-in-cheek and consciously imaginative with what they claim figures like Gregory to do or be, and are well aware of the limitations of projecting onto them across such a distance of time, culture and communication. For example, Michael Nausner's study of Gregory of Nyssa's 'transgendering' as part of his transformative eschatology (Nausner 2002), whereby it is seen as a prefiguring of full unity in Christ, is distinctly self-aware. Nausner appeals to a 'transformative eschatology' in Gregory's writings, but one which implies 'a playful and mutual transgendering rather than transcendence of gender' (Nausner 2002, p. 56). Nausner argues that, in Gregory's commentary on the Song of Songs, there is a sense of ecstasy transcending order – of becoming drunk with wine and milk – to the extent that 'One wonders whether the orderly gender hierarchy can stay intact in all this *going out* of orderliness . . . As the imagery gets more conflated, the clear distinction into male and female becomes less convincing' (Nausner 2002, p. 64). It is easy to see how this gender-bending kind of reading might render Gregory a queer-friendly or even proto-queer figure, but Nausner still recognizes the limits attached to being able to claim such an identity of a historical figure who also (it must be said) lived in a culture-bound community and himself resorted at times to gender stereotypes: Burrus, for instance, notes Gregory's apparent belief that virtue is a 'male' quality and vice a 'female' one (Burrus 2007, p. 153). To image oneself as feminine in contradistinction to a male Christ – as the fathers and patriarchs of the church frequently do – is already, if one is male, disruptive of straightforward heterosexual norms. It is *already* queer, even without bringing an explicitly homosexual element into it. Richard Rambuss comments, 'The convention is no more conventional – no more heterosexually conventional – than the deviation from it . . . Christian desire – the desire for Christ – remains other than straight and straitening' (Rambuss 1998, p. 68). The element of playfulness might be considered particularly important given that, as Karma Chávez shows, play marks a transcendence of normativity (and, therefore, a questioning of the often-unquestioned status quo) (Chávez 2008, p. 9). Something like this is going on in the phenomenon of camp, which, by appropriating a behaviour, mode of dress or pattern of speech in an exaggerated and overdone manner, calls into question its initial, and often unremarked, meaning and significance.

What is queer in an ancient text like Jerome's *Life of Paul the Hermit*, suggests Burrus, is not just the strikingly romantic and erotic bent of some of its language and imagery, but also, just as significantly, 'the fact that the text will not, finally, *settle* at all, will not settle upon an *object of desire*' (Burrus 2001, p. 459). As a result, 'as readers we are destined to remain uncertain'; objects of desire are 'productively unlocatable' (Burrus 2001, p. 474). It is exactly through recognizing that the ancient narratives are interrupted, inexact and incomplete, believes Burrus, that we must recognize that this also applies to us as readers; for 'where the object of desire is infinitely dispersed, so too is the subject' (Burrus 2001, p. 475). Importantly, this is not a wholly positive realization:

> Sliding into the tale of a captive monk, I have indeed found my tongue again, now a woman's tongue unambiguously interpellated into the text . . . And yet, where the path leads from there, I cannot say. I see only the doublings of duplicity, a multiplication of possibilities that may or may not cancel each other out . . . Shattered by so much freedom, so much constraint, I am swallowed up by a text that can scarcely hold a place for me, can scarcely hold me in place. It is from elsewhere that I will return, again and again. (Burrus 2001, pp. 478–9).

Queer, feminist, postcolonial and other readers may be suspicious indeed about the good of being 'swallowed up' – justifiably so, especially for those who have found their narratives and voices all too often quashed and swallowed by various incarnations of empire. This is discomfiting, perhaps the more so for some of Burrus' readers than for she herself. Nonetheless, this uncomfortable relationship with ancient texts might still be understood as queer, as Burrus suggests: it is precisely in their lack of co-operation with domestication that they resist annexation in the service of closed human ends, but this comes with the sometimes-unwelcome qualification that not even deserving readers can finally colonize them.

Similarly ambiguous is Amy Hollywood's attempt to find possible queer ancestors in the beguines, the thirteenth-century lay women who lived lives dedicated to prayer and service without having taken formal vows. These women are known for the strikingly erotic character of their descriptions of their mystical experiences. Mechthild of Magdeburg, for example, writes in *The Flowing Light of the Godhead*, 'That is child's love, that one suckle and rock a baby. I am a full-grown bride. I want to go to my Lover' (Mechthild 1998, p. 61, quoted in Hollywood 2007, pp. 166–7). Female desire for a male other might not seem particularly queer, as we noted earlier. Nonetheless, when the male in question is God, the erotic transcends purely reproductive and economic meaning. The work of Hadewijch of Anvers, in which she describes herself and Christ mutually melting away into each other, breaks down distinctions between God and humanity as well as male and female (Hollywood 2007, p. 169). What is particularly interesting, however, says Hollywood, is that 'we find accounts of insane love and endless desire in which gender becomes so radically fluid that it is not clear what kind of sexuality – within the heterosexual/homosexual dichotomy most readily available to modern readers – is being metaphorically deployed to evoke the relationship between humans and the divine' (Hollywood 2007, p. 165). In this way, she suggests, the beguines 'de-naturalize and de-stabilize normative conceptions of human sexuality in potentially radical ways' (Hollywood 2007, p. 166). But as Hollywood herself notes, there is also something problematic about the priority of souls over bodies and the loss of distinct bodily experience here: the beguines wish to transcend their bodies and to lose any sense of division between themselves and God, but this is also to efface their own particularity. This 'both queers heteronormative desire and sacrifices the bodies and desires from which, in their multiplicity, contemporary queer theory and practice emerge' (Hollywood 2007, p. 172). If the beguines are indeed queer ancestors, then, they are bleary and slightly embarrassing ones, like aunts who have become drunk at Christmas.

Other examples of queer readings of historical theological texts include several grounded in a Latin American context, such as Martín Hugo Córdova Quero's queer reading of Aelred of Rievaulx and his theology of friendship (Córdova Quero 2004) and 'The Prostitutes also go into the Kingdom of God: A Queer Reading of Mary of Magdala' (Córdova Quero 2006). In the latter piece, Córdova Quero asks why, in historical theological interpretation, women like Mary Magdalene must be made decent, and denied their carnality, before they can be considered exemplary. He suggests that it is necessary to 'undress' readings of Mary Magdalene and other women via queer theological analysis, to acknowledge their sexualities and their corporeal natures, in order to truly appreciate the ways in which queer sexuality flows through the Christian tradition. In this way, he believes, the dichotomous characterization of women as either sexual prostitutes, or as decent wives whose sexuality is the 'property' of their husbands, will stop being forcefully played out on the bodies of women across Latin America.

Reading the Christian tradition queerly might also necessitate a reinterpretation of certain Christian doctrines or concepts. For example, Mary Elise Lowe proposes that queer theologians should produce alternative models of sin, wherein women and non-heterosexual people are not scapegoated for being peculiarly (or excessively) sexual – that is, for engaging in sexual activity beyond the perimeters sanctioned by males. Such reworkings, she suggest, would do well to draw on secular queer theory's insight that the subject is constructed by social discourse and interaction, and that identity is a work in performative progress, not something stable or completed. The doctrine of sin rests on the twin notions of free will and autonomy, but, suggests Lowe, queer theory disrupts these, by emphasizing humans' constitution in and through dubiously motivated language structures and material conditions (Lowe 2009, pp. 55–6). A Butlerian understanding of the process of subjection is, therefore, a more helpful metaphor for understanding sin than that of bondage, and gives due emphasis to complicity and social sin (Lowe 2009, p. 56). Lowe comments,

> A queer definition of sin as subjection and as a subject position has several advantages. Sin need not have an historical origin, and it is not located in the disordered will of a stable subject . . . [It] accounts for the way humans are constituted by and complicit within sinful structures, and yet maintain the ability to resist these powers . . . [It] does not require the familiar binaries of gay/straight, or even the fixed identities of gay/lesbian. Consistent with the foundational commitments

of queer theory, sin – like meaning itself – emerges within relationships. (Lowe 2009, p. 57)

We might identify this reworking of the notion of sin as having echoes in
work by authors whose work has been important within feminist theology, like that of Daphne Hampson. Hampson suggests that the paradigm
of the ideal self being sacrificial and broken for others too easily feeds
into a downtrodden 'martyr-complex' already present in some women.
Conversely, what is virtuous for the powerless is the courage to claim
power and to speak up for themselves (Hampson 1996, pp. 130–1). Sin,
for women, might therefore be more usefully understood not as pride or
self-assertion but as a *lack* of pride or self-assertion. Hampson's account
has been criticised from feminist as well as other quarters: Sarah Coakley
suspects that Hampson is too essentialist in her demarcations of all males
as powerful and all females as powerless, and too unproblematically
considers power a 'good' (Coakley 2002, pp. 22, 32). Moreover, queer
theology cannot be simplistically understood as a descendant of feminist
theology. Nonetheless, Hampson's creative expansion of the concept
of sin via a resistance to what she perceives as an anti-female legacy in
Christian doctrine might act as a model for similar queer reframing of
sin and justice.

Queer traits and affiliations

We have so far seen that queer streams may be identified in several aspects
of the Christian tradition, including its scriptures, its devotional art and
some of its historical writings. I now suggest, from a slightly different
angle, that there may be certain character traits, behaviours or affiliations, which some have identified as especially queer, which resonate
with broader Christian goods. It is thus conceivable that, far from being
a distortion of 'true' Christianity, there are some aspects of queer which
might be understood as particularly indicative of its emphasis on love
and justice. Some writers have spoken of particular qualities or characteristics central to the Christian tradition and which seem, in fact, to
be peculiarly well executed within gay and lesbian relationships. These

include hospitality and friendship. Could there be a case for saying that, since gay and lesbian people might be understood to have lived out these qualities particularly faithfully, they are thereby especial bearers or prophets of this particular aspect of the tradition? In this way, some gifts or traditions might be figured as 'queer' precisely because it is queer people who have carried them forward.

Friendship and hospitality

For example, Kathy Rudy (1996b) has written on the concept of friendship, and has suggested that people who are not involved in monogamous heterosexual relationships or nuclear families may be better placed to extend friendship and welcome to others, since they are not tied into discrete, inward-looking units in the same way. Rather than 'mimicking' heterosexual couples and families by campaigning for marriage rights, she suggests, gay and lesbian people should embrace the fact that their difference allows them more easily the kind of community envisaged by Christ, grounded in friendship and loyalty to many members of a community, not just one's partner and biological children. Rudy suggests that polyamorous relationships, or the 'casual sex' practices of some gay men who have sex with multiple partners, are profoundly challenging to the assumption that the nuclear family model is the best and even most Godly way. She rejects the notion that such acts of sex are anonymous or non-relational, asserting rather that they initiate those concerned into a larger community identity into which, in turn, they wish to invite others (Rudy 1996b, p. 10). This involves not only sexual activity, but mentoring and friendship for young or naïve men. Of course, this polyamorous vision is somewhat idealistic, as Rudy herself acknowledges (Rudy 1996b, p. 92); and as others have noted, it may negate the potency of intimacy in same-sex relationships which sex with multiple partners risks eliding (Clark 1994, pp. 217–9). However, Robert E. Goss makes a particularly interesting reading of the gender codes in Ephesians 5 in light of polyamory:

The model of Christ as bridegroom is limited as long as we accept the notion of church as bride without comprehending the collectivity of the church. When the church is understood as a collective of countless men and women, married and unmarried, with a variety of sexual orientations and gender expressions, then Christ becomes the multi-partnered bridegroom to countless Christian men and women ... Christ is polyamorous in countless couplings and other erotic configurations ... The lover is a sexual outlaw, not a bridegroom as the sanitized Jewish and Christians read the text. (Goss 2004, p. 61)

Perhaps the most fully outworked queer theology from friendship is that by Elizabeth Stuart (1995). She, too, insists on querying the assumption that 'promiscuity' is inherently bad: indeed, *God* loves 'promiscuously', even if, as she notes, 'many Jews and Christians ... would prefer their God to be strictly monogamous' (Stuart 1995, p. 190). Stuart notes that heterosexual marriages have often repeated unhelpful patterns that are an overhang from times when wives were literally counted as part of their husbands' property. Indeed, she believes that the metaphor of marriage as used in Scripture for the relationship of God with humanity always assumes an unwelcome model of female submission (Stuart 1995, p. 173). By contrast, relationships rooted in friendship can bypass this built-in inequality, overcoming matrices of authority and submission (Stuart 1995, p. 43). Only friendships, rather than marriages, are shown in the Bible to be 'equal, mutual and just relationships' (Stuart 1995, p. 173). The small number of women who claim the label 'lesbian' without any actual sexual eroticism for other women 'are saying something about the most important people in their lives: their nurturers and supporters, their friends' (Stuart 1995, p. 72). (This seems to be informed by Adrienne Rich's concept of the 'lesbian continuum', whereby close friendships between women, and woman-based experiences, are valuable as part of a schema of female commitment, in which eroticism is incidental. See Rich 1980.) Of course, this does not mean that friendships are *never* sexual; indeed, as Rowan Williams comments in his review of the book, 'the apparently clear line between *eros* and friendship is illusory; we are looking at different forms of one passion – the passion for life-giving interconnection' (Williams 1996, p. 124). This erotic force and desire propels us both to reach out in friendship and to touch sexually (Stuart 1995, p. 81). If, as Williams suggests, Stuart does not go far enough in exploring theologies and philosophies of friendship in the Christian tradition, as in the works of Aquinas (Williams 1996, p. 126), this only goes to demonstrate that such a queer reframing of friendship as central to Christian relationship and Christian understanding of eroticism is by no means a stretch of Stuart's imagination. I would also want to make a claim for the capacity of (heterosexual) marriage relationships to contain true friendship and mutuality, particularly where the spouses have consciously rejected historical and contemporary dynamics of power, submission and stereotypically gendered work. Nonetheless, I take Stuart's point that queer relationships may be more easily oriented to equalities of friendship, since they carry less of the particular baggage associated with heterosexual marriage (even if they also have plenty of baggage of their own).

There are echoes in Stuart's work of that of Michael Vasey, who suggests that part of what makes certain men gay is their openness to male–male intimacy and gentle friendship, qualities which may be devalued or denied in British culture (Vasey 1995, p. 232). Vasey is keen to emphasize that relationships need not be marital to be covenantal, and that gay people may have particularly strong networks of friends precisely because they are less likely to be split up into nuclear family units (cf. Stuart 1995, p. 49). He believes that Christ's words from the Cross, beseeching Mary to recognize John as her son and John to recognize Mary as his mother, 'embody an essential principle of church life – the love of friends creating bonds of kinship' (Vasey 1995, p. 234).

From a very different angle, the trope of friendship and hospitality is expanded further by Goss in the context of the culture of bare-backing, the practice among gay men with HIV/AIDS of deliberately engaging in anal sex without using condoms. This hugely increases the risk of transmitting HIV, and 'threatens ... gay sustainable and survivable sexual ecology' (Goss 2002, p. 75). Indeed, Isherwood and Althaus-Reid comment of the custom, 'As liberation theologians it is natural that an initial reaction to men seeking death and others willing to oblige has to be sadness and even horror' (Isherwood and Althaus-Reid 2004, p. 12). Why does such an apparently injurious practice persist? Goss runs through a familiar list: there may be some men who simply enjoy the thrill of the danger, feel guilty that they are not already HIV-positive having lost partners or friends to AIDS-related diseases, or who have an unhealthy psychological death-wish;[13] younger men in particular may feel that they are invincible to illness. Others might simply be unwilling to have their level of sexual sensation compromised by condom use (Carballo-Diéguez 2001, p. 230) – a motivation often figured as both selfish and self-destructive. Other scholars have suggested that bare-backing is done as an act of rebellion against 'antiseptic' views of sex (Berg 2009, p. 755; cf. Crossley 2002; Forstein 2002), or that improved treatments for HIV/AIDS mean that men no longer consider it a death sentence or the risk of contracting HIV an overwhelming deterrent (Berg 2009, p. 755; cf. Mansergh et al 2002; Halkitis et al 2003; Elford et al 2007). (For a detailed overview of the recent sociological literature on barebacking see Berg 2009.)

However, bare-backing is also sometimes figured as exhibiting especial hospitality and intimacy: Berg notes, 'For some gay and bisexual men, semen is a gift, which shows the giver's devotion and a partner's refusal would be seen as rejection and distrust' (Berg 2009, p. 759; cf. Mansergh et al 2002; Yep et al 2002). Pippin and Clark note that the apocalyptic connotations of bare-backing are heightened by the characterization of the anus as an abyss – 'It plays out as an interesting place for the sowing of seeds (semen), even if that could also be sowing the seeds of death' (Pippin and Clark 2006, p. 765). Goss bravely suggests that there may also be an important spiritual element to bare-backing which is not usually recognized. Goss cites men who speak of the elevated level of communion felt when they have unprotected sex with their partners – of the feeling that there is nothing whatsoever coming between them, the sense of holding nothing back. In other words, condom use might somehow impede hospitality, by not allowing one to invite a partner into full intimacy with one's body. (This is not a million miles from the Roman Catholic argument that contraceptives are a barrier to complete self-giving in the openness of a relationship which should always be open and welcoming to a potential third person, that is, the child who may be conceived as a result of the act.) For some people there is a sense that they are actually being *selfless* by bare-backing, in exposing themselves to the risk of infection in order to achieve heightened intimacy and exchange; Jesus, says Goss, did not consider his own survival the highest possible good, but sacrificed his bodily integrity for the sake of love (Goss 2002, pp. 80–1). For some couples where one partner is HIV-positive and the other negative, there may be conflict present about whether or not to use condoms; Goss recounts how his own HIV-positive partner, Frank, wanted to use condoms in order to protect HIV-negative Goss, whereas Goss himself felt the intimacy and trust expressed in bare-backing was crucial to a full expression of their love (Goss 2002, p. 86). Given that plenty of heterosexual couples face similar tensions surrounding the loss of intimacy or sensation that may occur with condom usage, Goss suggests that gay men 'need to have a space to grieve the loss of unprotected sex and dream of a day when they can once again engage in unprotected anal sex' (Goss 2002, p. 87). He believes that queer churches might be able to be sites of such openness and support.

Issues of bodily hospitality, then, have profound overlaps with the ways in which queer couples and families might welcome people in other, less overtly sexual ways. For example, if sexual intimacy is designed not only to draw a couple closer together but also to turn them outward to their communities and to God, then this should go just as much for gay couples as for heterosexual ones. Not only can gay couples contribute just as much to the non-procreative fecundity which renews society, argues Goss (Goss 2002, p. 108), but the fact that they may be less likely than heterosexual couples to have their own children means that same-sex couples often have a particularly strong sense of wanting to 'include others and work for their social welfare' (Goss 2002, p. 109), and may 'collect' their own waif-and-stray communities of alienated and marginalized people. (This chimes with the observation by many scholars that Christ himself seems to have had at least an ambivalent relationship with biological kinship structures, calling a group of men to leave their families behind and seeming to suggest that communities were made by commitment that transcended the purely familial, as in Matt.

12.46–50.) Similarly, Nancy Wilson appeals to the extensive and informal hospitality she believes is common to lesbian culture characterized by open homes and shared tables frequented by a miscellany of adults, children, friends and strangers who may or may not be related (compare Althaus-Reid's description of *rejunte* theology in Althaus-Reid 2004, pp. 146–62).[14] Wilson suggests,

> Perhaps our neediness or loneliness has made us almost 'promiscuous' in our desire to provide hospitality. Being shut out has made us want to *include* with a vengeance . . . I don't mean that straight people don't do this. But there is something, perhaps, about being 'unhinged' from the conventional family constructs that opens up the opportunities, the desire both to deconstruct and reconstruct this aspect of our lives. (Wilson 2000, pp. 144–5)

In fact, she suggests, there is *something specific to being lesbian* which encourages people to support and nourish others through the sharing of food, homes, time, love and so on (Wilson 2000, p. 145), perhaps as a legacy of the radical women's separatist movement. As a result, lesbian people may be particular bearers of this central biblical ethic of hospitality. This can be *physical* without being *sexual*: Wilson says,

> We exchange bodily fluids at our communion rail – tears, sometimes perspiration, and the Blood of Christ . . . By the end of the day, my vestments and sometimes my shirts and jackets have accumulated tears (and sometimes a little snot for good measure), sweat, makeup – as people have cried with me, laughed, touched, hugged, and kissed me, especially all day Sunday . . . The experience is at once very holy, very tactile, and very demanding. It is a way in which I can provide bodily hospitality to strangers and friends, colleagues and family alike. (Wilson 1995, p. 256)

Again, this is not necessarily something limited to lesbian priests; but Wilson's congregation of the Metropolitan Community Church includes individuals who may be severely lacking in physical touch or affection because of a disability, HIV-positive status or another form of social alienation. As a result, Wilson considers that this aspect of her ministry is particularly necessary to and grounded in the specificities of the lives and bodies of her congregants.

Counter-cultural Catholicism

The Metropolitan Community Church provides a particularly welcoming denominational home for Christians who publicly profess a non-heteronormative sexuality or variant gender. It may, however, be considered 'lacking' by those for whom a sense of long-term history or a grounding in historical apostolic succession is important. Is there a case for arguing that, even within the mainstream historical Christian churches, there are some denominations or traditions with more affinity to non-standard sexuality and gender than others?

It is noteworthy, for example, that, as Patrick R. O'Malley discusses, both Roman Catholicism and Anglo-Catholicism within Britain have sometimes been understood as particularly tolerant of homosexual orientation in particular, even where this goes against the official tenets of church teaching (O'Malley 2009, pp. 541–2). O'Malley draws on the work of David Hilliard, who suggests that, for many gay men in the late nineteenth century, Anglo-Catholicism provided 'a set of institutions and religious practices through which they could express their sense of difference in an oblique and symbolical way' (Hilliard 1982, p. 184), since there was 'an affinity in outlook between a sexual minority and a minority religious movement' (Hilliard 1982, p. 209). Homosexuality and Catholicism in the English context might both be understood as closeted or cloistered non-normative identities 'outside the gaze of the dominant culture' (O'Malley 2009, p. 544). It has been suggested that the poetic and literary bent of much Anglo-Catholic culture in the nineteenth century may have been especially satisfying to aesthetically inclined homosexual men and that such educated and middle- or upper-class individuals were more likely to be able to express artistic, 'effete' characteristics since their cultural milieu afforded them more social freedom (Hilliard 1982, p. 182). The intense same-sex friendships common between members of the early Oxford Movement, suggests Hilliard, may have made Anglo-Catholicism attractive to closeted homosexuals who could not otherwise risk openly expressing their deep affection for other men (Hilliard 1982, p. 185). The acceptability of celibacy within the movement also meant there was less likely to be pressure to marry a woman for the sake of social respectability. It has been mooted that some of the central early Anglo-Catholic figures, such as John Henry Newman and Richard Hurrell Froude, may themselves have been homosexual (a suggestion discussed at length during the period surrounding Newman's beatification in September 2010, occurring as it did only a few months after Pope Benedict XVI's right-hand man and Vatican secretary of state, Cardinal Tarcisio Bertone, had asserted that homosexuality was responsible for clerical sexual abuse of children) – though this may rest, in part, on stereotypes of gay men as effeminate and unmanly, in contrast with the vigorous, virile 'muscular Christianity' of contemporaneous popular Protestantism (O'Malley 2009, p. 541; Hilliard 1982, pp. 188–9).

All this is, perhaps, hardly surprising, particularly given Catholicism's especial well-attested non-kinship community leanings, whereby celibacy and monasticism are just as foundational to social stability as are heterosexual families. Eve Kosofsky Sedgwick, for instance, writes of the way Catholicism provides 'the shock of the possibility of adults who don't marry, of men in dresses, of passionate theatre' (Sedgwick 1990, p. 140; quoted in O'Malley 2009, p. 542). In other words, Catholicism 'offers a public excuse for experiencing the sorts of images and emotions that the secretly queer child always already privately wants' (O'Malley 2009, p. 557). Thomas Lawrence Long concurs that, in the predominantly Protestant environments of nineteenth- and twentieth-century England and the USA, 'membership in the Roman Catholic communion was always already perceived as anti-social and deviant and thus served as a "subtle antinomianism" for the sexual dissident' (Long 2007, p. 20). Long suggests that for gay men in these societies, conversion to Catholicism may have provided a means by which to 'externalize their repudiation of mainstream erotic sensibilities' (Long 2007, p. 27) – that is, to redirect attention from one aspect of their difference to another, and move the emphasis from the Protestant focus on the interior self and personal morality to a focus on ritual and externalized practice.

As Long notes, however, even this subtle rejection of Protestant social 'rules' is not entirely antinomian, since it involves immediate submission to the rules of another kind of authority (in this case, Catholic doctrine). Anglican Catholicism, then, might likewise be figured as almost a rebellious identity, as for Newman whose Catholic faith stood 'as essential and as distinct from the religion of his parents' (O'Malley 2009, p. 549) – particularly since both celibacy and homosexuality might be figured as other than what is 'genealogically expected' (O'Malley 2009, p. 550; see also Long 2007, p. 21). Anglo-Catholicism and homosexuality could both be read as rejections of a particular model of governance – of Protestant Christianity and heteronormativity respectively. Indeed, argues O'Malley, nineteenth-century Anglo-Catholicism might be understood as in some sense an anticipation of the solidifying of 'homosexuality' as a distinct identity in that century and after, since the former pre-empts the latter in undergoing a shift 'from understanding itself as a set of performed actions to understanding itself as an internalized and essential subjectivity' (O'Malley 2009, p. 558).

As such, however, Anglo-Catholicism might find itself accused (in common with other strikingly male gay clusterings) of anti-femaleness, particularly where its proponents are vocally opposed to ordaining women or to using feminine language for God; Siobhán Garrigan comments, 'Such high-church Anglo-Catholic worship may be queerer than most but we have to be careful not to settle for a version of queer that harbors contempt for the female body and voice' (Garrigan 2009, p. 225). Indeed, in 1988 Kenneth Leech asserted, in no uncertain terms,

It does seem clear that there is some correlation between the [Anglo-Catholic] clerical ghetto (gay and straight) and the most extreme and pathological forms of hostility to the ordination of women, and indeed the deeply-rooted gynophobia which is endemic to much [Anglo-Catholic] life. The contrast between the attitudes to women in this group and those among the post-1960s more openly gay Christians (represented, for example, in Britain in the Lesbian and Gay Christian Movement) is very striking. Gynophobia and the dread of women is, of course, by no means restricted to sections of the 'gin and lace' fringe of the [Anglo-Catholic] movement: but it does seem there to have been exalted into a way of life in a very extreme form. (Leech 1988)

From a slightly different (and somewhat cynical) angle, Long suggests that (Roman) Catholicism may 'in a perverse way [foster] sexual promiscuity' (Long 2007, p. 20), since its system of regular and anonymous confession provides a mechanism for the absolution of non-marital sexual activity – '[tolerating] carnival excesses prior to Lenten austerities and [offering] daily sacramental confession after libertine nights' (Long 2007, p. 21). His contention that it is the Catholic focus on the material realm which makes it particularly appealing to queer people is perhaps less persuasive, smacking of the problematic assumption that queer people are somehow more embodied or more earthly than others. Nonetheless, it might be that, for the other reasons outlined, Roman and Anglo-Catholicism exemplify a strand of Christianity which is actually peculiarly hospitable to queer sensibility rather than alien to it.

Martin Stringer suggests that the Anglo-Catholicism prevalent in early- to mid-twentieth-century Britain was attractive to many people because of its focus on physically embodied, enacted liturgical worship, which might be contrasted with a more cerebral Protestantism sometimes suspicious of the body and physicality. Despite twentieth-century Anglo-Catholicism's sensuousness, notes Stringer, many of its adherents denied that a specifically sexual element was present, and it was, 'after all . . . ideally led by celibate practitioners' (Stringer 2000, p. 38). Moreover, 'the use of the body in Anglo-Catholicism may well be stylized and even, in some cases, oppressive' (Stringer 2000, p. 37). Nonetheless, Stringer suggests that Anglo-Catholic liturgy is a crucial window onto 'the potential role of the sexual body in worship' (Stringer 2000, p. 38). He believes that it is also significant that many of the prominent Anglo-Catholic parishes between the 1920s and 1950s (which he considers Anglo-Catholicism's heyday) had unmarried and celibate priests, which may have made this kind of priestly lifestyle more attractive to young gay men than the Protestant version with its focus on marriage and fatherhood alongside ministry (Stringer 2000, p. 41).

Stringer identifies a 'camp' element to Anglo-Catholic worship which may also have been particularly appealing to some homosexual men – a theatricality and exaggerated style, which may, especially in parishes where the majority of worshippers came from poor and underprivileged backgrounds, have been designed to evoke a richness of experience beyond the realm of their everyday lives:

> The liturgy was consciously presented as something outside of the experience of the people. It was constructed as a 'taste of heaven' in a life of drudgery. Anglo-Catholic worship pulled out all the stops to create the illusion of heaven. It was rich. It was colourful. It sounded heavenly with choirs and organs and occasionally even a full orchestra. It was shot through with gold and silver, with jewels and damask. It was dripping with lace. It was engulfed in clouds of incense. It was 'out of this world' . . . Anybody who has attended Benediction in a top Anglo-Catholic church, with the yards of lace, the flowing copes of cloth of gold, the cherub-like servers amid billowing clouds of incense, the glistening jewels, the slick precision of its choreography, and all the panache and style of a Busby Berkeley musical, could not but recognize that there was something 'camp' about this worship. (Stringer 2000, p. 44)

The camp elements of Anglo-Catholic worship and culture in the mid-twentieth century are not unproblematically positive, however, and nor are they unequivocally useful for models of queer liturgy: Stringer, like Garrigan and Long (though in stronger terms), points to 'the probably inevitable misogyny of the whole community' (Stringer 2000, p. 53). He also suggests that the secrecy attached to Anglo-Catholic clergy homosexuality led to much loneliness and tragedy, and that it would be better 'to move beyond the camp and to find alternative ways of expressing much more openly and directly our sexual selves in our worship' (Stringer 2000, p. 54). For this reason, even if it is a Christian tradition that seems in some respects to be more open to a queer aesthetic and dynamic than some others, Anglo-Catholicism should not be figured as somehow inherently, exclusively or unproblematically queer.

O'Malley's, Long's, Hilliard's and Stringer's analysis focuses on the nineteenth century and early- to mid-twentieth century (for further discussion of which see Hanson 1997, Roden 2003 and O'Malley 2006), but even today there appears to be a noteworthy correlation between homosexual orientation and Catholic (Roman or English) denominational affiliation. Much of the best-known queer theology done since the 1980s in Britain has come from established Catholic scholars such as Elizabeth Stuart and Gerard Loughlin, and recent collections such as *Queer and Catholic* (Evans and Healey 2008a) represent ongoing creative tensions generated by Catholic identification (as, also, throughout the canon of Marcella Althaus-Reid). The essays in Evans and Healey's collection suggest a playful and bittersweet relationship between queer and Catholic identities, since several of the authors note that Roman Catholic schools and congregations could be dangerous as well as exciting places to grow up queer. For Jane M. Grovijahn, her dual lesbian and Catholic identities were complicated by her experience of childhood sexual abuse, which rendered her vagina a site of pain and shame as well as of incarnated salvation (since even Christ was borne into the world by this route):

> My flesh knew opposing or contradictory realities simultaneously ... My God-consciousness was wrapped around terrible threads of abuse and a deeply buried desire for women's bodies ... This visceral battle is where God remains: thoroughly Catholic, complicated, embodied, sensual, and connected across a wide expanse of my own sexual hunger and healing. (Grovijahn 2008, p. 255)

A Catholic upbringing which communicated a fear and suspicion of female sexuality and female embodiment also, simultaneously, instilled Grovijahn with a strong sense of both wounded and blessed embodiment, and an awareness that, were it not for a female body – and a vagina – God would not have been embodied at all (Grovijahn 2008, pp. 256, 260).

In her study of gay Roman Catholic priests in Britain in the early 1990s (Stuart 1993), Elizabeth Stuart found that, although the question of homosexuality was not particularly well handled in seminaries and there was not enough formational training given which discussed priestly sexuality and celibacy in any depth, there still seemed to be a significant number of gay men who had been led to the priesthood (Stuart estimated that as many as 20 per cent of Roman Catholic priests at the time were homosexual, with many of these being sporadically or consistently sexually active; more recently, Donald B. Cozzens has suggested a figure of between 30 and 60 per cent, though this was for priests in the USA rather than Britain – see Cozzens 2000, pp. 98–101). In some cases, this was specifically because being a priest allowed a legitimate context in which not marrying a woman was acceptable. One of Stuart's respondents said, 'God does seem to like choosing gays to be priests. This must say something' (anonymous priest quoted in Stuart 1993, p. 105). Some of Stuart's interviewees, who had already been priests or seminarians in 1986 when the Vatican Congregation for the Doctrine of Faith (overseen by Cardinal Joseph Ratzinger, later to become Pope Benedict XVI) issued the *Letter to the Bishops of the Catholic Church on the Pastoral Care of Homosexual Persons*, said they had felt hurt and angry when the *Letter* repeated the assertion that to be homosexual was to be objectively disordered as a human being (since homosexual inclination was very likely to lead to homosexual activity, figured as an intrinsic moral evil). Nonetheless, they did not feel it compromised their vocation to the priesthood or their identity as Christian:

> The letter did not really change my attitudes. It seemed to confirm me in my determination to be Catholic and gay. Also it strengthened my conviction that the Church has got the question of homosexuality wrong.

> I think the Church's teaching on homosexuality is ill-informed . . . and very little to do with what I understand my relationship to be with Christ . . . My reaction to the 1986 letter on the pastoral care of homosexual persons was fatalistic. Nothing seemed to have changed, I am still considered to be an 'intrinsically disordered person'. It did not change my behaviour or attitudes in any way whatsoever.

> (Anonymous priests, quoted in Stuart 1993, pp. 73–4)

I suspect that the principal effect Ratzinger's letter had on me was to make me more radically aligned with those who felt oppressed by it.

('Father Simon', quoted in Stuart 1993, p. 44)

There are other aspects of Roman Catholicism which have seemed particularly appealing to some queer groups, perhaps especially in a context of 'turning' familiar symbols and iconography. This is exemplified by the wearing of nuns' habits by the activist queer 'order' the Sisters of Perpetual Indulgence, who 'employ the sanctifying grace of camp humor as a survival strategy and for social and spiritual transformation' (Evans and Healey 2008b, p. 198). The Sisters, a group of 'gay male nuns', are involved in peace and social justice work, sexual health promotion, human rights activism, and fundraising for AIDS charities. Founding member Sister Soami[15] comments that the adoption of nuns' habits – which, according to the Order's 'sistory', came about as a result of a convent in Iowa lending out some retired habits for a production of *The Sound of Music* in 1976 (http://www.thesisters.org/sistory.html) – represents both an appreciation for such 'fabulous attire' and also a desire to cite and emulate the work and devotion of conventional Roman Catholic nuns (Evans and Healey 2008b, p. 199).

Conclusion

Queer Theology takes its place not at the centre of the theological discourses conversing with power, but at the margins. It is a theology from the margins which wants to remain at the margins. To recognize sexual discrimination in the church and in the theological thinking ... does not mean that a theology from the margins should strive for equality. Terrible is the fate of theologies from the margin when they want to be accepted by the centre! (Althaus-Reid and Isherwood 2007, p. 304)

Cherry Smith has asserted that queer activists desire to 'fuck up the mainstream', and that queer 'marks a growing lack of faith in the institutions of the state, in political procedures, in the press, the education system, policing the law' (Smith 1996, p. 280). As such, the Christian Churches, particularly where they are established churches in a given nation, might be read as institutions which are inherently non-queer. It might therefore seem unlikely or even impossible that queer people should wish to be associated with them. As Greta Gaard shows, although Christian culture has tended to oppose homosexuality in particular because it is 'unnatural', that is, non-procreative (even as it also sees itself as a force of culture existing in tension with and *opposing* 'chaotic' nature), queer discourse makes clear that heteronormativity is itself a constructed phenomenon, not an unproblematically 'natural' one, and might recover the groups and phenomena written out of masculinist history (Gaard 1997). However, this might be mitigated by the argument set out by Loughlin and others that *Christianity itself* is counter-cultural and anti-hegemonic. In this account, even an established Church is never unproblematically simply in the service of the state, for it has a higher referee and arbiter, a God who stands over against all human ideology.

In another account, however, Christianity has never adequately resisted being allied to social, sexual, religious and conceptual norms which are leary of difference and ambiguity. Althaus-Reid has incisively critiqued Christianity's apparent alliance with heterosexual normativity; Jeremy Carrette, too, shows that Christianity tends actually to resist queerness, because of its need to be confessional and to lay bare 'truths' about identity (which, as we have seen time and again, broader queer theory usually attempts to subvert). Built in to the very concept of monotheism, believes Carrette, is a commitment to a single truth and (by association) a single kind of sanctioned sexual identity (Carrette 2004, p. 218). Even where theology embraces brokenness and fragmentation, it does so in the context of appeals to a greater, wholer, united God: salvation, he believes, is too neat a solution, and means there is always a convenient end-cap put onto the era of uncertainty and provisionality (Carrette 2004, p. 227). He asserts,

> Theology in the 'face' of . . . fragmentation still seems to insist on imposing a future unity because it holds a fundamental nostalgia for

a pre-modern imperialistic truth of what we are and what we may become. It appears to concede to 'looking through a glass darkly', but is never prepared to alter its central precepts in a blind hope of future victory in the unity of monotheistic truth and theological orthodoxy. (Carrette 2004, p. 228)

For Carrette, therefore, Christianity is not only decidedly *not* queer, it also reinforces an epistemology which prevents even seemingly 'rebellious' or 'subversive' identities from being properly queer themselves, since they perpetuate either/or, in-or-out dualisms (Carrette 2004, p. 220). For Christianity to become truly queer, believes Carrette, would necessitate its ceasing to hold to aspects of its creeds, which most people who call themselves Christian would deem irreducibly foundational:

Religion becomes queer when it breaks up the desiring self, when it refuses to confess an identity, when it refuses to say who we are, and acknowledges a plural self with polymorphous desires. To queer religion is to queer the foundations of theology, its monotheism, its monosexuality and its monopoly of truth. (Carrette 2004, p. 225)

Carrette's appeal to the Foucauldian 'solution' of identity without self-hood is itself not without its problems; quite apart from not addressing the fact that freedom to cede certainty of identity is a luxury good, it also fails to interrogate adequately the ease with which such giving-over of selfhood is often annexed by those brands of Christianity which are keen to keep women, homosexuals and other 'lesser' individuals in their submissive, self-emptying places.

The ambiguity of the Christian tradition means that it cannot be simplistically claimed by any one side. It is neither queer nor anti-queer: or rather, it is both. But the constant questioning and pushing of definition is characteristic of what has often been claimed to be pivotal for queer methodology: namely, its propensity to stand in opposition to conclusive, closed ideology. The presence of queer makes ideology hegemony, since the nature of hegemony is always to be resisted, but in doing so undermines any sense of finality or fixity even for itself. If queer shows up the apophatic thread running through the Christian tradition, it also, paradoxically, highlights its *own* apophasis, its own lack: which is its strength, and its resisting of strength, at one and the same time. The advantage queer might have over some other methodologies – although the very notion of claiming advantage betrays a problematic alliance with power and hierarchy embedded within our very language and grammar, as Butler and others have acknowledged – is that it is ever conscious of its own limitations and of the constraints brought about by particularity, contingency and context. This is not to say that it is more limited, particular, contingent or contextual than other theological ideologies, however; rather, it is perhaps merely more aware of it. If queer's awareness sometimes borders on hyper-awareness, rendering queerness incapacitated or stifled by its own self-analysis and self-reflection, then this might be figured as *both* a necessary counter to any methodology's tendency for aggrandizement and absolutization (and one which must therefore be ongoing in any methodology which seeks consciously to resist finality), *and* something which tells a story about queer's present particular historical point in its particular historical journey. Queer theology is still grappling with what it might mean to stand over against mainstream theologies, even while some of its proponents are simultaneously querying the very language of *againstness, opposition, abjection* and *binarization.*

It is therefore interesting that queer theologies are becoming more and more mainstream, studied by tenured academic theologians and written about in peer-reviewed journals and books, published by established, respectable academic publishing houses, and even engaged with at theological colleges. What does this mean for Althaus-Reid's assertion that 'queer theologians by definition belong to the margins of theology', since 'they work in a theology which is not part of the theological establishment' (Althaus-Reid 2008, p. 105)? Does the fact that queer theologies are appearing on the syllabi of theological colleges and seminaries as well as more historically liberal universities mean that they can no longer stand over against mainstream theologies, and can no longer really be considered 'outsider' discourses? Does the growing acceptance of queer theology as a serious theological discourse risk domesticating it, removing its 'teeth'? And to what extent should queer people continue to identify with a tradition that has been so damaging for them and many of their forebears? These and similar questions are addressed in Chapter 6.

Notes

1 Parts of this chapter originally appeared in Cornwall 2010c.

2 For a more recent collection informed by Heyward's notion of relational theology, see the essays in Isherwood and Bellchambers 2010.

3 Larkin, Philip (1977 [1955]), 'Lines on a Young Lady's Photograph Album' in Larkin, Philip, *The Less Deceived: Poems by Philip Larkin*, Hessle, East Yorkshire: The Marvell Press, pp. 13-14, here 14.

4 For unambiguous examples, see the workshop of Robert Campin's *The Virgin and Child in an Interior* (c. 1430); Sodoma's *Holy Family* (c. 1525); Antonio Carneo's *Holy Family Adored by Lieutenants and Deputies* (1667); Rogier van der Weyden's *Madonna and Child* (1460); Antonio Rossellino's *Virgin with the Laughing Child* (c.1465-75); Filippo Lippi's *Madonna and Child* (1445). For full discussion of these and other similar depictions, see Sturgis 2000, p. 56 and Steinberg 1996, pp. 22-51, 118-9, 180-3, 257-61, 279-80.

5 Steinberg explains, 'The English word "humanation", obsolete since it was ousted in the 17th century by "incarnation", deserves a place in the active vocabulary; it has at least some of the force of the German *Menschwerdung*. Italian never let go of the word; you hear it sung at Christmastide, "Cristo è nato e humanato"' (Steinberg 1996, p. 11). Bynum also picks up on the term, suspecting that Steinberg's use of it is too centred on the penis of Christ at the expense of other dimensions of his humanness.

6 For some of the examples Steinberg discusses, see Raffaelino dal Colle's *Madonna and Child with the Infant St John* (c. 1530); Perugino's *Madonna and Child* (1500); and Maerten van Heemskerck's *Man of Sorrows* pictures of 1532, 1525 and c. 1550.

7 Of course, as Steinberg discusses, the loincloths themselves display a certain oddness: they are hyperreal, artistic means to a less static composition: 'By means of a gorgeous flutter flaring forth from the center, the blanks are repleted and animated; and so felicitous is the solution that its aptness on grounds other than formal has never been challenged. No one has questioned the wisdom of making such pageantry of a breechcloth; or grudged its turbulence as a wind gauge where no other fabrics are stirred; nor its plausibility in a narrative that calls for the least covering of a victim whose garments had been the coveted loot of his executioners' (Steinberg 1996, p. 91, 94).

8 An interesting footnote arises from the controversy in 2010 surrounding Janet Jaime's altarpiece at St. Charles Borromeo Catholic Church in Warr Acres, Oklahoma, where the iconographic representation of the crucified Christ's abdominal muscles appeared to resemble an enormous erect penis – to the dismay of many parishioners, who described it as embarrassing, shocking, appalling and horrifying (Estus 2010a). The altarpiece is modelled after the famous San Damiano cross associated with Francis of Assisi; the original, in the Basilica di Santa Chiara in Assisi, also has prominent and arguably phallic-looking stomach muscles. The Oklahoma piece was subsequently removed from the church, and the priest who had commissioned it, Father Philip Seeton, transferred to a different parish (Estus 2010b).

9 Here I refer to the convention that women in religious orders are 'brides of Christ', some even wearing a wedding band – but their vow of chastity stands in tension with the imagery of marriage, since, between human partners, marriage is understood to be consummated only once sexual intercourse has taken place. As many commentators have noted, moreover, historically there has been a subversive note to women, in particular, choosing to live in a monastic community rather than fitting into the more conventional social structures afforded by marriage and motherhood. Even if there is an ambiguity attached to nuns requiring the presence of a male priest for the celebration of the Mass, by and large the special social and economic position of women living in all-female communities has been recognized as potentially subversive of the assumption that women are chattels and that they and their offspring are effectively the property of husbands or fathers.

10 See, for example, Friedrich Herlin's *Christ with Ears of Wheat and Grape Vine* (1469), Quirizio da Murano's *The Savior* (c. 1475), and Konrad Witz's *Man of Sorrows and Mary Intercede with God the Father* (c. 1450).

11 Although, as we have seen, depictions of the Christ-child's genitalia are relatively commonplace in medieval art, Ribas and others are right to note that this has not usually continued into more recent representation. Any depiction of Mary's own genitals would, of course, be extraordinary (and I would be pleased to hear of any extant example): her bared breasts are frequently seen, albeit less frequently than they once were, but these have a 'maternal' rather than a 'sexual' connotation (not that these can unproblematically be distinguished) since they are visible there specifically for the purpose of providing milk for the baby.

12 I am not sure that seeing 'alarm' here is quite fair, to Coakley at least – she acknowledges, for example, that Gregory's ideas of gender 'reversal' undercut and subvert notions of traditional married gender roles, and that 'the message Gregory evidently wishes to convey is that gender stereotypes must be reversed, undermined, and transcended if the soul is to advance to supreme intimacy with the trinitarian God' (Coakley 2002, p. 128). She notes, too, that Gregory's sexual imagery is intrinsic to the process rather than something incidental picked up from

the Song of Songs, simply making clear that a transformation of desire in Gregory is about more than *just* a transformation of gender or eroticism (Coakley 2003, p. 5). Coakley's appeal to asceticism and her reading of it in Gregory (Coakley 2002, p. 167) is not necessarily to do with Puritanism as Burrus suggests; rather, it points to a decisively queer refusal to assume that resisting a norm means adopting its opposite norm. To reject oppressive sex/gender roles does not necessitate advocating sexual libertinism.

13 The practice of HIV-negative men *deliberately* exposing themselves to HIV infection by engaging in unprotected sex with HIV-positive men is known as 'bugchasing' and is considered distinct from bare-backing (Berg 2009, p. 755).

14 *Rejunte* is the name given to the forms of 'family' which occur in the slum dwellings of Buenos Aires, where children, parents, step-parents, ex-partners and sundry unconnected individuals are forced to share cramped, vulnerable accommodation. Althaus-Reid says that indigenous rural peoples, already marginalized from affluent society, become further excluded when they migrate to urban zones to seek work (Althaus-Reid 2004, p. 147). Having lost contact with the traditional networks of family and community support in rural areas, the *rejunte* slip further and further into monetary poverty. Living under bridges, or in houses made of rags and detritus, there is a continual geographical nomadism, where people regularly return 'home' to discover that their dwellings have been bulldozed (Althaus-Reid 2004, p. 149-50). In such jeopardous circumstances, where promiscuity and incest are common, privacy scarce, and 'personal space' unknown, familial relationships are also always shifting. Althaus-Reid says, 'Exclusion makes families disperse under the weight of the struggle but the *rejunte* allows people to come back to the family or move on to another . . . People may be forgiven for old deeds or partners in disgrace may return not as partners, but as people who are in need of support' (Althaus-Reid 2004, p. 151).

15 The Sisters' adopted names reference sexual, political, cultural and religious imagery or a combination thereof, and generally involve humorous puns. Names of current members (as of 2009) include Ann R. Key, Anni Coque L'Doo, Bea Attitude, Bella de Ball, Celeste L. Powers, Constance Craving of the Holey Desire, Dinah Might (If You Ask Her Right), Holly Lewya, Lily White Superior Posterior, Meira-Meira Ondawall, Porn Again, Selma Soul, Sibyl Libertease, and Tilly Comes Again (http://www.thesisters.org/meet.html).

6

Should Queer Christian People Stay Christians?

> For many who have had the straight rule of christendom applied in hurtful and destructive ways, the answer is to slam the book shut altogether and have nothing more to do with this story. For some people that is surely a healthy response, not just 'understandable' in a condescending way, but a very good conclusion to the particular script they have been required to read. But for me that will not do. Part of the reason is that christendom has not only been the worst of my personal past but also the best of it; and the need to deal with the former requires a reappropriation and transformation of the latter. I will not become a more flourishing person by cutting off my roots. (Jantzen 2001, p. 276-7)

> To reiterate Foucault: to react against, to redefine, to 'queer' something or anything is to participate in that thing. (Haws 2007, p. 189)

> I have not left the church for reasons probably good and bad – and perhaps for reasons I do not know. (Heyward 1984, p. 10)

Many of the queer theologians with whom we have engaged thus far have expressed ambivalence and doubt about the Christian tradition, and some (like J. Michael Clark) are not sure that they wish to claim an overtly Christian identity at all. This chapter explores the ambiguities of the Christian tradition and asks to what extent it can be redeemed. I engage with the argument acknowledged by Stuart, Koch and others that queer people are colluding in their own continued oppression by remaining in a historically hostile tradition. I draw on work by Sweasey, Webster and Loughlin to demonstrate that, in fact, many queer people wish to hold onto or reclaim aspects of Christianity despite its problems. In particular, Webster's work on the tensions of standing in the tradition without accepting it all, and of the potential of queer to subvert Christianity as well as lesbian identity, is used to show that queer theologies can remain ambivalent about mainstream theology without entirely detaching from it. The chapter discusses the tensions of self-representation and the extent to which queer Christians may be accused of betraying the counter-cultural aspects of their identity. It also draws on Althaus-Reid and Isherwood's suggestion that queer theory is a new mediator science for all radical theologies.

Elizabeth Stuart, Alison Webster and others have written eloquently about the tensions bound up in retaining a Christian allegiance as someone whom many Christians would not recognize as a fellow-believer because of their publicly declared sexuality. Jeanette Mei Gim Lee says, 'My wielding the Bible, of all things, may appear as if I wish to bang my head against the walls of cathedrals of oppression' (Lee 2004, p. 82). Stuart notes the frequency with which queer Christians are asked why they do not leave and find something less oppressive or accused of colluding with their persecutors by staying in the religion (Stuart 1997a, p. 13). She retorts – after Janet Martin Soskice – that this is a little like asking someone why they are still in love, but acknowledges that even this might seem masochistic or delusional, akin to remaining in an abusive relationship because one insists that the violence and cruelty are not truly characteristic of one's partner. However, importantly, although neither aspect is necessarily fixed or absolute, for many queer Christians, their religion is just as fundamental to their identity as their sexuality is – so Stuart maintains that people who would not dream of suggesting that one should stop being homosexual and become heterosexual instead should also not suggest that one abandons one's faith, which is no more negotiable than one's sexual orientation (Stuart 1997a, p. 14).

Other queer theologians, too, have had to grapple with what it means to be in dialogue with a Christian tradition that might not recognize them as fellow Christians. This echoes, in certain respects, the moves made by feminist scholars such as Daphne Hampson and Mary Daly who eventually felt that they could no longer call themselves Christian at all because of the horrors and injustices inextricable from Christianity's history. Even for those who have chosen to continue to identify as Christian, the legacy of Christendom is a troubling one requiring acknowledgement and, sometimes, disassociation (as by those who claim that sexism, racism and imperialism are not 'really' inherent to Christianity but rather represent hegemonic distortions of its bias toward justice and freedom).

This raises its own problems: in some cases, the bent of queer theology has continued to appear more reactive to challenges and oppositions than constructive of a way forward. For instance, Angie Pears says of Althaus-Reid's 2000 book *Indecent Theology* – and her eponymous broader project – that it represents 'a moment of indecency rather than participation in any kind of constructive theological enterprise ... It does not really participate, or at least hasn't so far, in any kind of persistent constructive theological enterprise. And perhaps to ask of the relationship that it bears to the Christian tradition is to misconceive of the project entirely' (Pears 2005, p. 39). Althaus-Reid's untimely death in 2009 curtailed her continued outworking of these themes, though it is not quite fair to say, with Pears, that Althaus-Reid's thought was entirely non-participatory in productive theology. It is true to say that her work has a 'deconstructive, interruptive approach' (Pears 2005, p. 40), but I cannot agree with Pears that it is thereby not value-based. Pears seems to equate the rejection of monolithic truth and monolithic feminism in Althaus-Reid's work with a rejection of value-content (Pears 2005, p. 49), but I do not believe that this is either inevitable, or evident in Althaus-Reid's subsequent work.

Indeed, as we have already observed, Althaus-Reid has specifically noted that post-Christianity, a move beyond and out of Christianity, is not the only possible response to living with Christianity's problematic legacy. She says,

> Our identity as theologians is shaped somehow in relation to a certain sexual response. Therefore, post-Christians may have a point

in trying to break from that circle of subjection to a condition which limits exchanges and ways to do theology through the given authorized medium of expression. But so do queer theologians who have extended an alliance of different, plural sexual understanding to issues of Church tradition, ecclesiastical history and dogmatics. (Althaus-Reid 2004b, p. 103)

Althaus-Reid seems to suggest that a queering of theology does indeed 'free' people from mainstream theology's 'circle of subjection'. Importantly, though, this freeing does not mean walking away: it is a two-way process which, in turn, helps to show up for mainstream theology that its own tradition has been more plural and less 'straight' than it might realize, thus freeing it, too, from the tyranny of univocity. Indeed, a queer theologian who continues to identify as Christian is likely to present *more* of a challenge to the Church – and, conceivably, to make the Church more uncomfortable – than one who comes to identify as a complete outsider and can perhaps be more easily dismissed as a heretic or backslider, because they no longer stand in an obvious ongoing relationship with other Christians and the tradition.

'It may be that, as in the colonial experience, our Christian past negates us, but by doing so, it also affirms the production of new and multiple identities assumed in our communities', says Althaus-Reid (2004b, p. 109). This sounds positive, though at the same time she asserts that 'queer, indecent theologies are theologies of disruption which do not look for legitimization in the past or for a memory of a harmonious trajectory' (Althaus-Reid 2004b, p. 109). For Althaus-Reid, 'Even if the pursuit of sexual equality in the Church was the only objective of queer theologies, it should be encouraged as a worthy initiative' (Althaus-Reid 2004b, p. 103). But this is, in fact, *not* all that queer theologies are to do or to be: there is a fascinating at-once-ness to their charges. On the one hand, queer theology's task is to betray and show up – rather like the dental disclosing tablets which show up areas of plaque on one's teeth by dying them bright pink – the places where systematic theological norms are actually narrowly heterosexual–capitalist ones. (It is in this way, believes Gary David Comstock, that lesbian and gay people can be important 'critical friends' to Christianity, showing up the ways in which it falls short and prompting it to become better – Comstock 1993, p. 48). But at the same time, queer theology always *remembers*, rather than simplistically betraying and superseding, the problems in theology's past and present. Althaus-Reid says, 'Queer theology remembers the body of its former lovers, their departures and their contradictions . . . It is the theology that remembers the love that has been betrayed by dogmatic traditions and by the theological teaching of the church informed by ideologies of sexual exclusion' (Althaus-Reid 2006a, pp. 146–7). The dual meaning of *betrayed* is significant here: queer theology betrays (that is, it is disloyal to) theology's dubious alliance with heteronormativity, but it also betrays (that is, it shows up) the fact that this heterosexual dallying is not all that theology can do or be. Queer theological love comes about when 'the traditional theological places of love are betrayed, that is, if we become disloyal to the given ideological assumptions in theology that come from sexuality, racial and colonial understandings, and class biases' (Althaus-Reid 2006a, pp. 147–8). So in this account there is both continuity and discontinuity between theological history and the present queer theological task.

This is echoed by Elizabeth Stuart who asserts, after Robert E. Goss, that queer Christians must campaign for justice and freedom within their churches as well as outside it, in order to bring about the liberation which is central to the theological task (cf. Goss 1993, p. 124). Stuart says,

> Queer Christians are called not just to remember Jesus' basileia practice but also to imitate it. For Goss, this means, among other things, interrogating ourselves closely if we choose to remain within our Churches. Such a decision can only be justified if we engage in open and active challenges to Christian homophobic discourse. (Stuart 2003, p. 83)

It is from the place of 'exile' that comes about via public identification with and work for the rights of non-heterosexual people that queer Christians can most effectively testify to God's new order. In other words, Goss and Stuart are suggesting that queer people *should* remain within the Christian tradition, but that if they choose to do so, it is important that they carry on publicly resisting and querying its oppressive aspects. In some respects, this seems like too heavy a burden to place on queer people alone: I suggest that, rather than leaving resistance to those who have most to lose by making a stand, heterosexual and unambiguously sexed people should also assert publicly that there is no place for exclusion and homophobia in the Kingdom of God. In this way, queering theology will be shown to be a more than 'gay' concern and will more profoundly disrupt matrices of theological and ecclesiological discourse.

Queer theology repeats theology's problems exactly by showing up and resisting them, since it must continually remind us of (and thereby give voice to) precisely what it is opposing. It can therefore never be entirely 'post'-theological, since its very meaning is an oppositional, responsive one even as it seeks to do something new. This might be somewhat unnerving for those who would have queer theology as a way to escape theology's difficult past: in some sense, it is impossible to get away from it. This is not always acknowledged, as demonstrated in Karma R. Chávez's recent essay on the search for a queer women's spirituality. Chávez asserts that queer theology 'offer[s] little for those who seek freedom from Christianity, and yet are haunted by its teaching and condemnations' (Chávez 2008, p. 5), but her analysis risks being too uncritical in its suggestion that post-Christian queer spirituality is inherently less oppressive than Christianity. Moreover, Chávez insists that it is through figuring spiritual sexuality as specifically transcendent that the problematic 'haunting' legacy of Christianity can be overcome – but this gives too little credit to mainstream Christian emphasis on immanence and incarnation and seems to disallow an inhabiting of bodily specificity.

Robert E. Goss discusses a tendency for gay and lesbian spirituality to become more post-Christian as it becomes more postmodern, noting that although some queer post-Christian theologies have sought to be so because this allows them to get away from the 'stagnant doctrines and violent practices of the Christian churches' (Goss 1998, p. 193), the fact that such theologies by definition make no Christological claims and are also unlikely to manifest as actual churches, 'there is little connection between theological and communal practice' (Goss 1998, p. 193). This lack of confessional ritual outworking might be understood as leaving an empty space at the centre of Christian discourse, and appears to be what Pears identifies as the problem with Althaus-Reid's work. Goss concludes that, even so, post-Christian gay theologies such as that of Ron Long 'will become foundational for reformulating and re-envisioning new Christian queer theologies' (Goss 1998, p. 194). Goss may have overstated the subsequent influence of Long's work, and others have in fact figured his theology as exactly *opposite* to queer theology because it relies on such an essentialist conception of gay male experience (Spencer 2004, p. 273). Nonetheless, it is true that Long's imaginative outworkings of an ethics of sexual encounter (particularly between gay men) are refreshing in their creativity, figuring a penis which becomes erect at the sight or touch of a lover as a kind of greeting:

> One might say . . . that sexual arousal is a form of hailing and saluting another. And that might lead us into a poetics of sex which sees in sex a 'meeting and greeting'. On this basis, a one-night stand would not be a perversion of relation, but an incipient one, for the developed, even committed, relation could be seen as a repetition of, and deepening, of the one-night stand. Sex among committed lovers would not be different in form from a one-night stand, but in 'content' . . . What is blessed is when, having seen the other revealed in more and more dimensions of his being, that my dick still says, 'Hail.' (Long 2005, p. 42)

One issue with Long is that some of his work does not seem particularly post-*Christian*, but is rather informed by a broader sense of spirituality: indeed, it engages with ancient Greek, Buddhist, Native American and other indigenous spiritualities as well as the Hebrew Bible and early Christianity (Long 2004). There are many positive aspects to this wide engagement: nevertheless, it risks losing a capacity to critique Christian theology in particular, exacerbated by the fact that many Christians would find it impossible to recognize anything in their own tradition of Long's musings on his favourite porn scenes (Long 2002, pp. 24–5), or his conclusion that there must be gender in heaven, for 'how heavenly could a world without cock be?' (Long 2005, p. 37).

In some respects this is a pity, for many of Long's conclusions are actually strikingly similar to those of mainstream Christian sexual ethics: for example, he asserts that polyamorous relationships are likely to create pain and jealousy, and that 'It is the ideal of the monogamous couple that should be the hub around which our sexual practices are constellated' (Long 2005, p. 43). One-night stands and experiences of group sex, he says, are only stages on the way to the married state that is the ideal context for complete mutual self-giving; 'Every sexual encounter should be entered into as a kind of audition for its relational potential' (Long 2005, p. 44). This does not mean that every sexual encounter will lead to a permanent monogamous relationship, he continues, but every sexual encounter should at least be *open to the possibility* of this happening. Sex can be a vehicle for discovering people with whom we can grow in fulfilling relationship – of which sexual activity is an important part but should not be an end in itself. In short, even sex which starts off as 'just sex' should be respectful of the other and open to relational possibility:

> At the very least men should think of their erections . . . as a salute to another – so that their subsequent actions will accord with the spirit of that salute. Our bodies should stand for what our dicks stand up for – and what they indicate is what we appreciate. (Long 2005, p. 44)

My own problems with Long include his strong essentialism linked to sexual attraction, which seems to write out the experiences of intersexed, transgender and bisexual people. Long insists that eroticism is tied to gender because people are attracted to men or to women, not simply to individuals. However, this is only true for some people, and Long does not recognize that the existence of gender-variant or sexually ambiguous bodies undermines his assertions. His emphasis on *physical* responses to beauty also seems to be problematic, reinscribing a kind of body fascism in which 'hailing' and 'saluting' (and, by association, recognizing others as worthy of love and relationship) is too strongly linked to the capacity of bodies to arouse desire. Are ugly bodies or bodies which do not prompt arousal less deserving of affection or greeting? And what of bodies which are themselves no longer capable of physical arousal – because of age or illness? These concerns may be pressing Long's metaphor unfairly far; but the fact that norms of male beauty and attractiveness are already felt by some less conventionally attractive gay men (and some non-white men, as we saw above) to be exclusive and damaging means that Long and others must go further in formulating subversive, proactive, tenacious conditions of love.

Living with the tension

As we have been seeing, many queer Christian writers have expressly discussed the problems associated with their faith traditions. Some have decided they can no longer, in all conscience, call themselves Christian. Those who have fought for years to break down ecclesiastical injustice from the inside may come to a place where this feels untenable, where they cannot in conscience be seen to appear to accede to the horrors done in the name of God. Nonetheless, many people might choose to continue to seek identity and grounding in Christian tropes and communities even as they reject the official anti-queer teaching of their church authorities.

Andrew K. T. Yip, the sociologist of religion, suggests that this is linked to an increasing emphasis on individualism within society which means that 'individuals are increasingly empowered to actively construct their religious faith, rather than uncritically relying on views prescribed by authority structures' (Yip 2002, p. 201). Of Yip's study sample,[1] although 80 per cent attended mainstream (Roman Catholic, Anglican, Baptist or Methodist) Christian churches at least once a week, 'a vast majority of respondents held progressive views on human sexualities and relationships, which were contradictory to the churches' traditional teachings on such issues' (Yip 2002, p. 203). This was despite the fact that they considered their churches an important site of spiritual nurture otherwise. In fact, he suggests that church authorities are a *particularly* weak influence on non-heterosexual Christians in the area of sexuality, saying,

It is erroneous to assume simplistically that nonheterosexual Christians are inclined to leave institutional Christianity because of a lack
of affirmation and acceptance, and that there is no space within the
institution for them to engage with religious authority structures in
doctrinal and practical negotiations that could effect change. While
it is undeniable that a lot of self-defined gay, lesbian, and bisexual
Christians do distance themselves from churches because of their sexualities, many remain in this potentially stigmatizing environment and
persist in their spiritual journey, which seems to be at odds with what
the religious authority structures prescribe. (Yip 2002, p. 201)

Rather, Yip's sample tended to consider sexual morality a personal
issue rather than a communal one. Importantly, however, many of Yip's
respondents described the process of formulating 'dissident identities',
which could harmonize both their sexuality and their faith as a long and
complex process involving much psychological adjustment (Yip 2002,
p. 203). Interestingly, even those non-heterosexual Christians who did
leave church behind altogether, and cited negative responses to their
sexuality as a reason for doing so, often stated that they would like to
belong to a church or other religious community again in the future (Yip
2000, p. 139).

Along similar lines, Kimberly Mahaffy's earlier study of the cognitive
dissonance experienced by lesbian Christians showed that the majority
of them had chosen to remain affiliated with Christian churches[2] even if
they had experienced opposition from others within the church. When
asked to explain how they had resolved any tension arising from cognitive dissonance between their sexuality and their faith, most of Mahaffy's
respondents said that they had chosen either to live with the tension
or to change their cognitions (Mahaffy 1996, p. 395). 'Living with the
tension' was not necessarily a passive choice, and included fasting and
praying for those who opposed homosexuality, or appealing directly to
people for compassion, as well as simply ignoring one's detractors. Even
those lesbians who had initially left the church after coming out because
of negative responses to them by church leaders or other Christians
often returned later, usually remarking that 'after they recognised God's

acceptance of them and achieved a personal relationship with God, they returned to the church' (Mahaffy 1996, p. 395). This chimes with Yip's later assertion that many such individuals come to construct their faith personally rather than appealing to church authorities or other external authority structures; indeed, Mahaffy notes that although leaving church was the least likely means of reducing tension undertaken by her sample, even those who continued to identify as Christian sometimes moved to other congregations, or 'chose to remain affiliated with the Christian community but relied on other modes to manage their dissonance' (Mahaffy 1996, p. 400).

Mahaffy concludes from her data that, among her sample, women who had suspected from a young age that they were lesbians were fairly likely to remain in church membership, suggesting that they may have been able to put together beliefs that affirmed their lesbianism from the start. Those who had come to Christianity only after they had already embraced their lesbianism also tended to live with the tension that resulted: 'Possibly, they have come to the Christian community with a strong interest in what the church has to offer and are willing to tolerate others' discomfort with their homosexuality in order to reap the benefits of Christian fellowship' (Mahaffy 1996, p. 400). Importantly, she suggests, 'The act of coming to terms with a stigmatized identity early in life or choosing an affiliation voluntarily may in fact be a source of strength enabling the individual to affirm . . . both identities' (Mahaffy 1996, p. 401). Mahaffy's study is based on a relatively small sample and a mostly white North American context, but it points to a significant capacity for holding together apparently conflicting identities among non-heterosexual Christians, and to the fact that not every Christian wishes to leave the church just because their sex or gender orientation is opposed by others.

A 1998 article by Alison Webster explores in more detail the tensions bound up in standing in a given tradition without accepting it all, because, despite its problems, it still represents the most honest place for one to be. Like Elizabeth Stuart, she notes that many lesbians who express discomfort at elements of their Christian setting, for instance, are asked 'If Christianity's so awful, why don't you just leave?' (Webster

1998, p. 128). The tension of holding together lesbianism and Christianity, two identities often deemed by others to be mutually exclusive, is heightened by the fact that, says Webster, 'at a time when I have been challenged by new and exciting forms of thinking about the nature of my lesbian identity – or should I say, the nature of the signifier "lesbian" as applied to myself – I have found few analytical tools by which to do the same with the signifier, "Christian"' (Webster 1998, p. 28). In other words, while there may be many ways to be lesbian, it seems that there are fewer ways to be (acceptably) Christian.[3] Lesbians may be excluded in Christian discourse either overtly, or because their lack of acknowledgement, their 'unthinkability' for many people, brings about their abjection (Webster 1998, p. 29). But for Webster and others, 'closing the Christian chapter' of one's life is simply not a viable option. Choosing once and for all between Christianity and post-Christianity is too concrete and definite; most people are not that simple, but often hold seemingly incompatible beliefs or desires:

> It does not make sense that, as a lesbian, I enjoy romantic Hollywood heterosexual feel-good movies. But I do. Likewise, it does not make sense that I feel attracted to Christianity – enmeshed in and by religion, when intellectually I have decided that at many levels it is rubbish, and damaging rubbish at that. The truth is that I cannot leave it alone, intellectually or personally, and that is what I have to make sense of. (Webster 1998, p. 31)

To say that one has entirely left Christianity behind, to say one has moved definitively into the 'post-Christian' camp, requires a fairly fixed and monolithic definition of what Christianity actually is. Someone like Hampson, comments Webster, who has deemed feminism and Christianity to be incompatible for her, is operating with closed definitions of each phenomenon, and she thereby 'fails to interrogate the crucial issues of who has defined the boundaries, who maintains them, and for what purpose' (Webster 1998, p. 32). Moreover, as Webster explores in her earlier book (Webster 1995), leaving behind Christianity would not necessarily mean leaving behind the prejudices and patriarchal structures within it, since these exist more fundamentally within our culture (and, warns Althaus-Reid, 'the post-Christian discourse is still a much-gendered position, while in queer theologies there is a deeper problematization concerning sexual and gender categories' – Althaus-Reid 2004b, p. 103). In fact, the forces outside the Church include 'the unimaginative, anti-religious and fundamentalist forces which use the power afforded by their political supremacy to define who God is, what Christianity is, and what is ethical and unethical' (Webster 1995, p. 183). Jantzen concurs that 'secularism is not a satisfactory alternative', since 'western secularism is as sexist, racist and homophobic as the christendom that informs it' (Jantzen 2001, p. 277).

What might be truly queer, posits Webster, would be to continually interrogate how (after Butler) we 'perform' or 'play at' our Christianity. This would entail asking what it is that has constituted our religious subjectivity and what it is that we ourselves continue to bring and build through it (Webster 1998, p. 35). This focus on agency, she implies, would allow there to be more overlap and uncertainty in 'what it is to be Christian', 'what it is to be lesbian' and so forth. This openness would refuse identification by others, and is echoed by Sweasey, who suggests that, rather than letting homophobes establish and police all the boundaries of the game that is Christianity, queer people should say, 'We're already playing, and what makes you think you can set the rules here?' (Sweasey 1997, p. 79).

Stuart suggests that this is somewhat idealistic – that Christian identity simply cannot be as 'slippery' as Webster would like it to be (Stuart 2003, p. 106). But Webster is not unaware of the historicity and doctrinal character of Christianity. She is well aware, too, of the drawbacks of non-realist theology and philosophy (Webster 1998, p. 37). Even so, it is crucial to acknowledge the partial and situated nature of all experience, including Christian experience. If Christianity is historical, it is also contestable (Webster 1998, p. 36).

It is important to note at this point that Christians from evangelical church backgrounds may find that it is particularly difficult to reconcile their homosexuality and their Christianity, since conservative evangelical and charismatic congregations in recent years have been less accepting of homosexuality than theologically liberal congregations. Mahaffy notes that, of her study sample, almost three-quarters reported experiencing a tension between Christianity and lesbian identity, with most of these experiencing conflict between their *own* religious beliefs and their sexuality (Mahaffy 1996, p. 397). This was most common among those who had identified as evangelical before coming out as lesbian (Mahaffy 1996, p. 400). Although this may be exacerbated by a sense of vocal opposition to homosexuality within evangelical churches, especially those in the USA (over a third of Mahaffy's respondents felt a tension between others' religious beliefs and their own sexuality – Mahaffy 1996, p. 397), to paint evangelical congregations as entirely anti-gay or unwelcoming spaces would be overly simplistic. Even if some evangelical ministry to homosexual people has sometimes been dubious – particularly the 'ex-gay' movement which aims to 'heal' people of their homosexuality and help them find support as they marry, have children and lead 'normal' heterosexual lives – it would also be true to say that many evangelicals feel great compassion toward those whom they feel are somehow missing out on fullness of existence because of their sexuality.

In her sociological study of evangelical New Frontiers International (NFI; now known as Newfrontiers) congregations in the north of England, Kristin Aune found that many of her interviewees felt that male homosexuality represented a lesser or subordinate version of masculinity, but one which should be treated with sympathy, not condemnation (Aune 2009, p. 41). One interviewee, Simon, had been impressed with the concept that gay men may have had inadequate relationships with their fathers or lacked other male role models as children. This made Simon believe that, rather than assuming his more 'effeminate' or 'camp' workmates would not be interested in joining in with his 'laddish' conversation or activities, he should try to include and affirm them, because 'male affirmation is precisely what they need and have lacked', and 'I'm [that is Simon] exactly the kind of bloke they'd like affirmation from' (quoted in Aune 2009, p. 46). Aune comments that Simon is simultaneously both figuring his own heterosexuality as hegemonic by assuming homosexuality is somehow less adequate or legitimate, and attempting to act lovingly toward gay men by extending to them the 'benefit' of his own 'normal', 'healthy' male sexuality. Interestingly, several of Aune's interviewees suggested that gay men, who may be figured as effeminate, shy or camp (that is, those who exhibited non-hegemonic masculinity), were more likely to find love, acceptance and a 'place' in church (that is in evangelical congregations) than out in secular society (Aune 2009, p. 48). This points to a perceived space in at least some evangelical churches for acceptance and embrace of those who have homosexual inclinations, even if overt heterosexual activity (in common with other extramarital sexual activity) is much less likely to be accepted (Aune 2009, p. 49). It may belie the assumption that conservative evangelical congregations are likely to be less welcoming of queer-identified people than more theologically liberal ones are (though liberal congregations are much more likely to accept the sexual *activity* of non-heterosexual people).

Picking one's battles

Webster also draws attention to another, slightly different reason for questioning whether queer people should remain in the Christian tradition. That is, she asks what it means that Christianity is (at least in her own British context) the dominant religious tradition which is taken as the default against which 'other faiths' are contrasted (Webster 1998, p. 38). If Christianity signifies dominance culturally and, perhaps, politically, then to what extent should people who have rejected its dominance about pronouncements on sexuality still wish to be identified with it? Should they not reject allegiance with *any* dominant and culturally hegemonic institution – whether or not it does in fact presume to pronounce authoritatively on matters of sex specifically? In part, this assumption might be countered by a Loughlinian assertion that theology and the Church are strange because they seek the strange, and a body acknowledging the unknowability of God never can be wholly culturally mainstream. Moreover, Webster's characterization of the Church in Britain as politically and culturally dominant may simply no longer be true; even if half of Britons as of 2008 describe themselves as Christian (Voas and Ling 2010, p. 67),[4] this does not obviously equate to recognizably

Christian doctrinal or moral allegiances, or to church attendance. More-over, there is ongoing pressure for the Church of England to lose the historically entrenched political sway it does have, such as bishops hold-ing seats in the House of Lords. Nonetheless, it is true that, as Thomas Bohache says, the figure of Christ has been used as a weapon against non-Christian religions, and that a queer Christology 'must be vigilant to root out Christian imperialism' (Bohache 2003, p. 23).

For Stone, another part of the answer is that there is not actually any such thing as a clear distinction between inside and outside when it comes to the church. 'Church' versus 'world' is yet another binary distinction, and should be treated with the same suspicion levelled at any other binary. In fact, 'Perhaps the biblical stories that queer readers need to focus upon are not . . . stories that constitute religious identity in polarized terms or make absolute distinctions between insiders and outsiders' (Stone 2004, p. 132). There may well still be revolutionary, reforming work to be done before churches can be healthy, life-affirm-ing places for those who have been rendered outsiders; it may well be that campaigning for the legality of same-sex marriage is still a neces-sary goal. But importantly, for Stone, this kind of work is not the final goal, for simply moving from 'outside' to 'inside' signification does not sufficiently query the structures of outsideness and insideness. Rather, 'we may need to commit ourselves instead to the task of dissolving those very boundaries between "inside" and "outside"; or, like Tamar, using our marginality and proscribed sexual practices to turn those bounda-ries "inside out"' (Stone 2004, p. 134). Arguably, this cannot take place if queer people position themselves once and for all as outside, external to the speaking, acting theological community. Those who purport to speak on behalf of the entire Christian tradition and the whole of Christian his-tory when they claim that God hates queers, that women are created to be the helpers and completers of men, that homosexual relationships are somehow inherently less committed and more narcissistic than hetero-sexual ones, need to keep hearing others say that they are wrong and that this is not the whole truth. If no one within the church is making it clear that these people do not have the monopoly on God, if there is no-one within the church living out and demonstrating alternative stories, then it will remain too easy to dismiss queer people as hardened sinners, unfortunate backsliders, or people who are otherwise somehow missing the mark. The words of Sweasey are on point when he says, 'If the ranks of religious believers include not only homophobes but also queers, we steal their trump card' (Sweasey 1997, p. 79). Indeed, suggests Sweasey, it is just as problematic to assume that queer excludes Christian allegiance as to assume that Christian excludes queerness. Having battled not to allow one crucial aspect of their identity – their sexuality – to be negated, it would be ironic, says Sweasey, if queer people have subsequently colluded with their 'oppressors' in keeping their spirituality hidden, leading to the subsuming of another, equally momentous aspect of their identity (Sweasey 1997, p. 24).

Importantly, however, it will be just as important, if not more so, for allies to make themselves publicly visible as it is for queer people themselves, who might have compelling personal reasons for not wanting to put their heads above the parapet. Those who happen to enjoy the privilege of identities which are either outright endorsed or simply benevolently unremarked upon by the theological mainstream – those who are heterosexual, married, white, educated, financially solvent and so on – have *more* responsibility, rather than less, to stand with and speak with those who do not. This is not a question of speaking *for* or *on behalf of* others – except perhaps in specific interim situations and for a limited time – or this would be to deny the specificity and particularity of their own voices. (Dee Amy-Chinn's assertion that 'we are all potentially queer' and that queer theology should be brought 'out of the margins and into the mainstream' [Amy-Chinn 2009, p. 51] is therefore ambiguous and even dubious, as I explore further below.) Rather, it means standing by public alliances, refusing to be made complicit by silence in the discourses which wish that recalcitrant queer voices would be silent forever.

It is for this reason that Stuart is sympathetic to the strategy taken by Mary Daly, who continued to teach at a Roman Catholic college even after she had ceased to identify as Catholic, and Christian, herself. For Daly, this was possible because she felt she could resist and query patriarchy most effectively from a position somewhat *inside* this setting despite the institution's overt hostility to her. Stuart notes, however, that everyone is tangled up in oppressive systems, and that choosing 'where we stand our ground and what we walk away from' is a 'strategy for survival' (Stuart 1997a, p. 17). In other words, it is always expedient to pick one's battles. Stuart seems to be suggesting that not everyone can do everything: it might be legitimate for some queer people to continue to work within established Christianity, but it might be equally appropriate (and necessary for their own survival) for others to leave. It is not an either/or matter. Respecting someone else's choice to stay or go is part of demonstrating solidarity with them and acknowledging that not everyone has the same level of freedom to publicly speak out (Stuart 1997a, p. 18). In the same volume, however, Braunston suggests that behaving like 'house slaves' who never make a fuss or speak up for their rights 'might work for a time but will . . . lead to frustration as these terms will never be healthy or life-enhancing for us' (Braunston 1997, p. 103).

Stuart is also sceptical about the binary nature of a move beyond Christianity for all queer people. Stuart holds that her own Roman Catholic tradition was part of what *made* her queer – playfully through its acceptance of male priests' 'lavish frocks', but also through its emphasis on God's preferential option for poor and vulnerable people, boundless love and the provision of legitimate alternatives to marriage and parenthood. She also encountered feminist theology and a sense of equality and mutuality within Roman Catholicism. At the same time, she notes that she did not always take from the tradition what she was 'meant' to take, and is sympathetic to those who have 'found no life at all in the symbols of Christianity, only violence, dryness and death' (Stuart 1997a, p. 16). However, she is adamant that there is something within Christianity that is prior either to secular rationales for queer or oppressive anti-queer distortions, even though 'from the inside, as well as the outside looking in, our conviction that Christianity can be liberating can appear foolish and irrational' (Stuart 1997a, p. 19).

This appears to chime with Stuart Macwilliam's comments on queer subversion and his belief that theology must be fundamentally *redemptive*:

It is axiomatic of queer theory that the act of subversion is in itself valuable, because without it, we cannot see clearly how we have structured our lives. What happens post-subversion is more problematic; on the completion of a nice little bout of gleeful subversion, it is tempting for the queer theorist to slip away from the scene regardless. The queer theologian, however . . . must poke amongst the wreckage looking for, if not salvation, at least something salvageable. (Macwilliam 2002, p. 400–1)

For Macwilliam, a project of deconstruction is useless if it leads nowhere. This does not mean settling for neat pat answers if the realities of life are messier, however; rather, in Macwilliam's account, queer theologies, and queer biblical interpretations, will be an ongoing project of poring over and assessing strands of the tradition. These may have been charred, melted or all but destroyed in the fire of queer theoretical criticism; nonetheless, they might represent sources which can be reused in new ways and combinations. How might this occur? To use an example from Macwilliam's own work, it might involve *shifting the focus* of interpretation (Macwilliam 2002, p. 401). If a given biblical metaphor or liturgical image is deemed offensive in light of contemporary norms of equality and justice, suggests Macwilliam, this might prompt the reader to re-examine the assumptions which have led to the text or image in question being read or exposited only in this way. A metaphor like that of marriage in Jeremiah, for example, might be considered to reinscribe patterns of meek submissive obedient femininity and thereby to be an unjustifiably repressive text for women in particular. However, 'The queer point of view does not deny the offensiveness, but it sees it as not an incidental *effect* of the metaphor but a deliberate *device* intrinsic to the metaphorical process' (Macwilliam 2002, p. 400). A stereotyping of women as submissive and obedient is still problematic – but if male readers are *also* implored to become 'like women', this already begins to disturb the caricature, and to invite wider questions about the nature of power, dominance, authority and the ways in which these play out in marriage conventions and the divine–human relationship. Importantly, however, such rereadings and reconstructions should always be recognized as tentative and imperfect, not as wholesale 'rehabilitations' of images which might still often be used in violent and oppressive ways (Macwilliam 2002, p. 404). Macwilliam and those persuaded by him might therefore be sceptical of too-assimilationist attempts to find queer (rather than proto-queer) ancestors and 'trancestors' in the Jewish and Christian Scriptures.

Christophobia and counter-rejection

As we saw in Chapter 3, some scholars have found it particularly important to construct a queer Christology grounded in the assertion that Jesus cannot be unproblematically represented as white, heterosexual and so on. Some of these Christologies echo the early work of Robert E. Goss in formulating a notion of a queer Christ who stands with all oppressed people as a living sign of God's liberation. Elizabeth Stuart summarizes,

> Goss argues that at Easter Jesus became the queer Christ . . . Jesus' resurrection is . . . the hope for queer people for it is through it that God turns Jesus into a parable about God and so we know that God is on the side of the oppressed . . . For all time and space Jesus identifies with the oppressed. Just as it is possible for people to proclaim that 'Jesus is black' and women to relate to the image of the Christa, so it is that queer people can declare that 'Jesus is Queer'. Indeed, if Jesus is not queer then the gospel is at best irrelevant and at worst bad news for queer people. (Stuart 2003, p. 82)

Thomas Bohache also attempts specifically to trace a queer Christology, which he believes is necessary for demonstrating to queer people that the opposition and inhospitality they may have experienced in Christian churches does not stem from Christ himself, despite what they may have come to believe. He says,

> There is . . . [a] deep-seated feeling among many gays and lesbians that Jesus Christ is not an option for them, that he, as the embod-

ied representative of God, hates them, and that they have no place in either Christ's Church or the kingdom of God . . . This is a mindset that I call 'Christophobia'. It is as factually bankrupt as homophobia and just as pernicious, for it separates many spiritually focused and religiously gifted individuals from a path that could bring them the fulfilment they have sought and been unable to find elsewhere. (Bohache 2008, p. 178–9)

Like Peter Sweasey, therefore, Bohache believes that the Christophobia of the queer community and the homophobia of the non-gay Christian community are *both* deeply inadequate and must both be overcome. Moreover, he states, 'The queer consciousness . . . seeks to critique heteronormativity and heteropatriarchal patterns of domination. This is where a queer Christology intersects with biblical studies, for we can discern from Jesus' recorded words and deeds how he felt about power relations' (Bohache 2003, p. 19). Since, says Bohache, the 'Christ-presence' dwells in *all* people (Bohache 2003, p. 21), it is not limited to one historical figure, and therefore is not exclusively to be epitomized by that one historical figure. Gay and lesbian people must acknowledge that Christian homophobia does not originate in Christ himself (Bohache 2008, p. 183).

Bohache is emphatically not claiming that Christ was homosexual. Indeed, he says that a queer Christology 'will not try to argue for or against the gayness of Jesus, but will seek rather to determine what his Christ-ness says to marginalized peoples of all generations, including today's queer community' (Bohache 2003, p. 19). It is possible to say Jesus was queer *whether or not* we feel we can speculate on his sexuality, for his queerness inheres just as much and just as crucially in his social-political allegiances and his critique of power structures as it does in his sexual orientation. Bohache believes that Christ is the relational expression of God, and that all people have the potential to birth Christ via loving relationally (and there are clear echoes here of Carter Heyward, especially in Heyward 1982). This is an especially important thing to hear for queer people who may have been told that, even if they are able to, they should not birth or parent children. In fact, says Bohache,

A queer appreciation of the Nativity is the realization that Christ *will* be born, no matter what the circumstances. No matter how hard it is, no matter how perilous the journey, no matter that folks might not receive us, once we have agreed to give birth to the Christ in self-empowerment and creativity, Christ *will* be born. (Bohache 2003, p. 27)

Bohache's concept of 'Christophobia' chimes with Andrew K. T. Yip's politics of counter-rejection, whereby 'nonheterosexual Christians, having felt that they [are] rejected by the churches, [counter-reject] the churches' official teachings and, indeed, moral authority in the area of sexuality' (Yip 2002, p. 208; see also Yip 1999). The main difference is that Yip considers many of these individuals to have reinterpreted and reframed Christian teaching through a personal lens – still considering Christian teaching relevant to personal sexual morality, and still looking to the Bible even if non-mainstream interpretations are preferred – rather than having rejected it outright. Indeed, Yip notes that the construction of Jesus as a champion of marginalized people is often propounded as a central trope by non-heterosexual Christians (Yip 2002, 2003, 2005). Yip's survey respondents and interviewees figure Christ as a site of solidarity for non-heterosexual people, championing all who are marginalized (Yip 2005, p. 57). Yip notes that this chimes with Goss' assertion that Christ's suffering encompasses the suffering of all who are violated and assailed, including those who experience homophobic assault (cf. Goss 2002).

Andy Braunston suggests that queer people should not go along with the wishes of homophobic Christians by hiding who they really are, since, he claims, 'If we play by their rules we will always be betrayed' (Braunston 1997, p. 102). Using the model of women-church as propounded by Ruether (Ruether 1985),[5] Braunston notes the emergence of queer-church: for example, the congregations of the Metropolitan Community Church[6] and Unity Fellowship Church, and support and activism groups such as the Lesbian and Gay Christian Movement. He suggests that queer people should formulate their own liturgies and practices rather than going along with established ones that have proven crushing or inadequate. (He does also note, however, that not all queer congregations are immune from using sexist, racist or ableist language, and that there may be a danger of simply replicating the mistakes of what has been left behind – Braunston 1997, p. 102, 104.)

Queer worship

Siobhán Garrigan explores the notion of queer worship and liturgy in more detail, with particular mention of rites and liturgies formulated especially for queer people, such as formal blessings of same-sex partnerships, or renaming ceremonies for people who have undergone gender transition. Such ceremonies, she says, have proven useful symbols for LGBT people for 'living into their identities' (Garrigan 2009, p. 213). However, she suggests, focusing only on these special or 'extraordinary' events means too little thought is given to questions of how 'inclusive' or queer-friendly the ordinary, workaday life and liturgy of a given congregation really is. For example, it is rare even in 'open and affirming' churches for an ordinary anecdote or sermon illustration to be about a non-heterosexual person or a non-standard family setting. Unwitting heteronormativity (such as inviting the congregation to split into 'men and women' for singing the parts of certain hymns) may exclude transgender people even where this is not intentional (and Garrigan suggests that splitting into high singing voices and low singing voices might be a practical and low-key solution in this particular instance – Garrigan 2009, p. 215). Simply including gay and lesbian people in worship, she claims, does not do enough to unveil the extent to which all human sex is socially constructed and, therefore, contingent and unstable (Garrigan 2009, p. 217; McClintock Fulkerson 1997, p. 197) and does not, therefore, change the basic 'rules' of this gender-normative 'game'. This chimes with McClintock Fulkerson's assertion that 'conservative' and 'inclusive' theologies alike tend to go only so far in disrupting fixities of identity.[7]

Moreover, questions arise about whether special renaming or coming-out rituals are actually necessary: Garrigan asks pointedly, 'Are queer people's lives really so different from other people's lives that they need special rites for key events?' (Garrigan 2009, p. 213). As Garrigan herself acknowledges, many queer-identified people do *not* wish to have special mention or exception made for them: 'They claim that the liturgy is simply the liturgy: it is by its nature neutral and being gay, straight or anything else is irrelevant when it comes to how one worships' (Garrigan 2009, p. 215). However, Garrigan counters, after Teresa Berger (2008), that the 'neuter' of liturgy is a false one, and that 'LGBT people insisting that worship is "neutral" regarding gender are either blind to or in denial about the extent to which Christian liturgy is ... gendered' (Garrigan 2009, p. 216).

Of course, such an assertion can and should be problematized: to claim that all LGBT people who find mainstream liturgy unproblematic are simply failing to recognize how gendered, sexist or heteronormative it is might be deemed very patronizing. However, Garrigan's claim that some LGBT Christians who are members of mainstream denominations (as opposed to congregations like the Metropolitan Community Church which might be deemed exceptionally queer-friendly) may 'tone down' their queerness in order to fit 'respectably' into a worshipping community is an important one and bears consideration.[8] This is a question of recognizing liturgical worship as a 'game' with certain 'rules' and acknowledging that one must follow them to a greater or lesser extent in order to be playing the same game – which might entail 'muting' one's LGBT status (Garrigan 2009, p. 218–9). This arises even in churches where queer people are ostensibly welcome – because, says Garrigan, the churches themselves probably do not realize that the only queer people they are *really* willing to welcome are those who may be gay rather than straight but who otherwise fit into conventional patterns of dress, behaviour and family structure. Following Kenji Yoshino, Garrigan suggests that this comes about because gender 'normality' has not been sufficiently disturbed by the predominantly heterosexual mainstream (North American) churches, which means that even congregations deliberately and consciously open to LGBT people are often reinscribing gender norms – which, in turn, require other 'normal' behaviour and the 'covering' (that is, the concealment) of queerness (Garrigan 2009, p. 220–1; Yoshino 2007). Tolerance of a few queer people by a church does not equal their full integration (Garrigan 2009, p. 221); it might be that gay couples or transpeople, like many people with disabilities, are 'welcomed by' a church (and may become tokenistic specimens for how hip and inclusive the church in question is) rather than ever being fully recognized as *part of* the church that does the welcoming.

Garrigan acknowledges that there remains a tension here: it is problematic if queer people go along with being 'hidden', but if queer people behave *more* rather than *less* atypically in relation to their heteronormative church communities – if they 'flaunt' their queerness – then this itself may contribute to their increased 'othering'. Her conclusion is that if liturgical worship itself is to be queered, this must be a project of the whole congregation, not just its LGBT members:[9]

> LGBT people must not be the only people having to choose to do an 'unusual' thing, a thing that exposes them and their relationships in ways that others never have to experience … By enabling full (and unpredictable) LGBT participation, the whole church and its worship become 'queer', instead of a picture where the church is normal – where, in other words, normal behaviour is suggested of all who wish to feel accepted within it. (Garrigan 2009, p. 223)

This is positive, but I suspect it does not quite go far enough to engage the issues surrounding what 'normality' really is: if 'queer' behaviour (whether or not done by LGBT people) becomes typical within a community, in what sense *is* it really queer or subversive (if queer entails a positionality in opposition to the mainstream)? As Garrigan notes, 'there are no ready-made recipes for what will constitute queer worship in any given place (and relatedly, the "normal" that is being queered is different in every given place)' (Garrigan 2009, p. 228). In other words, do queer people *want* to reach a societal state where they no longer stand out because everyone else is like them – and if so, where does one get one's identity from when there is no longer any injustice to oppose? Is this not just another kind of assimilationism – something just as sinister and intolerant of multiplicity and difference as patriarchal heteronormativity has often been deemed? Is it that *churches* are uniquely called to be queer communities in contrast to a non-queer secular society? If so, is this not also exclusive because it means that people who do not belong to churches can never be 'really' queer – thus further marginalizing those queer Christians who have made a political/moral decision that they will not belong to church communities because of Christianity's blemished copybook on LGBT concerns?

As Loughlin's and Stuart's definitions of Christian theology as inherently queer might suggest, for Garrigan part of the answer is that 'worship can be claimed as queer by its very character as a perennially counter-cultural force, one of the key mechanisms whereby the endlessly changing divine–human alliance is established and developed, contested and investigated in this world' (Garrigan 2009, p. 225). Importantly, worship is not limited to undoing heteronormativity, but to standing over against 'any and every site of supposedly established earthly power' (Garrigan 2009, p. 225).[10] For this reason among others, simply acknowledging queer people's existence (even if it is often important to do so) cannot be the whole story of queering liturgy – 'add gay and stir' will not leaven the whole loaf (Garrigan 2009, p. 228). However, worship also cannot lose sight of the fact that LGBT people do have sexualities and sexual lives and that these should not be elided where they differ in some specific way from the sexual lives of others. It is therefore inadequate, suggests Garrigan, to say that *all* worship is inherently 'a structurally queer site in human living'; she says, 'It is not enough to talk about how Christian worship queers the pitch of a consumerist culture or even to rely on a self-satisfied queer ritual ethic: that is to spin the word "queer" out too poetically, if not to wholly (mis-)appropriate it' (Garrigan 2009, p. 226). Truly queer worship will involve all its participants in a culture of naming and endorsing difference, demanding an ethic of faithfulness and love from everyone, gay or not, and resisting individualism to press into a new kind of ecclesiology (and, indeed, a new kind of Christology) (Garrigan 2009, p. 227).

It is for this reason that the growing acceptance of queer theology as a serious theological discourse need not be its death-knell or render it inherently disempowered. It is true that seeing queer theology listed as a study topic alongside feminist, liberation and postcolonial theologies is a double-edged sword, because this both demonstrates that it has come to merit critical consideration by the theological academy, and risks its becoming just another methodology to be examined in passing rather than becoming transformative of method and practice more broadly. The fact that various feminist and liberation theologies have become so relatively mainstream in university and seminary settings is both positive and negative for queer theology: feminist, postcolonial and liberationist concerns do indeed underlie much of the theory and praxis in some such settings, showing that they are robust, incisive, tenacious, and more than marginal concerns. However, the insistence, by some queer theologians, that queer theology is more profoundly disruptive than these its close relations, means that its examination as just another mode of theological discourse may itself represent a failure to understand the radical nature of what its proponents believe it to be. But if queer theology never does receive exposure and academic scrutiny and come to inform the research and teaching practices of scholars, it risks being written off as a risible, easily dismissed phenomenon. The fact that Garrigan and others have shown queer discourse to be both profoundly transformative of ecclesiastical practice *and* profoundly in line with the strong precedent of theological over-againstness – as championed by Barth and other theological heavyweights – means that queer theology can continue to exist in this liminal state. It can carry on its existence as an insider–outsider discourse which will sometimes want to be recognizably Christian and sometimes not, but which is familiar enough with the Christian legacy and story to be able to comment on and critically appraise it.

Conclusion

To the extent that religion produces and legitimates coercive norms, queer theology must critique it and stand outside of it. To the extent that religion transforms fear into life and denial into risk, queer theology should articulate it and support it. As critical and engaged theory and prophecy, queer theology will have to wager on surrender and redemption but not assume too quickly or easily that a place for queer thinking will open up. Homosexuals engaged in religious communities are warring over a place at the table and so cannot devote much energy to anything beyond the polarizations and solidifications of identity that come in times of war. Queer theorists in religion have the task of complicating the warring positions without losing sight of the stakes that remain for those they would help. (Schneider 2000, p. 11)

Are 'queer churches' the answer to the exclusion and lack of welcome many queer people have experienced in their congregations? Only if they are more than specialist, partisan places. Troy Perry, the founder of the Metropolitan Community Church, was clear from the first addresses to his fledgling congregation that the church was to be in some sense 'mainstream', reflecting the Roman Catholic, Lutheran and Episcopal backgrounds of many of its early members:

> I made it clear that we were not a gay church; we were a Christian church, and I said that in my first sermon. I also told them that we would be a general Protestant church to be all-inclusive . . . It would have to be a church that most could understandably and easily identify with, and accept it as not being unusual or odd. It seemed to me that it should be traditional, almost like those they attended in childhood . . . I . . . had to re-establish old links with God, but do it in a new way that would be meaningful in our community. (Perry 1972, pp. 122, 126–7)

As Garrigan argues, what would be truly radical would be for entire congregations to talk together about what it is to queer particular norms – norms concerning social justice, economics, consumer habits, the environment, education and the media, and not just in terms of non-heterosexual sexuality or what might be deemed 'marginal' concerns (even if the realities of embracing a range of bodies and sexualities will remain crucial). The existence of specialist 'queer churches' has been historically expedient for those who have met overt or implicit hostility elsewhere; nonetheless, they are, perhaps, only an interim answer. The risk is that queer church enclaves repeat the figuring of queerness and queer theology as marginal, so that they are never visible enough to mean that mainstream denominations have to take any notice of them or recognize them. Such recognition is a two-edged sword; as Althaus-Reid, Isherwood and others realize, to be made 'central' rather than 'marginal' might simply rob queer of its oppositional energy and render it ineffectual. A church congregation comprised only of people who identify as queer – especially if this means queer in the sense of being a sexual minority – will provide important support and safety for those who need it. However, it may be at greater risk of homogeneity – and of being unifocal – than a more integrated church. This concern is not specific to queer churches: ecclesiologists working in the emerging church movement are still grappling with the implications of what it means when a congregation comprises only people in their teens and twenties, or only retired people, or only families with young children, and to what extent such a congregation can be considered synecdoche of the universal Church. In some cases, there may be convincing reasons for this homogeneity; Hannah Lewis, for example, has argued that Deaf-only churches might be necessary contexts for the best flourishing of Deaf Christians, since creating space for Deaf voices to be heard in theology and the Church means maintaining settings where they are consciously privileged over those of even sympathetic hearing people, in order to 'balance out the hearing-centred discourse that has dominated Deaf life' (Lewis 2007, p. 6). Nonetheless, by and large such 'interest-group' congregations might still be considered threats to catholicity. Of course, catholicity itself should not be assimilationist and force every congregation to fit the same mould.

If these questions seem circular – or rather, spiralling – then this is further evidence of how they repeat the uncertainties brought about in questions of the very nature of identity and belonging. In some sense, queer theologies raise as many new questions as they answer. However, Marcella Althaus-Reid and Lisa Isherwood have suggested that, just as reflections grounded in social-scientific and economic analysis have shown up the liberationist threads in theology, so might reflections grounded in queer theory draw out the queerness of the Christian tradition. In this way, they say, queer theory can be understood as a new 'mediator science' for radical theologies. Queer theory has disrupted theology in a way no other oppositional or postcolonial theory ever has, because queer 'has deregulated the binary myths of the subjects of theology, and in doing that, it has de-regulated our representations of God' (Althaus-Reid and Isherwood 2007, p. 306). Queer theory's emphasis on plurality and ambivalence does indeed seem quite opposed to what Althaus-Reid and Isherwood consider the kernel of mainstream theology, namely givenness, monotheism, and an authoritarian metanarrative (Althaus-Reid and Isherwood 2007, p. 307). The fact that this picture of mainstream theology is something of a caricature (of a tradition which also, let us not forget, contains apophatic philosophers, lactating Christs, gender-bending Church Fathers, and a profound concern for the excluded running through its holy book) is a pity. However, if binary desire-and-lack has *come* to underscore significant parts of the tradition endorsed, Althaus-Reid and Isherwood's point stands, at least in part – especially since they are willing to say, with Graham Ward, that it may be a Greek metaphysical overlay on the story of God made incarnate, rather than the queer instability of divinity-becoming-humanity, that is the real problem (Althaus-Reid and Isherwood 2007, p. 310).

As Gerard Loughlin has argued, even if certain churches are indeed (and unequivocally) guilty of perpetuating the exclusion and marginalization of queer people, of continuing to consider 'queer' an insult, churches also have the potential to render queer an insult *turned*. In this way, it is no longer a mark of shame (Loughlin 2008, p. 144). This is neither an unproblematically good or an inexorably unilinear thing: rather, it is likely that Christian churches, and the Christian tradition, will remain only contingently welcoming places for those who call themselves queer. It may be that some such people, therefore, conclude that Christianity is not worth the trouble, and that they deserve a more unambiguously safe and hospitable narrative alongside which to make their own journeys. It is likely that those of us who do not face regular opposition or, at best, find ourselves the targets of 'prayerful concern' (at least not on the grounds of our sexuality), will not blame them for doing so. Queer theology is not the 'answer' to theology's problems of homophobia, sexism, and too easy alliance with Western capitalist norms. It can critique and subvert these things, but not by providing a fixed, stationary answer of its own. As Stephen D. Moore has observed, '"Queer" is a supple cipher both for what *stands over against* the normal and the natural to oppose, and thereby define, them, and what *inheres within* the normal and the natural to subvert, and indeed pervert, them' (Moore 2001, p. 18).

Are queer Christians betraying the counter-cultural aspects of their identity by aligning themselves with an institution which has oppressed them and other marginal people? Only, perhaps, if both queerness and Christianity are understood as monolithic and mutually exclusive, and if narrow understandings of identity are maintained. Should all queer people remain in the Christian tradition? Perhaps not. For some, this will mean continuing to claim a personal Christian faith without participating in communal church worship; for others, it may mean ceasing to identify as Christian at all if the label is too replete with pain and compromise to be tenable. Laurel C. Schneider points to this difficulty when she remarks upon 'the tension between strategies of lesbian and gay liberation on the one hand and queer re-imagining of the world on the other':

> Lesbian and gay liberation may be about intense and intimate needs for inclusion, recognition, and identity that are worth the cost of some heteronormativity. Queer theology may be about creative re-imagining of possibilities in which we are no longer recognizable, but in which we no longer beg for recognition either. The cost of freedom and integrity seems so great on the one side and the risk of loss so real and impossible on the other. This tension is powerful, creative, and dynamic, but it is devastating as well. (Schneider 2000, p. 9)

Nonetheless, queer theologies more broadly can remain ambivalent about mainstream theology without entirely detaching from it. Indeed, their incisive, critical ambivalence makes them an important apophatic voice at the theological table. Remaining at least in *conversation* with the 'mainstream' tradition will oblige the tradition to recognize that it, too, is not unquestioned or unopposed – and, indeed, that questioning and opposition are not evidence of diabolical attack, but rather vital tools for keeping alive.

Notes

1 Yip's data is drawn from 565 postal questionnaires and 61 interviews with self-identified non-heterosexual Christians in the United Kingdom, conducted in the late 1990s (Yip 2002, p. 201).

2 Mahaffy notes that 33 per cent of her sample, based mostly in the north-eastern USA, identified their original church membership as Roman Catholic, while 65 per cent belonged to one of 32 Protestant denominations. Mahaffy's data is based on surveys of 186 lesbian women (Mahaffy 1996, p. 396).

3 However, Webster notes that the exclusion does not only happen one way: in some respects, she suggests, it is easier to come out as lesbian among Christians than to come out as Christian among lesbians (Webster 1998, p. 30). Similarly, Cheri DiNovo, a United Church minister in Canada, comments that when attending a queer studies symposium she wore her clerical dog-collar 'just so that I could feel "queer" among the queers . . . When the standard look was radical chic, a collar became the very symbol of queerness . . . To be an "out" Christian at a queer studies symposium was queer indeed' (DiNovo 2007, p. 105).

4 This data is drawn from the 2008 British Social Attitudes survey, which found that 50 per cent of Britons who responded identified as Christian in 2008 (as opposed to 66 per cent in 1983). 23 per cent of Britons identified as Church of England, 9 per cent as Roman Catholic, 3 per cent as Presbyterian, 2 per cent as Methodist, 1 per cent as Baptist, 2 per cent as another Christian denomination, and 10 per cent as non-denominational Christian. 7 per cent belonged to a non-Christian religion, including 3 per cent Muslim, 1 per cent Jewish and 3 per cent other non-Christian religions. 43 per cent of Britons said that they had no religion (Voas and Ling 2010, p. 67).

5 Ruether's book attempts to point to a processive understanding of liturgy and ecclesiology, and includes suggested rituals for 'forgotten' or excluded times and rites of passage in the lives of women and others. These include a rite of healing from an abortion, a coming-out rite for a lesbian, a liturgy of preparation for birth, a croning liturgy, and a ritual to mark the end of a marriage.

6 For an overview of the foundation and early history of the MCC, see Perry 1972 and Swicegood 1974.

7 For example, McClintock Fulkerson says, conservative Christians who oppose homosexuality often do so on the basis of appealing to 'natural' heterosexual gender relations as affirmed in Scripture. Inclusive liberal Christians refuse such a heteronormative natural theology, holding that gender is culturally constructed and contingent, *but* 'invoke the modern (read *new*) "natural" identity that comes from sexual orientation' (McClintock Fulkerson 1997, p. 196). But, she goes on, assuming that sexual orientation is fundamental to one's being leads to questions about why some people are homosexual rather than heterosexual, *not* about how stable these either/or categories of sexuality actually are. This in

turn leads to a mindset of 'inclusivism', wanting to ensure that homosexual people can be integrated into predominantly heterosexual churches and communities, but never adequately querying whether the predominantly heterosexual, stably gendered norm is itself 'real' or not. She concludes, 'I wonder whether . . . inclusion will ever be anything but denial of difference – homosexuals are the same as you and me – or implicitly support a mentality of the normal/deviant, real/imitation . . . However strongly we bless the "just-like-usness" of gay and lesbian sexual practice, the politics of inclusion is not a direct hit at the frame which regulates and rules – and defines this "us"' (McClintock Fulkerson 1997, pp. 200–1). See also the notion of ex-gay community as a 'queer space', since it does provide a designated place, albeit ambivalent, for those in the evangelical world who identify as homosexual: the ex-gay identity is in some sense unstable and resists polarization into homosexual or heterosexual (Erzen 2006, pp. 14–16, 89, 186; Aune 2009, pp. 44, 48–9; Gerber 2008). Erzen says,

> Although the political goals of the ex-gay movement and queer activists are radically distinct, by accepting that a person's behaviour and desire will not necessarily correspond with their new ex-gay identity or religious identity, ex-gay men and women enact a queer concept of sexuality when they undergo queer conversions. Although men and women in ex-gay ministries do not and cannot envision homosexuality as a positive way to be, their lives also exemplify the instability and changeability of their own identities rather than serve as a testament to heterosexuality. (Erzen 2006, p. 14)

8 Even the MCC does not escape similar tensions, however. Robin Hawley Gorsline, an MCC minister, notes that some members of his congregation are unhappy about the frequency with which he mentions the words 'queer', 'LGBT' or even 'our community' during services. He remarks that in his local LGBT community, 'queer is a fighting word' (Gorsline 2006, p. 730), and suggests three possible further reasons for his congregants' discomfort: first, specifying queer allegiance might exclude non-gay members of the congregation. Second, making an MCC congregation too easily identifiable as 'queer' might endanger those members who are not publicly 'out' as gay. Third, people who have been used for a long time to keeping their sexuality and spirituality separate may find it difficult to reunite them.

9 I have argued elsewhere that the same is true for intersex people (Cornwall 2008a, pp. 188–9).

10 For much more on theology as necessarily countering hegemony, see Gorringe 2004, p. 119, Gorringe 1999 and Cornwall 2009a, pp. 229–30. The scriptural witness is always other than 'the deafening clamours of conflicting ideologies', thereby testifying to God's resistance to being subsumed by human ideology (Gorringe 2004, p. 120).

7

Other Controversies in Queer Theology

The advent of queer theory and praxis, which seeks to dissolve all received conceptualizations of gender and sexuality, may also undermine any appeal to a common set of moral values on which claims for legal, social and theological change could be grounded. (Gill 1998b, p.176)

Queering theology is not a rhetorical pastime but a political duty. (Althaus-Reid and Isherwood 2007, p. 305)

This chapter addresses other accusations levelled at queer theologies, such as the suggestions that they are too nihilistic, idealistic or self-indulgent to be politically effective. This includes the argument by Claudia Schippert that queer is too empty of reference to lead to ethics, and that this fundamentally divides it from feminist and/or liberationist theological concerns; the suggestion by Robert E. Goss that queer's reputation as unrealistic is more damaging than its reputation as indecent or distasteful; and the suggestion by Christopher Hinkle that queer theologians are too naïve and do not realize the extent of secular queer theory's antipathy to religion. I draw on counter-currents within queer theology, such as Marcella Althaus-Reid and Lisa Isherwood's portrayal of queer theology as an agent for social transformation, and Malcolm Edwards' suggestion that a political project is less important to queer theology than talk about God is. I acknowledge the strikingly apolitical nature of some queer theologies, ask whether queer must always be political to be of value at all and suggest that there is space for both praxis and reflection within the movement.

Queer as an empty referent: is a 'queer ethics' possible?

> Queer theory . . . has . . . tended toward nihilism, the only hope it can hold out is the hope of an unending, subversive performance of identity, an endless drag show. And, perhaps most importantly, for many who are sympathetic to its aims as a project it seems hopelessly idealistic . . . Queer theology has to address these concerns. (Stuart 2003, p. 103)

As discussed above, one of the possible problems identified with queer theology may be that it is too vague or loose to offer any practical imperatives or guidelines for social action, so it does not actually advance the cause of those who continue to be marginalized in churches and in society at large. Queer has sometimes been figured 'as devoid of ethical meaning, as anti-ethical or as directly opposed to anything Christian' (Schippert 1999, p. 50). Kathy Rudy has written that queer 'offers us little insight for ethics', since 'queers in principle are opposed to any ethical program that passes judgment on any sexual behaviour' (Rudy 1997, p. 123, cited in Schippert 1999, p. 50). In recent years, scholars have debated the extent to which queer entails an 'end' or 'edge' to ethical thinking. Lee Edelman's suggestion that queer theory is profoundly about a rejection of a certain social future and that a 'death drive' is central to it (Edelman 2004) might be considered characteristic of this somewhat nihilistic or anti-normative bent. It is important to note that such objections to queer's abstract nature are levelled at Butler and other foundational queer theorists, not just at those who have built other methodologies on their ideas; for instance, Valerie Hey notes that Butler has been accused of 'obscurantism, wilful impenetrability, political quietism and intellectual elitism' (Hey 2006, p. 441), and says of her,

> Certainly Butler's psychoanalytically informed poststructuralism provides resources that deepen our understanding of the effects of power. But, to restate the obvious, her abstractions remain disconnected from the vibrancies of life. Yet, ironically it is only when this 'connection' is accomplished that we are given ways into better specifying what she

means by the 'sedimentation of the "we", in the constitution of the any I'. (Hey 2006, p. 451; quoting Butler 1993, p. 105)[1]

In this account, despite the supposed political importance of the denseness and difficulty of Butler's writing (see for example Salih 2003), it might be said that Butler actually prevents political connection and activist alliance from being made.

However, it has also been mooted that queer's abstractness, its lack of content and lack of ethical normativity might be essential to it, and that its distinction from other liberative theologies is significant and irreducible. This is the argument made by Claudia Schippert in her 1999 essay 'Too Much Trouble? Negotiating Feminist and Queer Approaches in Religion'. Schippert proposes that notions of power, resistance, and identity within queer theory are not necessarily identical with the concepts called by the same words within liberationist and feminist ethics. A major concern, she suggests, is that 'a queer active opposition to normativity raises questions for feminist ethicists as to how to conceptualize values and norms without relying on and reinscribing normativity' (Schippert 1999, p. 47). It is therefore not possible to say unproblematically that queer ethics (or queer theology) should take on the conceptual mantle of liberation and feminist theology, since queer subverts the very concept of promoting norms, whereas liberation and feminist theologians have often had clear ideas about the areas of praxis and action necessary to bring about a more just world. Moreover, suggests Marcella Althaus-Reid, queer theologies are often understood as perpetually placeless and in motion, existing in a liminal non-place of Deleuzian 'becoming'; as such, 'Queer theologies are not the "natural consequence" of feminist thinking but an option related to a different understanding of a theological trajectory and a different aim' (Althaus-Reid 2008, p. 108). Of course, notes Schippert, queer theory does have a genealogy in feminist criticism and cannot be figured as entirely other than it; however, there are real tensions in their differing methodologies and underlying conceptual frameworks (Schippert 1999, p. 47).[2] As we have seen, this is often understood as problematic by feminist as well as by queer scholars; Heather Walton comments,

Many feminists have argued that while the queering of identity offers a welcome challenge to essentialist understandings of gender and sexuality it also effectively undermines struggles to assert distinct spheres of knowledge, experience and resistance. It also tends to deflect attention away from contesting the economic, legal and moral boundaries that sustain heteronormativity. These can be safely held in place while we experiment with transgressive performance that may well call into question what is normal, natural or chosen in sexual identity but does little to shift the balance of power. (Walton 2004, pp. 39–40)

The linking of queer theologies and hermeneutics with liberationist praxis is evident even in recent work like that of Ibrahim Abraham (see for example Abraham 2007, p. 4.9), so it seems that Schippert's warning has not been fully heeded.

Interestingly, though, Schippert's problematization of feminist and liberationist normativity does not, in fact, necessarily mean that there can be no such thing as a queer ethics. Schippert says,

I focus on the question of norms and their potentially automatic implication in normalizing operations of power. I argue that we should not 'choose' between one or the other, that is opt for ethical norms versus queer resistance to normativity in general. Rather, we need to address and reconfigure the relation of norms and normativity itself, for example, develop tools to recognize and differentiate between the specific effects norms and their deployment have in particular contexts and practices. (Schippert 1999, p. 44)

As a matter of fact, Rudy and others are wrong, suggests Schippert, to suppose that either queer theory or queer people are opposed to notions of ethics or moral value on principle (Schippert 1999, p. 50). Schippert asserts, after Janet Jakobsen and David M. Halperin, that norms need *not* automatically become normativities, and that 'we can describe specific practices that enact and deploy norms but do not depend on negative screens or the casting out of some to constitute the subjectivity of dominant positions' (Schippert 1999, p. 53). Rather, queer people, by actively choosing to live out of abjected or somehow 'incoherent' embodied positionalities – *while still proactively resisting their own abjection* – might disrupt the appearance of coherence which underlies and supports normativity (Schippert 1999, p. 62). In so doing, they might demonstrate that the abject is not simply the inverse or absence of subjective normativity, but has a grammar (Schippert says a 'geometry') all its own. The tension between normativity and norms will not be 'solved' by finding 'better' norms; and actually, the troubling nature of this tension is important in itself, since it traces the complexities of power and authority bound up in the notion of ethics itself.

In 'Turning On/To Ethics' (2006), which draws heavily on her earlier paper and its primary interlocutors (Judith Butler, Katie Geneva Cannon and Evelynn Hammonds), however, Schippert explicitly asserts that 'queer theoretical work, instead of turning *on* ethics (in the sense of evading, defying, or betraying), can enact a turn *to* ethics' (Schippert 2006, p. 158) – and that this is exactly what Butler foresaw when, in *Bodies That Matter*, she appealed to 'a radical resignification of the symbolic domain' (Butler 1993a, p. 22, cited in Schippert 2006, p. 159). It is precisely the (ethical) act of 'reading from within shifted correlations' (Schippert 2006, p. 160) that continues to resist normativized (and normativizing) structures of power. Cannon's act of resistance in writing her womanist ethics, claims Schippert, is nothing less than 'doing ethics from a place in which no ethics can be done' (Schippert 2006, p. 165). This process is not one of garnering recognition or inclusion, but one which questions the structures which rendered black women's voices unrecognized and marginal in the first place – yet *without* seeking their assimilation into unqueried 'discourse'. But Schippert now reads Cannon slightly differently from the way she did in 1999, recognizing that the ideals and imperatives Cannon proposes *are* ethical ones and *do* demand lived responses. Abjected bodies are still *bodies*, and still undergo lived, bodily experiences with an ethics and morality of their own (Schippert 2006, pp. 167–8). The most striking difference between this essay and the earlier one is that, despite its largely similar focus and content, Schippert no longer utilizes the motif of making trouble (after Butler's *Gender Trouble*), whose recalcitrant, rebellious bent grounds the 1999 piece. In short, she no longer seems quite so sceptical of ethics as an interim move for queer, despite still recognizing its provisionality: 'The position affirmed and taken would be simultaneously dissolved. However, this paradoxically does not negate its reality' (Schippert 2006, p. 172). Since queer has shown itself to be to do with 'multiple starting points and alliances of contradictory norms' (Schippert 2006, p. 172) – what Butler calls 'provisional unities' – its dynamism and constant movement makes the norms less likely to petrify into concrete normativities. Schippert is still wary of systematic or *constructive* ethics, however, precisely because it is not possible to know what living under the rules of a very different grammar, or geometry, would be like. The focus should be on small and temporary alliances and norms, which may fade away before they can even be described, rather than attempting to draw out a grand and 'truthful' ethical system with no contradictions or tensions.

Schippert's concerns about the extent to which queer theology can be ethically prescriptive are perceptive, and deserve more consideration by queer theologians, since they seem to disturb the very nature of ethics more profoundly than many writers acknowledge. Althaus-Reid and Isherwood affirm that queer theology 'pertains to the exploitation but also to the solidarity and cooperation of people at the margins of society and theology. Therefore, it is not correct to say that Queer Theology lacks agency. Queer Theology is an agent for transformation' (Althaus-Reid and Isherwood 2007, p. 308). In this account, queer theology is inherently concerned with social justice and the transformation of human relationship: it cannot afford to be anything else, since it stands as a clearly prophetic voice over against solidified capitalist and heteronormative manifestations of theology (what Althaus-Reid sometimes calls T-theology – see for example Althaus-Reid 2003, p. 172). Interestingly, Stuart believes that, since the categories of experience and activism are clearly so important to Althaus-Reid, 'it would be better to characterize her work as liberation theology informed by queer theology than as queer theology as such' (Stuart 2003, p. 103). There is certainly a tension here: Althaus-Reid, Isherwood and others assert that queer theology is uncertain, open-ended, moving, in process and so on, and yet they still want it to be somehow directional. But perhaps this argument is not quite so far from Schippert's as it might appear: Althaus-Reid and Isherwood note that one of queer's major strategies 'is to read theology dismantling dualist readings and plays of oppositions' (Althaus-Reid and Isherwood 2007, p. 309). Importantly, therefore, we might say that they recognize that queer theology *cannot* set out to be totally non-normative – *even where normativity as a rule is regarded with suspicion* – since this would be to close off an area of possibility and render it irredeemable. Queer theology 'challenges the boundaries and wishes to propel us into a much wider paradise' (Althaus-Reid and Isherwood 2007, p. 310) – an assertion about incarnation, but one which also pertains to discourse and seems to repeat Schippert's endorsement of Hammonds' 'new geometry' wherein simple binary negation of what is known in the rules of the present realm cannot be assumed to describe the yet-unknown queer (dis)order. Shutting off ethical discourse because it is contaminated with normativity is too dualistic and negates queer's capacity to be transformative even of this.

Althaus-Reid acknowledges that queer's insistence on the rejection of identity and definition is still an ambivalent good, since 'if we cannot define the "queer subject" (otherwise it would not be queer) how can we then define the struggle and unify a reader–believer through a textual strategy of self-identification?' (Althaus-Reid 2008, p. 115). Althaus-Reid and Isherwood note that queer has also been criticized in liberation-ist perspective, because it views the main problem with capitalism 'as one of access and not the system itself' (Althaus-Reid and Isherwood 2007, p. 313). However, they believe that there is potential to expand the scope of both theologies, through an analysis which profoundly recognizes and critiques the connections between sex, gender, money, labour and power. This is where meta-questions about the very notion of queer theology as a genre come to the fore: can queer theology ever be more than a discursive exercise? For Althaus-Reid, the key is that, whereas feminist and other liberationist discourses have figured themselves as oppositional to certain phenomena and thereby inevitably *exclusive*, queer theological discourses might allow for a plethora of political acts which cannot be represented along binary lines of opposition but, rather, via multiple differentiation (Althaus-Reid 2008, p. 115).

Other scholars have also insisted that queer which is not political is useless. This is the basis for Sheila Jeffreys' critique of 'transgression' based simply on gender-bending dress, unusual sexual practices and so on. These are not inherently resistant, she suggests, unlike political protest and campaigning (Jeffreys 2003, p. 42; see also Weeks 2000). As we noted above, Lee Edelman suspects that queer theory's rejection of normativity and certain futures might mean that ethical speech can go no further and that queer represents an untraversable boundary (Edelman 2004). Nonetheless, others have held strongly to the conviction that queer must contain and perpetuate ethical momentum since it is concerned with the abjected and oppressed nature of real lives. All this goes to restate an assumption we have seen arise again and again throughout this book: queer is provisional, ambiguous and in flux. Its conscious uncertainty might be considered to rend it impotent and divorced from reality. However, its resistance to assimilation by other normativities is also its strength, and it is precisely in and through its constant reframing and restating that it is methodologically and politically vital.

Queer self-indulgence

Another controversy surrounding queer theology stems from the suggestion that it is somewhat self-indulgent, linking sex too strongly with transcendence and subsuming God within sexual pleasure. Christopher Hinkle asserts that, to accord too much significance to the sensual or erotic aspects of religious experience, as occurs in much queer theological writing, is unwarranted (Hinkle 2007, p. 193). He suggests that likening orgasm to mystical experience is dangerous not because these things are in fact *not* similar, but precisely because they are. Experiencing the divine via human sexual congress is not unthinkable, but all *too* thinkable. It is therefore possible that 'one will become overly attached to these [sexual] experiences, gradually allowing the pursuit of them to replace the desire for God' (Hinkle 2007, p. 194). Hinkle believes that conflating the two is an especial risk for people whose experience occurs in a context alienated from institutional authority and in a highly politicized sphere. He claims, 'Taken to its extreme, this tendency makes of queer theology a technology for better sex, an erotic spiritual dimension to supplement the strictly secular pursuit of pleasure' (Hinkle 2007, p. 194). But this is where his discontinuity with someone like Althaus-Reid becomes particularly evident: the latter might have said that there is no such thing as better sex unless it is more just sex, sex always aware of how it affects and is affected by its broader socio-economic context. Economics might not be everyone's fantasy of choice – indeed, some people might consider it to have a distinctly dampening effect on their ardour – but Althaus-Reid recognizes that sex is always already bound up with discourses of money and power and that nothing kills the mood quite as much as having to worry about whether or not to forgo condoms in order to earn some extra cash or whether one can afford the next meal. Hinkle's analysis does not adequately recognize that, while queer theology is indeed distinctly playful and joyous in its reading of sexual pleasure, this does not render it inherently or necessarily self-indulgent. For Althaus-Reid, it cannot afford to be self-indulgent, precisely because it is aware of its own implication in broader economic and political discourses. Hinkle criticizes queer theology for privileging the erotic as a source of sacred experience and thereby privileging something which tends 'to equate unity with God with the satisfaction of one's own desire' (Hinkle 2007, p. 195); Althaus-Reid recognizes that desire is muddied and its motives are mixed but that a politicized understanding of sex in the context of a God who is also sexual need not be an individualistic or narcissistic one as Hinkle seems to suspect.

A separation of God from sexual desire might, however, be useful in another way. Hinkle observes,

> As a spiritual director, John of the Cross would often insist that one of his charges give up, at least for a while, a favourite cross, some specific prayer practice, or a distracting pleasure. In part this self-denial helps strengthen and prepare the soul for greater trials ahead, but more basically it works to distinguish desire for God from those habits . . . with which it has become too closely associated. (Hinkle 2007, p. 195)

If we recognize that God is not actually identical with the sexed and gendered desires and practices often sanctified and endorsed by mainstream theology – the desires for power, control, and demarcation – then we allow God to 'come out' of the heterosexual closets in which God has often been 'decented' and hidden (Althaus-Reid 2003, p. 37). Favourite crosses and prayer advice hardly seem sinister – but neither, at first sight, do moralities of hard work, family values, and paternalistic care. They, too, however, can get in the way of God, if God is only sought in these certain regulated and authority-sanctioned places. It is necessary to travel outside approved 'paths' or routes, to form alliances beyond those sanctioned by the 'colonizers' who have made theology a project of heterosexual imperialism, and to seek God in unfamiliar places (Althaus-Reid 2003, p. 31–2).

Althaus-Reid herself notes, of course, that queer theologies have had accusations of self-indulgence levelled at them from other quarters. Discussing the tendency of historical feminist liberationists to focus on issues of social justice and women's ordination, Althaus-Reid says, 'In a sense they see queer theologies as a luxury which only privileged women in academia can afford to pursue' (Althaus-Reid 2008, p. 106). Queer and more generally sexual theologies have been accused of having moved away from 'common sense' in their emphasis on sex rather than economics (Isherwood and Althaus-Reid 2004, p. 1). In other words, issues of sexuality must be secondary to issues of economic survival and religious status, and the only people who can balance the cost of reflecting 'rebelliously' on sex are those who have economic security and social/intellectual status via other avenues. But as Althaus-Reid and others have argued (Althaus-Reid 2006b; Maduro 2006; Petrella 2006; Carvalhaes 2006), liberation theologies are of limited use if they do not engage with the real and continued sexual and gender oppression of those whose identities do not 'fit' theologically sanctioned patterns. Classic Latin American theologies of liberation, she suggests, have failed fully to engage with issues of the sexuality of poor people as well as their specifically economic marginalization. In this account, queer theologies could assist in the sexual 'undressing' of liberation theology – not to *detract* from the important issues surrounding socio-economic safety, but to *enhance* them, since those who are sexually marginal often tend to be economically marginal too. The pressure faced by a woman who works as a prostitute out of economic necessity but who can make more money by allowing her clients not to use condoms – or who, in a Roman Catholic country, cannot access condoms easily or inexpensively – is 'about' both sex and economics. Sexuality is not a secondary or 'luxury' issue, but inextricably bound up with questions of survival.

Indeed, sex underlies much other discourse; Althaus-Reid says, 'Queer theologies interrogate much more than sexuality: sexual episte-mologies are seen as the foundation of current political and economic systems that have generated the external debt and trade agreements which produce hunger and oppression' (Althaus-Reid 2008, p. 107). Importantly, Isherwood and Althaus-Reid figure queer theology as fundamentally being about *love,* and the ways in which both individu-als and societies can speak and act more lovingly. They assert that love is central to all theologizing, because it must prompt questions about the legitimacy of systems and discourses which receive theological sanc-tion (Isherwood and Althaus-Reid 2004, p. 2). Nonetheless, as Deryn Guest notes, queer theology and queer biblical criticism's propensity for affinity with 'controversial' sexual practices or behaviours might leave them always unpalatable to a Christian mainstream uncomfortable con-templating phenomena such as kink/BDSM. Since non-heterosexual sexual activity is often characterized as similarly 'controversial' even when it is exclusive and faithful, Guest fears that 'Queer readings may, in fact, further the breach between those arguing for pro-lesbian and gay interpretations of Scripture and those refuting them' (Guest 2005, p. 45).

Queer as anti-Christian

Hinkle states that 'queer theological writings seem with a few excep-tions unaware or uncritical of queer theory's antipathy towards the most basic Christian commitments' (Hinkle 2007, p. 196). He considers much queer theory aggressively anti-religious, and is keen to make clear that he himself does not go along with the 'secularizing conclusions' of queer theory. Hinkle suspects that secular queer theory does not adequately interrogate the sources of desire – because it is so hyper-keen to avoid essentialism that it reduces everything to social forces. By contrast, suggests Hinkle, queer theology might speak to a God who is simultaneously a source of desire and a purpose for desire, who is 'beyond all the cultural artifacts and processes' (Hinkle 2007, p. 196). Goss, too, notes that queer theorists often condemn the Christian tradition as irrelevant, violent or oppressive (Goss 2002, p. 247; Hinkle 2007, p. 197) (and compare Sweasey's and Bohache's observations on Christophobia), and Rollan McCleary claims that queer theory's rationalist bent is already evident in queer theology: 'Queer theology is not as adventurous or mystical as it could be, but simply critical and hyper-rationalist' (McCleary 2004, p. 102). As we saw above, there is much debate over whether queer Christians should bother with the Christian tradition.

But the notion that theology stands over against other discourses and can reject human ideologies means that, despite its own muddied history, theology is able to critique and queer oppressive human systems (Gorringe 2004, p. 117–18) and to exist in an inside–outside relationship with other disciplines. Moreover, importantly, Hinkle believes that queer theology can be prophetic, demonstrating to secular, pragmatist queer theory something of which it is already aware, namely that secular queer theory is itself muddied by mixed motives and a Foucauldian will-to-power which have in the past rendered it too dismissive of religion. This built-in awareness of its own problems means, suggests Hinkle, that 'queer theory has the tools (and perhaps . . . even the desire) to rise above a self-promoting dismissal of Christian claims and even in some cases to be transformed by them' (Hinkle 2007, p. 196). Whether or not this hope will prove realized remains to be seen.

Sarah Coakley suspects that queer, in the form posited by Butler, may have another problem in terms of its use by theologians. Coakley believes that Butler's approach to destabilizing gender through highlighting the dubious nature of sex binaries or the fixity of gender is 'vibrant'; however, she says, 'it has very little time for the kind of transformations that arise out of patient practices of vulnerability before God. It tends to take such practices as merely re-enshrining forms of subjugation' (Coakley in Shortt 2005, p. 77). For this reason, suspects Coakley, queer theology itself – if modelled along Butler's lines – might be unable to take sufficient account of the *multiple* areas of transformation necessitated by human interaction with God. Transformation requires grace (Coakley 2002, p. 159). Importantly, this is attributed not to the anti-Christian bias noted by Hinkle, but rather to a case of queer theory and Christianity speaking in different languages, where the language-game of Christianity – with its talk of soteriology, sacrament and sacerdotalism – simply does not make sense to theorists who are not themselves grounded in it. Furthermore, this time like Hinkle, Coakley insists on a confessional basis as the best ground on which to do the work of resistance and reframing – making space for God to be God (Coakley 2002, p. 34). If this is missing, then a crucial dimension of understanding the *contingency* of human ideology is absent. We might take as an example Coakley's insistence that, since desire is even more of a fundamental category for interrogation than gender, gender is 'always in renegotiation' (Coakley in Shortt 2005, p. 79); but that, importantly, *both* desire and gender (and their treatment by Butler and other secular gender theorists) must be considered in terms of their *a priori* secondary relationship to what Coakley considers the central doctrines of Christianity, namely incarnation and God's triune nature (Coakley in Shortt 2005, p. 79). The existence of Christ as an expression of God's desire comes first, the existence of gender second, and it is for *this* reason that gender must be seen as provisional or fluid. Queerness is contingent on God, not vice versa.

It might be countered (against both Coakley and Hinkle) that Christian doctrinal expressions about Christ and God did not arise in some kind of gender vacuum, but were always already informed in their accidental and deliberate formulations and disseminations by pre-existing social understandings of the meaning and efficacy of human sex and gender. Importantly, when Coakley expresses doubt about queer's usefulness or appropriateness for theology, she does so with Butler's gender 'trouble-making' very clearly in mind; and, for Coakley, a 'protest' act often means a somewhat immature and dead-ended one – using queer 'to sanction various forms of previously unacceptable pleasure' (Coakley in Shortt 2005, p. 80), but with no further *theological* purpose. It is here that Coakley's understanding of queer theology might perhaps be limited by her solely sexual reading of it. She is well aware that desire in Butler is always about loss, the loss of a narrative which is more than heterosexual, which hegemony has written out of possibility (Coakley 2002, p. 160). However, Coakley's lack of engagement with the broader and especially socio-economic expressions of queer theology as outlined above (and developed by commentators other than Butler) means that sex and gender remain isolated from other matrices of power. She can point to a priest's movements from behind the altar to in front of the altar during the Eucharist as profoundly disruptive of gender stasis and hierarchy (as indeed it may be), while not adequately acknowledging the other kinds of hierarchy and subordination repeated in both the priest's relationship to the laity and the God–human relationship that this echoes. This is ironic, since Coakley is critical of the late twentieth-century (and presumably early twenty-first-century) obsession with gender liberation not informed by eschatology (Coakley 2002, p. 161) but does not seem adequately to explore eschatological queering of class and economic norms in this connection. In fact, although she might not recognize them as such, there are those more explicitly doing queer theology who are travelling companions of Coakley: Althaus-Reid and others have insisted strongly that what they seek to do in 'queering' or 'indecenting' theology is not an invention of something new, but a recovery of something always already present in God.

The point stands, however, that queer and Christianity are often read as possessing a mutual antipathy: 'On the one side there are Christians who think that queer studies offends Christianity, while on the other there is a suspicion that a too close association with Christianity will contaminate queer studies' (Althaus-Reid 2008, p. 107). If secular queer theory believes Christians are inherently conservative, homophobic, proselytizing or narrow-minded, then queer theology is an 'outsider' discourse just as much among secular queer theorists and activists as among mainstream theologians (as DiNovo and others note above). But this liminality, this placelessness, might itself be understood as prophetic:

The 'no location' of queer theology between theology and queer theory is symptomatic of the site of revelation that queer theology has come to represent, that is, the in-betweenness of a liminal theology the aim of which is to continue to speak about God, beyond the closures produced by the heterosexual epistemology of western discourses. (Althaus-Reid 2008, p. 107–8)

It is for this reason that Althaus-Reid is suspicion of the 'domestication' of queer theology – even though she herself taught in 'decent' academic contexts as well as marginal ones.

I was recently asked whether queer theology might be significant for formulating a new kind of systematic theology, the questioner suspecting that it tended to perpetuate its own marginalization via its frequent emphasis on issues of sex and sexuality. As I showed above, queer theology is certainly beginning to speak to multiple and various subject areas. However, it is also important to note that there is something tenaciously *un*systematic about much queer theology, occasionally even named as such; its suspicious bent tends to render it inhospitable either to grand narratives or to the neat categorizations which order and demarcate Christology, pneumatology, eschatology and so forth. To engage in confirmed 'systematic' theology might besmirch queer's cherished freedom from being boxed in, toeing a party line or being on the payroll of perceived oppressive systems. It might be felt that a systematic treatment of doctrine along traditional lines would be too limiting, though it should be noted that queer theologians have (as we see throughout this book) already addressed some of the most commonly treated doctrinal areas – such as Christology, soteriology, ecclesiology, the nature of God, eschatology, hermeneutics, pneumatology, Mariology and theological anthropology – in queer perspective.

Queer on the ground: preaching, praxis and pragmatism

Another perceived problem with queer theology and queer biblical criticism is that they are too intellectual and therefore too removed from 'theology on the ground' and the everyday lives of those Christians not involved in academic theological and/or theoretical study. Ken Stone gives a pragmatic warning about the use of queer theology and exegesis by those who preach and teach in churches, noting that if such readings are too controversial or simply too abstractly intellectualized for the average hearer's tastes, they are unlikely to be recognized as important methodological tools 'on the ground', *even if* a concern for democratic and anti-hegemonic hermeneutics is built into them theoretically. Moreover, the perceived controversial nature of queer may lead to ministers who draw publicly on queer readings losing their positions – and thereby their platforms – so that such readings may not receive public airing at all. Noting queer's propensity to disturb, subvert and overturn, Stone says,

> [The] ministry of 'making others uncomfortable' does present certain challenges to the livelihood of the Preacher, not to speak of the seminary fundraiser. These challenges may cause some to object that the biggest problem with queer reading is not that it makes others uncomfortable, but that it seems (perhaps like the rhetoric of queer professors) so thoroughly unrealistic. For if we are concerned about what some folks at my seminary like to call 'ministry for the *real* world', what shall be the point of preaching sermons so controversial that we may soon no longer have a pulpit? In the real world – it will surely be said – only preachers who can keep a pulpit have any chance to effect transformation. (Stone 2007, p. 164)

Of course, this raises much larger questions about the extent to which preachers should challenge and exhort their listeners rather than just telling them what they want to hear or what they can comfortably fit into their existing theoretical framework. But there might certainly be a case for arguing that, in a congregational setting, it would be appropriate for preachers to help their audiences consider more explicitly *how* the implications of queer theoretical hermeneutics affect 'real world' situations. Importantly, this does not mean doing away with theory, or glossing over the theoretical underpinnings in which queer political-religious resistance might be based; rather, it means helping Christians to find and articulate robust theological bases for their praxis. Is this abstractly intellectualist, and thereby somehow inherently 'anti-queer', if 'queer' means working to a less goal-oriented, forward-thrusting agenda, perhaps rejecting the very notion of straight-line trajectories as oppressively prescriptive? Not necessarily; an important element of queer theology is its emphasis on respecting a multiplicity of voices, contexts and experiences. It would be ironic indeed if a voice from a pulpit were to say 'But, of course, *this* is what you really mean and *this* is why' (for even if that voice is advocating queer, anti-hierarchical outworkings of theory, there is still a problematic aspect to the fact that the speaker has to have some externally validated authoritative legitimacy in order to be standing in the pulpit in the first place). Nonetheless, it may be that the preacher's (and, more generally, the minister's) tasks include facilitating access to existing vocabulary and reflection in order to help members of the congregation *enrich* their own description of – and critical reflection on – their situations.

Something of the kind happens, for example, in contextual Bible study, a methodology which is very consciously plural and anti-hierarchical. One of its proponents, Gerald West, comments that the facilitator of contextual Bible study discussions has only one voice among several, and should therefore 'defer to the group, even if what the group is saying does not appeal to the facilitator' (West et al 2007, p. 12). He goes on,

> It is important to be committed to reading the Bible in community with others whose contexts are different to our own. And this 'in community with' means that the facilitator recognises that in the group, he/she may have power which comes from a privileged background. It also means that the facilitator's role is to empower the group participants during the Bible study process to discover, acknowledge and recognise their own identity, and the value and importance of their contributions. (West et al 2007, p. 17)

It seems to me that the same should be true for preachers who seek to draw on queer theologies and queer biblical criticism (who may have had the privilege of access to academic training and theory which some members of their congregations have not), and that this will necessitate a balance between encouraging consciously democratized discursive reflection on practical situations and critiquing the questionable power-structures and social systems which may be evident within them. This begins to be seen in the sermons collected and evaluated by lesbian minister Olive Elaine Hinnant in *God Comes Out* (Hinnant 2007), which are variously by heterosexual, publicly homosexual and privately homosexual preachers, and which are analysed in a context of broader reflections on what 'coming out' might mean for both God and the preacher. As Stone insists, a Christian concern for eschatology – which is also, and simultaneously, a queer concern for a more just society – means that 'We should . . . not allow ourselves to be trapped into deciding between pragmatic decisions in the real world, and that future toward which we are already trying to order our lives' (Stone 2007, p. 165).

Dee Amy-Chinn also fears that outworkings of queer theology have thus far often been deemed too intellectual (and, by association, too abstract) by those who may be less familiar with – or less convinced by – the critical theory in which it has been grounded. She says,

> My concern is that the way queer theology has sought to use Butler and Laqueur may leave any reader unsympathetic to the queer project with the sense that, particularly in the case of Butler, this work is no more than an intellectual exercise, a set of thought experiments that form the basis for an idealized and unrealizable project. (Amy-Chinn 2009, p. 50)

Sara Salih, Valerie Hey and others have written at length on the importance of the 'difficulty' of Butler's writing, noting that it means Butlerian analysis cannot easily be 'smoothed out' or made accessible to beginning readers. But, as Salih notes, criticizing Butler for not writing clearly misses the point. The challenging nature of reading Butler might itself help to shape readers who are not content with easy answers from either their texts or their cultures, and who are therefore willing and critically equipped to query all aspects of discourse – even those as naturalized and 'invisible' as syntax and grammar (see Salih 2003, p. 43; Hey 2006, pp. 443–4). Amy-Chinn suggests that criticizing Butler for idealism actually arises from a misreading of Butler, and is therefore not an insurmountable problem. Although it might sometimes seem as though Butler is advocating a transcendence of the binary sex/gender model, with its solely feminine females and solely masculine males, actually what she proposes is far more concrete that that. Amy-Chinn notes that Butler is calling not for a 'freeing' of gender from sex so that one's gender can be whatever one wants *despite* one's sex, but for a recognition that *sex itself* is multiple and recalcitrant – so she calls not for a rejection of bodily particularity, but for a proliferation. In some respects, I think Amy-Chinn is too generous to Butler, who has spectacularly failed on at least one occasion to understand the real lived specificity of atypically sexed bodies.[3] Nonetheless, the highlighting of bodily particularity which is often overlooked by Butlerian scholars is important, since it means an amorphously abstract concept of embodiment is not possible. For Amy-Chinn, this means that queer theologies drawing on Butler must also, inherently, take stock of bodily multiplicity as expressed in *individual* bodies, and acknowledge that their similarity and difference runs along for more than dually sexed lines.[4]

Finally, as Rollan McCleary remarks, it is important to note that it is not only heterosexual Christians who may be unfamiliar with queer theory and thus turned off by the intellectual, abstract quality of some queer theology: 'Queer theology may even be unwittingly, irrelevantly elitist towards the majority of gay Christians left struggling to establish themselves and whose position is normally more theologically conservative' (McCleary 2004, p. 105).

Queer as apolitical

A further criticism sometimes levelled at queer theology is that it fails to engage at an activist level with lived queer concerns, and that by remaining theoretical (as in the previous criticism) it fails to muddy its feet with the specificities of agitation and protest as played out on the ground. One of Deryn Guest's motivations for championing lesbian, rather than specifically queer biblical hermeneutics is her belief that queer readings, at least prior to the early 2000s, are insufficiently political. While some queer biblical critics have explicitly spelled out the importance of their work for grassroots politics, too many others 'leave it for readers to see the relevance of the work and apply it' (Guest 2005, p. 49). For Guest this is problematic, because social justice and political action are too pressing and urgently necessary to leave to chance, and the issue of identity is not somehow 'over', or no longer relevant, if one's gender or sexual orientation means that one still faces very real and tangible threats to one's safety. Guest believes that there might still be pressing ethical reasons for actively privileging the women's movement, for example, as a site of transformative action and discourse, rather than dismantling any grouping based on a category like 'woman' or 'lesbian' – since women and lesbians still experience disproportionate danger and marginalization.

As we saw above, any project as ethically normative as Guest's might be considered too directional in a context of queer anti-prescriptivism; however, for Guest, abstract apolitical intellectualism is too expensive a luxury on the ground, and queer theology is, therefore, unjustifiable. Conversely, we have seen throughout this book the assertion by Isherwood and Althaus-Reid that queer theology is indeed political, because it is committed to sexual and social justice: in its exposure of unjust social, economic and religious systems, they insist, it *is* political theology and *is* an 'agent for transformation' (Isherwood and Althaus-Reid 2004, p. 6). Even if someone like Schippert might counter that Isherwood and Althaus-Reid are incorporating queer too unproblematically into their existing feminist–liberationist agenda without taking enough account of its necessary lack of ethical prescription, their honest attempt goes far to mitigate the concerns of Guest, Jeffreys and others.

But must queer *always* be political? Does using queer as an interesting methodology – rather than one necessarily grounded in activism and political action – enfeeble it, erasing its genealogy in civil rights and praxis? Malcolm Edwards asserts that, while the political project is important for those who do queer theology, it should not become their focus to the exclusion of talk about God (Edwards 1997, p. 74). This is not dissimilar from Coakley's criticism above: politics must be secondary to theology.

Gerard Loughlin's 2007 edited collection, *Queer Theology: Rethinking the Western Body*, is strikingly apolitical in many respects. This might seem an odd thing to say of a book which endorses same-sex marriage and erotic friendships, appeals to a biological basis for homosexuality, rejects the notion that homosexual bodies are 'disordered' heterosexual bodies and likens the Eucharist to sexual intercourse, all in its introduction. Overall, however, the volume's essays appear to exist on a plane safely distant from grassroots struggles and homophobic violence: even if some of the authors have faced such oppression themselves, they do not (with a few exceptions, like Kathy Rudy) draw on it explicitly here, unlike the very confessional and experiential North American queer theologians of the previous decades.[5] Of course, in part this is because not all the contributors would even claim to be rooted in theological praxis: Linda Woodhead, for instance, is a sociologist of religion, and her essay represents a decidedly sociological analysis of Christian concern with sexual regulation and social power (Woodhead 2007). Nonetheless, even the out-and-out theologians represented here are not quite in the Goss and Wilson tradition. This change is not insignificant: Loughlin notes that Virginia Burrus' essay in the volume 'raises important questions about the appropriation of queer theory by theology, a supersessionist tendency – not entirely avoided in this introduction – to find theology in advance of a theory that only that theory has made possible' (Loughlin 2007b, p. 19). The shift itself is important, since Loughlin himself recognizes a swing from 'uncovering' queerness with an assumption that it has historically been hidden, quashed and abjected, to discovering that queer interests 'have always already been at play in the dominant, supposedly straight culture' (Loughlin 2007b, p. 8). Loughlin quotes Henry Abelove, himself paraphrasing his students:

[Don't] focus on histories that require the trope of marginalization for their telling . . . Focus on the musical comedies of the 1950s. What could be queerer? . . . [These] cultural productions were central rather than marginal. By ignoring or neglecting them, we misconceive the past and unwillingly reduce our presence in and claim to the present. (Abelove 2003, p. 47; Loughlin 2007b, p. 8)

Abelove, writing in the early 2000s, explains that his self-proclaimed queer students, who might have identified themselves as lesbian or gay had they been born twenty years earlier, now call themselves queer but *without* an inherent suggestion of struggle, marginalization or abjection attached to this description. Abelove says,

> They do not typically experience their own subjectivity as marginal, even in those moments when they feel most oppressed by homophobic and heterosexist discourses and institutions. Marginalization isn't their preferred trope. It doesn't seem to them to be cogent as a narrative device for organizing the telling of their own lives or, for that matter, of their history. What these queers prefer to say and believe or try to believe instead is that they are both present and at the center. (Abelove 2003, p. 45)

Is this part of what is going on in Loughlin's *Queer Theology*? The political struggles have not disappeared, but nor are they, any more, definitional. Queer does not always have to be belligerent; it can also afford to relax enough to be more casually reflective. Of course, this cannot be anti-historical: it is probable that without the political struggles of earlier generations, openly identifying as queer, and making queer readings, would not be even so relatively safe as it has become. But as Loughlin explains, if queer 'betokens something other than political and sexual identity' (Loughlin 2007b, p. 9) – if it is, indeed, after Halperin, a positionality rather than a positivity – then this emptiness of content must encompass an emptiness of political content too. Undoing identity must also imply undoing politics. Loughlin suggests that the collection is consciously 'inclusive' in terms of politics, while always aware that such inclusiveness can 'occlude the differences between queers, the tensions of taste and politics that drive them apart' (Loughlin 2007b, p. 9). Even if this consciousness does not come through in each individual essay, then – Rudy's has already been mentioned, and Gavin D'Costa insists that 'theology is an ecclesial practice while queer theorizing is not' (D'Costa 2007, p. 270) – the whole collection is set in this light.

This helps make sense of the way the theological tradition can be said to be queer without anachronism and without reading queer figures into the past in the way that has been criticized by Koch and others. For, says Loughlin,

> Queer theology . . . has an interest in reminding the church of its remarkable early antipathy to sexual congress, which was, of course, an antipathy to sexual reproduction. The interest is not to advocate a return to such extreme sexual abstinence, but to relativize modern obsessions with heterosexual marriage. (Loughlin 2007b, p. 14)

So the theological mainstream can queer the theological mainstream, *as well as* sex-gender 'dissidents' critiquing and subverting it. It is in this way that queer need not be always or inherently about marginality or abjection: queer also represents shifts in affiliation and emphasis that are not a product of hegemony so much as a reflection of a discursive climate which recognizes multiple, changing sites of power and prominence. 'The point is not to queer an ostensibly straight tradition, but to show that the tradition's doctrinal heart is already queer, and that as a named undertaking "queer theology" is already belated', says Loughlin (Loughlin 2007b, p. 27).

The point might stand that the authors in the *Queer Theology* collection tend to endorse physical specificity and locatedness (see for example Beattie 2007, pp. 297–8) but without openly situating their discussions in their own situated contexts, and may thereby risk a kind of universalizing theoreticism which more overtly political queer theologians have sought to resist. However, there is another sense in which this is actually less prescriptive (and more queer?) than situating queerness in only *one* kind of experience and one kind of overtly activist outworking, in which proponents may appeal to strikingly similar testimonies, allegiances and political affiliations as one another and thereby, ironically, perpetuate a new normativity. This is significant, too, for negotiating the ways in which 'outsiders' might act as allies, by blurring further the boundaries concerning who can speak queerly. Schippert comments,

Asserting that things operate in terms of a different geometry posits that it is not obvious what things look like inside. Simultaneously, it is not necessarily the case that only those who have been or are inside can participate in the resistant engagement. Rather, being part of a resistant engagement is a continual process; being an ally is not an a priori position but the result of engaging or being in alliance. (Schippert 2006, p. 172)

Conclusion

The kinds of criticisms levelled at queer theology are by no means exclusive to it: accusations of obfuscatory intellectualism, apoliticism and self-indulgence might be applied just as much to other critical theories. Indeed, although these criticisms mean that queer theology should not be taken on uncritically (which would be ironic indeed), they in no way point to its failure as a phenomenon.

Many of the scholars who ascribe to queer theological tenets want to say that queer strands can be traced back to creation itself, and that queer theology is in no way separable from the Christian tradition. That said, queer theology as a distinctly named, discrete academic and ecclesiastical stream is barely twenty years old. For much of that time, it has sought to negotiate if and how it differs from its close cousin, gay theology, and still exists to some extent in that cousin's shadow. What this means is that queer theology is still negotiating what it might become, all the while going through the existential journey of asking whether it can 'become' anything at all, or whether that is too prescriptive and fixed for a resisting, deconstructivist methodology. Just as bright-eyed, idealistic (and sometimes naïve) twenty-year-olds often become disillusioned, settled (and sometimes cynical) fifty-year-olds, it is possible that queer theology will not manage to retain its apophatic strand and will be content to take its place alongside other twentieth- and twenty-first-century contextual theologies as important but ultimately niche phenomena. Alternatively, as queer theology becomes better known, and gains in familiarity with lay and ordained Christians, it may manage something more devastating, upturning theology's relationship with the rest of the world as well as with its God. Always, though, queer theology exists in an important tension, not trying to impose itself as a definitive norm, but rather showing that the definitive norms of other discourses are false ones.

As we have seen, queer theology's 'emptiness' is therefore an important aspect of its deconstructive bent, and makes clear that it is not a simple replacement for other kinds of theology. Queer's 'anti-Christian' strand is a problem only if queerness and Christianity are artificially held apart, rather than being acknowledged as interacting and mutually critiquing, especially in the lives of those who call themselves both Christian and queer. The criticisms that queer theology is apolitical, and that it is self-indulgently abstract, are, perhaps, more problematic ones; if these tendencies do not go unchecked, queer may retreat to a closet which is safely removed from the messiness and difficulty of life lived in a way often excluded, abjected or delegitimized. Nonetheless, as we have seen, this does not mean that identity politics are incontrovertibly positive, or that eliding the difficulty of even theoretical critical analysis is an unproblematic good. Queer theology will be most incisive if it continues to speak into *both* academic theological contexts (in all areas, not just those concerning sexuality and gender) *and* more pragmatic, everyday ones – even while continuing to question and query why Christians are so often keen to keep theology out of churches altogether.

Notes

1 David Nixon brought Hey's article to my notice, for which I am grateful to him.

2 Laurel C. Schneider, writing at almost the same time as Schippert, makes it clear that this is also the case for tensions between queer theology and specifically gay liberation theology: 'Gay and lesbian liberationist attempts to challenge, reform, and reframe Christian faith to value, bless, and incorporate queer experience are, in the perspective of more radical queer theory, simply ludicrous. The gay/lesbian liberationist and the queer theorist positions rest on very different key assumptions about Christian faith and its contents. For the liberationists, Christian faith is fundamentally about something true and real, although it can be (and has been) distorted . . . But in much of queer theory, indebted as it is to postmodern literary criticism, the objects of religious faith can never be resolved enough to matter in the ways that the subjects of faith can' (Schneider 2000, pp. 10–11).

3 In a 2001 *GLQ* article, Butler considers intersex and transgender accounts of selfhood and self-description. Unfortunately, she seems to have a rather loose grasp on the material she cites. Butler has misunderstood or misrepresented the thrust of Milton Diamond's argument about the extent to which chromosomes, rather than environment, determine gender identity: she says, 'Diamond argued . . . that intersexed infants . . . generally have a Y chromosome, and that possession of the Y is an adequate basis for concluding that they ought to be raised as boys' (Butler 2001, p. 625); and, later, asks 'Why is the Y chromosome considered the primary determinant of maleness, exercising preemptive rights over any and all other factors?' (Butler 2001, p. 628). However, this is not quite what Diamond says. It is not as simple, as Butler claims, as saying that Diamond sees the Y chromosome *in itself* as a basis for raising a child as a boy; rather, identification of a Y chromosome in karyotyping usually (though not always) means that increased androgen levels have already been experienced *in utero*. To say that Diamond claims that it is simply the Y chromosome that 'cannot be constructed away' (Butler 2001, p. 626) or 'does not need to "appear" in order to operate as the key feature of gender identity' (Butler 2001, p. 626) is to oversimplify Diamond's argument. This weakens Butler's own rhetorical tack of pitting Diamond against John Money in an impasse where each is as essentialist as the other despite starting from opposite corners. By pushing Diamond's position to this extreme, Butler has eroded her own project of forging a 'third way', for she is arguing against a stand which Diamond does not actually take. Her attempts to read the 'discourse of self-reporting and self-understanding' are useful in terms of considering the extent to which the sexed self-determination of transgender and intersexed people is always already tempered by their background and by the positive and negative gender messages that have been received from earliest infancy and which affect the reading of their own 'innate' impulses. There is, however, no need to base this on caricatured versions of Diamond's or Money's positions. In Butler's 2004 book *Undoing Gender* she includes a reworking of the 2001 paper, not significantly different from the earlier version, except for one paragraph influenced by Cheryl Chase's assertion that 'although a child should be given a sex assignment for the purposes of establishing a stable social identity, it does not follow that society should engage in coercive surgery to remake the body in the social image of that gender' (Butler 2004, p. 63); rather, any surgery or hormone treatment should occur only when the (older) child has requested it. The earlier version stated, 'There is no reason to make a sex assignment at all; society should make room for the intersexed as they are' (Butler 2001, p. 626). This demonstrates Butler's unfortunate lack of engagement with Chase and other intersex activists prior to the publication of the 2001 piece.

4 Although Amy-Chinn asserts that one of the major goals of the queer theological project has, in fact, been to query the 'biological fundamentalism' of the

existence of two distinct biological sexes (Amy-Chinn 2009, p. 49), I wonder if this is overstating the case. The majority of scholars working in queer theology until the turn of the twenty-first century did not, in fact, for example, engage in any great depth with the theological implications of the existence of biological intersex conditions; *Sex and Uncertainty in the Body of Christ: Intersex Conditions and Christian Theology* (Cornwall 2010b) was the first full-length theological treatment of the phenomenon. Earlier engagements with intersex, like that of Virginia Ramey Mollenkott (2007), did not adequately recognize the specificities of intersex or the ways in which many people with intersex conditions reject a notion of inevitably queer or problematic gender identity (Mollenkott 2007; see also Cornwall 2010b, pp. 8–10). The important intersex-based work by Gross, which Amy-Chinn cites, is not particularly representative of queer theological discourse, which – as Amy-Chinn herself is aware – has tended to draw more on proto-*transgendering* in the tradition rather than anything to do with variant sex specifically. The work of Ken Stone and others in demonstrating the ways in which queer Butlerian analysis disrupts fixities of interpretation and iteration of, for example, the Genesis creation narrative (see for example Stone 2006b) does undermine biological fundamentalism, but more as it plays out in discourses of heteronormativity and *a priori* gender complementarity.

5 It is significant, too, that Rudy's essay, the most experiential, is also the least hopeful in the collection (Loughlin 2007b, p. 11).

Conclusion

Most queer people have gone through periods of their lives when they have felt lost or alone or abandoned by God; but often, a stranger comes into our path, announcing to us, 'God is with you!' The queer person, based on past experience, is perplexed by a greeting such as this; doesn't God hate queers? Past hurts and internalized oppression bring up a wall of fear. At this point, often the queer person turns away and goes off on his or her own. But there are just as many who face their fear and listen to the next message, 'Don't be afraid.' The messenger from God tells us, 'Walk out of your past. Do not give the past the satisfaction. There is a whole future awaiting you, if you will receive it.' The messenger assures us, 'You will do great things because God is with you.' I can love queer people if I want to, God says; no church or state can place a boundary upon my love. I created every person in my very own image. I am a queer kind of God; I stir up and spoil what humans create with their agendas of power and oppression. Turn to me, allow me to queer you. (Bohache 2003, p. 25)

The existence of so many controversies within queer theology and the theory in which it is grounded, should be taken as evidence not of their imminent failure, but of their potential to provoke questioning and resistance to the 'given'. Queer theology does not often present itself as the 'answer' to the problems of exclusion, prescriptive normativity, or human sin – and, where it does so, I would suggest that it is failing to be truly queer. Rather, queer theology recognizes its own limitations and provisionalities, as well as pointing to those of other discourses. This is deeply disturbing, and it is intended to be: it is all very well to whisk away the rug from under mainstream theology's feet, but mainstream theology might reasonably expect there to be some kind of floor or other foundation under *that*.

Queer theology does not, however, venture to suggest that it, itself, is the floor or the foundation; rather, it poses odd and subversive questions: Why does there need to be a floor at all? How do we know that gravity isn't just an illusion? What happens when a 'firm foundation' stops life from growing up beneath it and breaking through it? What injustices and abuses are swept under those prettily patterned theological carpets? Nor does queer theology suggest that even God is the 'floor', or at least not in any unproblematic way. In this case, queer theology's questions might run something like: What historical phenomena have led Christians to affirm God's qualities as including solidity and immovability? In what ways might the affirmation of those qualities have come to shut down, rather than encourage, imaginative dialogue about God's vulnerability, elusiveness and frequent apparent absence?

Whisking away the rug of theological incontrovertibility is not a one-off or a once-and-for-all activity on the part of queer theology. Rugs tend to creep back into people's homes, even where the inhabitants purport to prefer minimalist clean lines and clear vistas. Rugs are comforting when we feel cold and vulnerable; they are soft and warm underfoot; they prevent wobbly new walkers from bruising themselves too violently; they soak up bathwater from bare feet and stop the floor from buckling. However, rugs can also be trip-hazards; they can harbour cat hair and dust mites lethal to asthmatics; they can become torn and stained; sometimes, they just begin to look embarrassingly dated. Queer theology does not allow any rug to be left unturned; it insists that it is worthwhile to ask questions about even something as innocent-seeming as a carpet. In this way, it shows up for mainstream theology the built-in querying and resisting strands which it possesses but which have sometimes been lost (theology has been settled down for a long time; when you move house only infrequently, you acquire a lot of clutter). Queer theology throws open the shutters, allowing the sun to stream in, and showing up just how dusty and threadbare some of those theological rugs really are. What doctrines and assertions about God do we keep around just because they are comfortable?

But queer theology is not a purgative wet-and-dry vacuum cleaner; it does not bluster in and 'fix' theology, or purport to be a definitive methodology leading to definitive answers. Rather, it helps us to look at our theological surroundings differently, and to interrogate how and why certain normativities (especially, but not exclusively, those relating to heterosexuality and the other norms based on its championing) are often taken for granted or placed beyond contradiction. And this stirring up, this spoliation of the unquestioned, is (as Bohache notes above) precisely a divine quality. It is an appropriate activity for those who seek God and who know that God is not easily knowable; for those who assert that God is other than human ideology, and who continue to generate this God, and the divine love valued by this God, through their right relationship.

Laurel C. Schneider suggested in 2000 that queer theology had not yet really started to be written, because even those writers who purported to be doing it were not, at that time, fully entering into queer theory's project of querying identity. Schneider was sympathetic to this conundrum, acknowledging that it was difficult fully to embrace a ceding of identity when one's identity as lesbian or gay was probably an important site of political and personal community, and when one's religious belonging might well also rely on being (acceptably) lesbian or gay rather than 'queer':

> Organized religions still function to determine 'good' and 'bad' identities and still demand of their good homosexuals a set of heteronormative behaviors and commitments, like marriage, or monogamy (which is a linguistic problem for gay men). Queers will remain queer – and outside of the communion – to the extent that they do not fulfil these demands. Queerness does not have to mean incommensurate difference, but in current debates it does tend to mean that. Incommensurate difference is not the bread many hungry gay and lesbian Christians want. Belonging, affirmation, blessing, and sanctification – all signifiers of inclusion – are the loaves they demand. (Schneider 2000, p. 11)

In the intervening years, some writers have, as we have seen, engaged more directly with the implications of radical queer theory for queer theology – though questions about identity are ongoing and continue to present difficulties. As we saw in Chapter 7, tensions between lofty, intellectual, theoretical queer theology, and the kinds of queer Christianity and community life worked out 'on the ground', are still perceived to exist. It is all very well to argue that these kinds of distinctions are just as insidious – and possibly destructive – as other things set up as binary oppositions, but that does not mean that resentment is not still felt by those on each 'side' (as well as those who attempt to navigate a third way, informed by critical analysis and real-life pragmatism).

This book began with a remark on vuvuzelas. As I come toward its end, they are being heard once again. Here in the first weeks of the academic year in my university city, vuvuzelas have become the accessory of choice for sports clubs and other student societies as they herald their presence around its streets and campuses. Their loud, carrying note seems to signal a desire to communicate manifestation, existence, identity, *there*ness on the parts of these students, many of whom are living away from home for the first time. As I watch them finding their feet and their places, however, I am acutely aware that some students will never return to university (or, in some cases, never even register for the first time). A sickening roll has had name after name added to it over the summer of 2010: that is, the tally of young people enrolled at schools and colleges, in the USA and elsewhere, who have taken their own lives due to their misery at having suffered bullying because of their open or suspected homosexuality. In a piece for *The Huffington Post*, Patrick S. Cheng made clear that the deaths of these young people was precisely and profoundly a theological issue, saying,

> I believe this recent string of suicides by LGBT young people is, at root, a *religious* problem. For me, there is a clear and indisputable link between these horrible deaths and the rhetoric espoused by anti-gay Christians who continually condemn lesbian, gay, bisexual, and transgender (LGBT) people as sinners worthy of divine punishment . . . Regardless of one's view about sexual ethics, family values, or

same-sex marriage, I believe that encouraging or contributing to violence against LGBT people, either directly or indirectly, is the true sin against nature and creation . . . I challenge all people involved with anti-gay faith-based groups to practice what they preach and condemn all forms of violence, self-inflicted or otherwise, against LGBT people. They can no longer remain silent and wash their hands of responsibility, as Pontius Pilate did with Jesus of Nazareth, in the face of the growing number of deaths of LGBT young people. Regardless of what these groups may believe about sin, they need to speak out against this violence. (Cheng 2010b)

Even where it prefers to be theoretical, queer theology can never take place in a context entirely divorced from the reality in which children and adults suffer and commit suicide because their sexualities are considered illegitimate. Queer theology will continue to be debated, and to generate controversy, precisely because so much is at stake in showing up sin and injustice. Queer theology is at once a critical friend to the theological tradition, and a kernel of creative disorder right on the inside, exploding and showing forth what is within – just as popping corn does when things get agitated and heated.

Queer theology, then, is a popcorn kernel; it is a disclosing tablet; it is a conjuror who whips away the rug from beneath theological feet. It might also, as we end this part of our journey, be characterized as a grain of sand inside an oyster's shell. The critical irritation and discomfort it produces might, like this grain of sand, be transformed, becoming prophetic harbingers of a new way of justice and peace. This new way will be something so precious that whole lands and vineyards of belief and dogma are given up and given over for its sake: a pearl of great price which makes what used to seem final and ultimate pale into insignificance in the light of divine love. In this new order, justice will roll down like rivers and righteousness like an everlasting stream, as God is shown to live with those who are shut out and cast aside: a stranger at the gates whose love and mercy will not be limited by any human ideology.

Like any eschatological vision, this will not be cheap or easy to come by, and will not unfold without its problems and struggles. Indeed, the controversies and tussles explored above might be understood as part of this process of coming-into-being – like the hours of labour prior to transition in childbirth, or the many thousands of words crossed-out and discarded before a fair draft is achieved and a book can be completed. For this reason, controversies in queer theology point to dynamism, vibrancy, and the generation of a new mode of theological life which is long overdue. At the same time, however, they reach back into the deepest history of the theological tradition, to connect with modes of resistance which should be at the heart of all theologies, as they seek more and more of God's way and refuse to be shut down by small and unyielding certainties.

Works Cited

Abelove, Henry, 2003, *Deep Gossip*, Minneapolis, MN: University of Minnesota Press.

Abraham, Ibrahim, 2007, '"On the Doorstep of the Work": Ricœurian Hermeneutics, Queer Hermeneutics, and Scripture', *Bible and Critical Theory* 3.1 (2007), pp. 4.1–4.12.

Abraham, Ibrahim, 2010, '"Everywhere You Turn You Have to Jump Into Another Closet": Hegemony, Hybridity, and Queer Australian Muslims', in Habib, Samar (ed.), *Islam and Homosexuality, Volume 2*, Santa Barbara, CA: Praeger, pp. 395–418.

Ahmad, Aijaz, 1995, 'The Politics of Literary Postcoloniality', *Race and Class* 36.3 (1995), pp. 1–20.

Akinola, Peter, 2004, 'Statement on Windsor Report', 19 October 2004, archived online at http://www.episcopalchurch.org/3577_53238_ENG_HTM.htm.

Alpert, Rebecca, 1994, 'Finding Our Past: A Lesbian Interpretation of the Book of Ruth', in Kates, Judith A. and Gail Twersky Reimer (eds), *Reading Ruth: Contemporary Women Reclaim a Sacred Story*, New York, NY: Ballantine, pp. 91–6.

Alpert, Rebecca, 2000, 'Do Justice, Love Mercy, Walk Humbly: Reflections on Micah and Gay Ethics', in Goss, Robert E. and Mona West (eds), *Take Back the Word*, Cleveland, OH: Pilgrim Press, pp. 170–81.

Alpert, Rebecca, 2006, 'Exodus', in Guest, Deryn, Robert E. Goss, Mona West and Thomas Bohache (eds), *The Queer Bible Commentary*, London: SCM Press, pp. 61–76.

Althaus-Reid, Marcella, 2000, *Indecent Theology*, London and New York: Routledge.

Althaus-Reid, Marcella, 2003, *The Queer God*, London and New York: Routledge.

Althaus-Reid, Marcella, 2004, *From Feminist Theology to Indecent Theology: Readings on Poverty, Sexual Identity and God,* London: SCM Press.

Althaus-Reid, Marcella, 2006a, 'Feetishism: The Scent of a Latin American Body Theology', in Burrus, Virginia and Catherine Keller (eds), *Toward a Theology of Eros: Transfiguring Passion at the Limits of Discipline,* New York, NY: Fordham University Press, pp. 134–52.

Althaus-Reid, Marcella (ed.), 2006b, *Liberation Theology and Sexuality,* Aldershot: Ashgate.

Althaus-Reid, Marcella, 2006c, 'Mark', in Guest, Deryn, Robert E. Goss, Mona West and Thomas Bohache (eds), *The Queer Bible Commentary,* London: SCM Press, pp. 517–25.

Althaus-Reid, Marcella, 2008, 'The Bi/girl Writings: From Feminist Theology to Queer Theologies', in Isherwood, Lisa and Kathleen McPhillips (eds), *Post-Christian Feminisms: A Critical Approach,* Aldershot: Ashgate, pp. 105–16.

Althaus-Reid, Marcella and Lisa Isherwood, 2007, 'Thinking Theology and Queer Theory', *Feminist Theology* 15.3 (2007), pp. 302–14.

Althaus-Reid, Marcella and Lisa Isherwood (eds), 2009, *Trans/Formations (Controversies in Contextual Theology),* London: SCM Press.

Amy-Chinn, Dee, 2009, 'Is Queer Biology a Useful Tool for Queer Theology?', *Theology and Sexuality* 15.1 (2009), pp. 49–63.

Ansell, Amy E., 2006, 'Casting a Blind Eye: The Ironic Consequences of Color-Blindness in South Africa and the United States', *Critical Sociology* 32 (March 2006), pp. 333–56.

Anzaldúa, Gloria, 1991, 'To(o) Queer the Writer: Loca, Escrita y Chicana', in Warland, Betsy (ed.), *InVersions: Writing by Dykes, Queers and Lesbians,* Vancouver: Press Gang, pp. 249–63.

Ariès, Philippe, 1962, *Centuries of Childhood,* translated by Robert Baldick, London: Jonathan Cape.

Armour, Ellen T., 2003, 'Review of Jones, Serene, *Feminist Theory and Christian Theology: Cartographies of Grace*', *Journal of the American Academy of Religion* 71 (March 2003), pp. 212–15.

Armour, Ellen T. and Susan M. St.Ville (eds), 2006, *Bodily Citations: Religion and Judith Butler,* New York and Chichester: Columbia University Press.

Art in Defense of Humanism (AIDOH): http://www.aidoh.dk/ (accessed 23 March 2010).

Atay, Ahmet, 2010, '*Touch of Pink*: Diasporic Queer Experiences Within Islamic Communities', in Habib, Samar (ed.), *Islam and Homosexuality, Volume 2*, Santa Barbara, CA: Praeger, pp. 445–62.

Aune, Kristin, 2009, 'Between Subordination and Sympathy: Evangelical Christians, Masculinity and Gay Sexuality', in Hunt, Stephen (ed.), *Contemporary Christianity and LGBT Sexualities*, Farnham: Ashgate, pp. 39–49.

Bal, Mieke, 2005a, 'Grounds of Comparison', in Bal, Mieke (ed.), *The Artemisia Files: Artemisia Gentileschi for Feminists and Other Thinking People*, Chicago, IL and London: University of Chicago Press, pp. 129–.67.

Balboa, Jaime Ronaldo, 2003, 'The Word Made Queer: Implications for a Liberationist Imago Dei', PhD thesis, Graduate Theological Union (Berkeley, CA).

Barnard, Ian, 1999, 'Queer Race', *Social Semiotics* 9.2 (1999), pp. 199–211.

Barnard, Ian, 2004, *Queer Race: Cultural Interventions in the Racial Politics of Queer Theory*, New York, NY: Peter Lang Publishing.

Barth, Karl, 1933, *The Epistle to the Romans*, translated by Edwyn C. Hoskyns, London: Oxford University Press.

Barth, Karl, 1956a, *Church Dogmatics I/2: The Doctrine of the Word of God*, translated by G. T. Thomson and Harold Knight, Edinburgh: T&T Clark.

Beattie, Tina, 2007, 'Queen of Heaven', in Loughlin, Gerard (ed.), *Queer Theology: Rethinking the Western Body*, Oxford: Blackwell, pp. 293–304.

Beckford, Robert, 1996, 'Does Jesus Have a Penis? Black Male Sexual Representation and Christology', *Theology and Sexuality* 5 (1996), pp. 10–21.

Berg, Rigmor C., 2009, 'Barebacking: A Review of the Literature', *Archives of Sexual Behavior* 38 (2009), pp. 754–64.

Berger, Teresa, 2008, 'The Challenge of Gender for Liturgical Traditions', *Worship* 82.3 (May 2008), pp. 243–61.

Berlant, Lauren and Michael Warner, 1999, 'Sex in Public', in During, Simon (ed.), *The Cultural Studies Reader,* 2nd edn, London and New York: Routledge, pp. 354–67.

Bhabha, Homi K., 1994, *The Location of Culture*, London and New York: Routledge.

Blevins, John, 2005, 'Broadening the Family of God: Debating Same-Sex Marriage and Queer Families in America', *Theology and Sexuality* 12.1 (September 2005), pp. 63–80.

Bohache, Thomas, 2003, 'Embodiment as Incarnation: An Incipient Queer Christology', *Theology and Sexuality* 10.1 (2003), pp. 9–29.

Bohache, Thomas, 2006, 'Matthew', in Guest, Deryn, Robert E. Goss, Mona West and Thomas Bohache (eds), *The Queer Bible Commentary*, London: SCM Press, pp. 487–516.

Bohache, Thomas, 2008, *Christology from the Margins*, London: SCM Press.

Bong, Sharon A., 2006, 'Post-colonialism', in Sawyer, John F. A. (ed.), *The Blackwell Companion to the Bible and Culture*, Oxford: Blackwell, pp. 497–514.

Bonilla-Silva, Eduardo, 2006, *Racism Without Racists: Color-Blind Racism and the Persistence of Racial Inequality in the United States*, 2nd edn, Lanham, MD: Rowman and Littlefield.

Boone, Joseph A., 2000, 'Go West: An Introduction', in Boone, Joseph A. et al (eds), *Queer Frontiers: Millennial Geographies, Genders, and Generations*, Madison, WI: University of Wisconsin Press, pp. 3–20.

Bornstein, Kate, 1994, *Gender Outlaw: On Men, Women and the Rest Of Us*, New York, NY: Routledge.

Boyarin, Daniel, Daniel Itzkovitz and Ann Pellegrini (eds), 2003, *Queer Theory and the Jewish Question*, New York, NY: Columbia University Press.

Braunston, Andy, 1997, 'The Church', in Stuart, Elizabeth (ed.), *Religion is a Queer Thing: A Guide to the Christian Faith for Lesbian, Gay, Bisexual and Transgendered People*, London: Cassell, pp. 96–104.

Brenner, Athalya, 2000, '"My" Song of Songs', in Brenner, Athalya and Carole R. Fontaine (eds), *The Song of Songs (A Feminist Companion to the Bible, Second Series)*, Sheffield: Sheffield Academic Press, pp. 154–68.

Brenner, Athalya and Carole R. Fontaine (eds), 2000, *The Song of Songs (A Feminist Companion to the Bible, Second Series)*, Sheffield: Sheffield Academic Press.

Brock, Rita Nakashima, 1997, 'Interstitial Integrity: Reflections Toward an Asian American Woman's Theology', in Badham, Roger A. (ed.), *Introduction to Christian Theology: Contemporary North American Perspectives*, Louisville, KY: Westminster John Knox Press, pp. 183–96.

Burrus, Virginia, 2001, 'Queer Lives of Saints: Jerome's Hagiography', *Journal of the History of Sexuality* 10.3/4 (July/October 2001), pp. 442–79.

Burrus, Virginia, 2007, 'Queer Father: Gregory of Nyssa and the Subversion of Identity', in Loughlin, Gerard (ed.), *Queer Theology: Rethinking the Western Body*, Oxford: Blackwell, pp. 147–62.

Burrus, Virginia and Catherine Keller (eds), *Toward a Theology of Eros: Transfiguring Passion at the Limits of Discipline*, New York, NY: Fordham University Press.

Butler, Judith, 1990, *Gender Trouble: Feminism and the Subversion of Identity*, New York and London: Routledge.

Butler, Judith, 1993a, *Bodies That Matter: On the Discursive Limits of 'Sex'*, New York and London: Routledge.

Butler, Judith, 1993b, 'Critically Queer', *GLQ* 1 (1993), pp. 17–32.

Butler, Judith, 2001, 'Doing Justice to Someone: Sex Reassignment and Allegories of Transsexuality', *GLQ* 7.4 (2001), pp. 621–36.

Butler, Judith, 2004, *Undoing Gender*, New York and London: Routledge.

Bynum, Caroline Walker, 1986, 'The Body of Christ in the Later Middle Ages: A Reply to Leo Steinberg', *Renaissance Quarterly* 39.3 (Autumn 1986), pp. 399–439

Bynum, Caroline Walker, 1992, *Fragmentation and Redemption: Essays on Gender and the Human Body in Medieval Religion*, New York, NY: Zone Books.

Bynum, Caroline Walker, 1995, *The Resurrection of the Body in Western Christianity, 200–1336*, New York, NY: Columbia University Press.

Cannon, Katie Geneva, 1988, *Black Womanist Ethics*, Atlanta, GA: Scholars Press.

Carballo-Diéguez, Alex, 2001, 'HIV, Barebacking, and Gay Men's Sexuality, circa 2001', *Journal of Sex Education and Therapy* 26 (2001), pp. 225–33.

Carden, Michael, 2001, 'Remembering Pelotit: A Queer Midrash on Calling Down Fire', in Stone, Ken (ed.), *Queer Commentary and the Hebrew Bible*, Sheffield: Sheffield Academic Press, pp. 152–68.

Carden, Michael, 2004, *Sodomy: A History of a Christian Biblical Myth*, London: Equinox.

Carden, Michael, 2006, 'Genesis/Bereshit', in Guest, Deryn, Robert E. Goss, Mona West and Thomas Bohache (eds), *The Queer Bible Commentary*, London: SCM Press, pp. 21–60.

Carrette, Jeremy, 2004, 'Beyond Theology and Sexuality: Foucault, the Self and the Que(e)rying of Monotheistic Truth', in Bernauer, James William and Jeremy R. Carrette (eds), *Michel Foucault and Theology: The Politics of Religious Experience*, Aldershot: Ashgate, pp. 217–32.

Carvalhaes, Claudio, 2006, 'Oh, Que Sera, Que Sera. . . A Limping A/Theological Thought in Brazil', in Althaus-Reid, Marcella (ed.), *Liberation*

Theology and Sexuality, Aldershot: Ashgate, pp. 51–69.

Chávez, Karma R., 2008, 'Breaking Trances and Engaging the Erotic: The Search for a Queer Spirituality', *Liminalities: A Journal of Performance Studies* 4.2 (2008), pp. 1–16.

Cheng, Patrick S., 2001, 'Jesus, Mary, and the Beloved Disciple: Towards a Queer Asian Pacific American Christology', MA thesis, Union Theological Seminary (New York).

Cheng, Patrick S., 2002, 'Multiplicity and Judges 19: Constructing a Queer Asian Pacific American Biblical Hermeneutic', *Semeia* 90/91 (2002), pp. 119–33.

Cheng, Patrick S., 2006a, 'Galatians', in Guest, Deryn, Robert E. Goss, Mona West and Thomas Bohache (eds), *The Queer Bible Commentary*, London: SCM Press, pp. 624–9.

Cheng, Patrick S., 2006b, 'Reclaiming Our Traditions, Rituals, and Spaces: Spirituality and the Queer Asian Pacific American Experience', *Spiritus* 6 (2006), pp. 234–40.

Cheng, Patrick S., 2010a, 'Rethinking Sin and Grace for LGBT People Today', in Ellison, Marvin M. and Kelly Brown Douglas (eds), *Sexuality and the Sacred: Sources for Theological Reflection*, 2nd edn, Louisville, KY: Westminster John Knox Press, pp. 105–18.

Cheng, Patrick S., 2010b, 'Faith, Hope and Love: Ending LGBT Teen Suicide', *The Huffington Post*, 6 October 2010, online at http://www. huffingtonpost.com/rev-patrick-s-cheng-phd/faith-hope-and-love-endin_ b_749160.html.

Cherry, Kittredge, 2007, *Art That Dares: Gay Jesus, Woman Christ, and More*, Berkeley, CA: AndroGyne Press.

Chung Hyun Kyung, 1990, *Struggle to be the Sun Again: Introducing Asian Women's Theology*, Maryknoll, NY: Orbis Books.

Clague, Julie, 2005a, 'The Christa: Symbolizing My Humanity and My Pain', *Feminist Theology* 14.1 (September 2005), pp. 83–108.

Clague, Julie, 2005b, 'Divine Transgressions: The Female Christ-Form in Art', *Critical Quarterly* 47.3 (Autumn 2005), pp. 47–63.

Clague, Julie, 2005c, 'Symbolism and the Power of Art: Female Representations of Christ Crucified', in Bird, Darlene and Yvonne Sherwood (eds), *Bodies in Question: Gender, Religion, Text*, Aldershot: Ashgate, pp. 29–56.

Clark, J. Michael, 1989, *A Place to Start: Toward an Unapologetic Gay Liberation Theology*, Dallas, TX: Monument Press.

Clark, J. Michael, 1994, 'Men's Studies, Feminist Theology, and Gay Male Spirituality', in Nelson, James B. and Sandra P. Longfellow (eds), *Sexuality and the Sacred: Sources for Theological Reflection*, Louisville, KY: Westminster/John Knox Press, pp. 216–29.

Clark, J. Michael, 1997, *Defying the Darkness: Gay Theology in the Shadows*, Cleveland, OH: Pilgrim Press.

Clines, David J.A., 1995, *Interested Parties: The Ideology of Writers and Readers of the Hebrew Bible*, Sheffield: Sheffield Academic Press.

Coakley, Sarah, 2002, *Powers and Submissions: Spirituality, Philosophy and Gender,* Oxford: Blackwell.

Coakley, Sarah, 2003, 'Introduction – Gender, Trinitarian Analogies, and the Pedagogy of *The Song*', in Coakley, Sarah (ed.), *Re-thinking Gregory of Nyssa*, Oxford: Blackwell, pp. 1–13.

Coleman, Monica A., 2006, 'Roundtable Discussion: Must I Be Womanist?', *Journal of Feminist Studies in Religion* 22.1 (Spring 2006), pp. 85–96.

Comstock, Gary David, 1993, *Gay Theology Without Apology*, Cleveland, OH: Pilgrim Press.

Comstock, Gary David, 2001, *A Whosoever Church: Welcoming Lesbians and Gay Men Into African American Congregations*, Louisville, KY: Westminster John Knox Press.

Comstock, Gary David and Susan E. Henking (eds), 1997, *Que(e)rying Religion: A Critical Anthology*, New York, NY: Continuum

Cone, James H., 1989, *Black Theology and Black Power,* twentieth anniversary edn, New York, NY: Harper and Row

Cone, James H., 1997, *God of the Oppressed,* revised edn, Maryknoll, NY: Orbis Books

Cone, James H. and Gayraud S. Wilmore (eds), 1993, *Black Theology: A Documentary History, Volume II: 1980–1992*, Maryknoll, NY: Orbis Books.

Constantine-Simms, Delroy (ed.), 2001, *The Greatest Taboo: Homosexuality in Black Communities*, Los Angeles, CA: Alyson Publications.

Córdova Quero, Martín Hugo, 2004, 'Friendship with Benefits: A Queer Reading of Aelred of Rievaulx and His Theology of Friendship', in Althaus-Reid, Marcella and Lisa Isherwood (eds), *The Sexual Theologian: Essays on Sex, God and Politics*, London and New York: T&T Clark, pp. 26–46.

Córdova Quero, Martín Hugo, 2006, 'The Prostitutes Also Go Into the Kingdom of God: A Queer Reading of Mary of Magdala', in Althaus-Reid,

Marcella (ed.), *Liberation Theology and Sexuality*, Aldershot: Ashgate, pp. 81–110.

Cornwall, Susannah, 2008a, 'The *Kenosis* of Unambiguous Sex in the Body of Christ: Intersex, Theology and Existing "for the Other"', *Theology and Sexuality* 14.2 (Jan 2008), pp. 181–200.

Cornwall, Susannah, 2008b, 'Ambiguous Bodies, Ambiguous Readings: Reflections on James M. Murphy's "Christine on the Cross"', in Davy, Zowie et al (eds), *Bound and Unbound: Interdisciplinary Approaches to Genders and Sexualities*, Newcastle: Cambridge Scholars Publishing, pp. 93–110.

Cornwall, Susannah, 2009a, 'Theologies of Resistance: Intersex, Disability and Queering the "Real World"', in Holmes, Morgan (ed.), *Critical Intersex (Queer Interventions)*, Aldershot: Ashgate, pp. 215–43.

Cornwall, Susannah, 2009b, 'Apophasis and Ambiguity: The "Unknowingness" of Transgender', in Althaus-Reid, Marcella and Lisa Isherwood (eds), *Trans/Formations (Controversies in Contextual Theology)*, London: SCM Press, pp. 13–40.

Cornwall, Susannah, 2010a, 'Queer theologie: Sporen van een vreemde God' ['Queer Theology: Traces of a Strange God'], translated by Adriaan van Klinken, *FIER (Feministisch Inspirerend Eigenzinnig Religieus)* 13.1 (Jan–Feb 2010), pp. 24–5.

Cornwall, Susannah, 2010b, *Sex and Uncertainty in the Body of Christ: Intersex Conditions and Christian Theology*, London: Equinox Press.

Cornwall, Susannah, 2010c, 'Stranger in Our Midst: The Becoming of the Queer God in the Theology of Marcella Althaus-Reid', in Isherwood, Lisa and Mark D. Jordan (eds), *Dancing Theology in Fetish Boots: Essays in Honour of Marcella Althaus-Reid*, London: SCM Press, pp. 95–112.

Cozzens, Donald B., 2000, *The Changing Face of the Priesthood: A Reflection on the Priest's Crisis of Soul*, Collegeville, MN: Liturgical Press.

Crawley, Ashon T., 2008, 'Circum-Religious Performance: Queer(ed) Black Bodies and the Black Church', *Theology and Sexuality* 14.2 (Jan 2008), pp. 201–22.

Crossley, Michele L., 2002, 'The Perils of Health Promotion and the "Barebacking" Backlash', *Health* 6.1 (2002), pp. 47–68.

Daly, Mary, 1986, *Beyond God the Father: Toward a Philosophy of Women's Liberation (with Original Reintroduction)*, London: The Women's Press.

D'Costa, Gavin, 2007, 'Queer Trinity', in Loughlin, Gerard (ed.), *Queer*

Theology: Rethinking the Western Body, Oxford: Blackwell, pp. 269–280.

Derrida, Jacques, 1976, *Of Grammatology*, translated by Gayatri Chakravorty Spivak, Baltimore and London: The Johns Hopkins University Press.

DiNovo, Cheri, 2007, 'Queer Theology, Queer Evangelism', Doctor of Ministry Thesis, Toronto School of Theology (Ontario, Canada).

Donaldson, Laura E., 2006, 'The Sign of Orpah: Reading Ruth Through Native Eyes', in Sugirtharajah, R. S. (ed.), *The Postcolonial Biblical Reader*, Oxford: Blackwell, pp. 159–70.

Doty, Alexander, 1993, *Making Things Perfectly Queer: Interpreting Mass Culture*, Minneapolis, MN: University of Minnesota Press.

Douglas, Ian T. and Kwok Pui-lan (eds), 2001, *Beyond Colonial Anglicanism: The Anglican Communion in the Twenty-First Century*, New York, NY: Church Publishing Incorporated.

Douglas, Kelly Brown, 1994, *The Black Christ*, Maryknoll, NY: Orbis Books.

Douglas, Kelly Brown, 1999, *Sexuality and the Black Church: A Womanist Perspective*, Maryknoll, NY: Orbis Books.

Duncan, Celena M., 2000, 'The Book of Ruth: On Boundaries, Truth, and Love', in Goss, Robert E. and Mona West (eds), *Take Back the Word*, Cleveland, OH: Pilgrim Press, pp. 92–102.

Ebrahim, Amreen Mohamed Jamal, 1997, 'The Story of Lot and the Qur'ān's Perception of the Morality of Same-Sex Sexuality', MA thesis, University of Calgary (Alberta, Canada).

Edelman, Lee, 2004, *No Future: Queer Theory and the Death Drive*, Durham, NC: Duke University Press.

Edgardh, Ninna, 2009, 'Difference and Desire – a Queer Reading', *Dialog* 48.1 (March 2009), pp. 42–8.

Edwards, Malcolm, 1997, 'God', in Stuart, Elizabeth (ed.), *Religion is a Queer Thing: A Guide to the Christian Faith for Lesbian, Gay, Bisexual and Transgendered People*, London: Cassell, pp. 67–75.

Elford, Jonathan, Graham Bolding, Mark Davis, Lorraine Sherr and Graham Hart, 2007, 'Barebacking Among HIV-Positive Gay Men in London', *Sexually Transmitted Diseases* 34.2 (February 2007), pp. 93–8.

Eng, David L. and Alice Y. Hom (eds), 1998, *Q&A: Queer in Asian America*, Philadelphia, PA: Temple University Press.

Ephrem the Syrian, 1989, *Hymns*, translated by Kathleen E. McVey, Mahwah, NJ: Paulist Press.

Erzen, Tanya, 2006, *Straight to Jesus: Sexual and Christian Conversions in the Ex-Gay Movement*, Berkeley, CA: University of California Press.

Estus, John, 2010a, 'Controversial Crucifix Creates Rift at Warr Acres Church', *The Oklahoman* 15 April 2010 (online at http://newsok.com/warr-acres-catholic-church-has-crucifix-some-say-shows-exposed-genitals-of-jesus/article/3453833?custom_click=rss).

Estus, John, 2010b, 'Warr Acres Catholic Priest who Commissioned Controversial Crucifix Reassigned', *The Oklahoman* 11 May 2010 (online at http://newsok.com/warr-acres-catholic-priest-who-commissioned-controversial-crucifix-reassigned/article/3460353).

Eugene, Toinette, 1998, 'How Can We Forget? An Ethic of Care for AIDS, the African American Family, and the Black Catholic Church', in Townes, Emilie M. (ed.), *Embracing the Spirit: Womanist Perspectives on Hope, Salvation, and Transformation*, Maryknoll, NY: Orbis Books, pp. 247–74.

Evans, Amie M. and Trebor Healey (eds), 2008a, *Queer and Catholic*, New York, NY: Routledge.

Evans, Amie M. and Trebor Healey, 2008b, 'Good Habits to Hang Onto: An Interview with Sister Soami of the Sisters of Perpetual Indulgence', in Evans, Amie M. and Trebor Healey (eds), *Queer and Catholic*, New York, NY: Routledge, pp. 197–209.

Evans, James H., 1992, *We Have Been Believers*, Minneapolis, MN: Augsburg Fortress.

Exum, J. Cheryl, 2000, 'Ten Things Every Feminist Should Know About the Song of Songs', in Brenner, Athalya and Carole R. Fontaine (eds), *The Song of Songs (A Feminist Companion to the Bible, Second Series)*, Sheffield: Sheffield Academic Press, pp. 24–35.

Exum, J. Cheryl, 2005, *Song of Songs (The Old Testament Library)*, Louisville, KY: Westminster John Knox Press.

Farajajé-Jones, Elias, 1993, 'Breaking Silence: Toward an in-the-Life Theology', in Cone, James H. and Gayraud S. Wilmore (eds), *Black Theology: A Documentary History, Volume II: 1980–1992*, Maryknoll, NY: Orbis Books, pp. 139–59.

Fausto-Sterling, Anne, 2000, *Sexing the Body: Gender Politics and the Construction of Sexuality*, New York, NY: Basic Books.

Ferguson, Roderick A., 2003, *Aberrations in Black: Toward a Queer of Color Critique*, Minneapolis, MN: University of Minnesota Press.

Fiddes, Paul S., 1990, 'The Status of Woman in the Thought of Karl Barth', in

Soskice, Janet Martin (ed.), *After Eve: Women, Theology and the Christian Tradition*, London: Marshall Pickering, pp. 138–55.

Ford, Michael, 2002, *Wounded Prophet: A Portrait of Henri J. M. Nouwen*, New York, NY: Image Books.

Forstein, Marshall, 2002, 'Commentary on Cheuvront's "High-Risk Sexual Behavior in the Treatment of HIV-Negative Patients"', *Journal of Gay and Lesbian Psychotherapy* 6 (2002), pp. 35–43.

Foucault, Michel, 1979, *Discipline and Punish: The Birth of the Prison*, translated by Alan Sheridan, Harmondsworth: Penguin.

Foucault, Michel, 1990, *The History of Sexuality: Volume 1: An Introduction*, translated by Robert Hurley, London: Penguin.

Gaard, Greta, 1997, 'Toward a Queer Ecofeminism', *Hypatia* 12.1 (Winter 1997), pp. 114–37.

Gallagher, Lowell, Frederick S. Roden and Patricia Juliana Smith (eds), 2007, *Catholic Figures, Queer Narratives*, Basingstoke: Palgrave Macmillan.

Garrard, Mary D., 1982, 'Artemisia and Susanna', in Broude, Norma and Mary D. Garrard (eds), *Feminism and Art History: Questioning the Litany*, New York: Harper and Row, pp. 146–71.

Garrigan, Siobhán, 2009, 'Queer Worship', *Theology and Sexuality* 15.2 (2009), pp. 211–30.

Gearhart, Sally and William R. Johnson (eds), 1974, *Loving Women / Loving Men: Gay Liberation and the Church*, San Francisco, CA: Glide Publications.

Gerber, Lynne, 2008, 'The Opposite of Gay: Nature, Creation, and Queerish Ex-Gay Experiments', *Nova Religio* 11.4 (May 2008), pp. 8–30.

Gibel Mevorach, Katya, 2007, 'Race, Racism, and Academic Complicity', *American Ethnologist* 34.2 (2007), pp. 238–41.

Gill, Sean (ed.), 1998a, *The Lesbian and Gay Christian Movement: Campaigning for Justice, Truth and Love*, London and New York: Cassell.

Gill, Sean, 1998b, 'Doing Your Own Thing: Lesbian and Gay Theology in a Postmodern Context', in Gill, Sean (ed.), *The Lesbian and Gay Christian Movement: Campaigning for Justice, Truth and Love*, London and New York: Cassell, pp. 175–86.

Gillibrand, John, 2010, *Disabled Church – Disabled Society: The Implications of Autism for Philosophy, Theology and Politics*, London and Philadelphia: Jessica Kingsley Publishers.

Goldenberg, David M., 2003, *The Curse of Ham: Race and Slavery in Early*

Judaism, Christianity, and Islam, Princeton, NJ: Princeton University Press.

Gopinath, Gayatri, 2005, *Impossible Desires: Queer Diasporas and South Asian Public Cultures*, Durham, NC: Duke University Press.

Gorringe, T. J., 1999, *Karl Barth: Against Hegemony*, Oxford: Clarendon Press.

Gorringe, T. J., 2004, *Furthering Humanity: A Theology of Culture*, Aldershot: Ashgate.

Gorsline, Robin Hawley, 2006, '1 and 2 Peter', in Guest, Deryn, Robert E. Goss, Mona West and Thomas Bohache (eds), *The Queer Bible Commentary*, London: SCM Press, pp. 724–36.

Goss, Robert E., 1993, *Jesus Acted Up: A Gay and Lesbian Manifesto*, San Francisco, CA: HarperSanFrancisco.

Goss, Robert E., 1998, 'Sexual Visionaries and Freedom Fighters for a Sexual Reformation: From Gay Theology to Queer Sexual Theologies', in Gill, Sean (ed.), *The Lesbian and Gay Christian Movement: Campaigning for Justice, Truth and Love*, London and New York: Cassell, pp. 187–202.

Goss, Robert E., 2002, *Queering Christ: Beyond Jesus Acted Up*, Cleveland, OH: Pilgrim Press.

Goss, Robert E., 2004, 'Proleptic Sexual Love: God's Promiscuity Reflected in Christian Polyamory', *Theology and Sexuality* 11.1 (2004), pp. 52–63.

Goss, Robert E. and Amy Adams Squire Strongheart (eds), 1997, *Our Families, Our Values: Snapshots of Queer Kinship*, Binghampton, NY: The Haworth Press.

Goss, Robert E. and Mona West (eds), 2000, *Take Back the Word*, Cleveland, OH: Pilgrim Press

Gray, Mary L., 2009, '"Queer Nation is Dead/Long Live Queer Nation": The Politics and Poetics of Social Movement and Media Representation', *Critical Studies in Media Communication* 26.3 (August 2009), pp. 212–36.

Greer, Rowan A. (ed.), 1979, *Origen: Selected Writings*, New York, NY: Paulist Press.

Griffin, Horace, 2001, 'Their Own Received Them Not: African American Lesbians and Gays in Black Churches', in Constantine-Simms, Delroy (ed.), *The Greatest Taboo: Homosexuality in Black Communities*, Los Angeles, CA: Alyson Publications, pp. 110–21.

Griffin, Horace, 2006, *Their Own Receive Them Not: African American Lesbians and Gays in Black Churches*, Cleveland, OH: Pilgrim Press.

Gross, Sally, 1999, 'Intersexuality and Scripture', *Theology and Sexuality* 11 (1999), pp. 65–74.

Grosz, Elizabeth, 1994, 'Experimental Desire: Rethinking Queer Subjectivity', in Copjec, Joan (ed.), *Supposing the Subject*, London and New York: Verso, pp. 133–58.

Grovijahn, Jane M., 2008, 'Reclaiming the Power of Incarnation: When God's Body is Catholic and Queer (With a Cunt!)', in Evans, Amie M. and Trebor Healey (eds), *Queer and Catholic*, New York, NY: Routledge, pp. 249–61.

Guest, Deryn, 2005, *When Deborah Met Jael: Lesbian Biblical Hermeneutics*, London: SCM Press.

Habib, Samar (ed.), 2010a, *Islam and Homosexuality, Volume 1*, Santa Barbara, CA: Praeger.

Habib, Samar (ed.), 2010b, *Islam and Homosexuality, Volume 2*, Santa Barbara, CA: Praeger.

Halkitis, Perry N., Jeffrey T. Parsons and Leo Wilton, 2003, 'Barebacking Among Gay and Bisexual Men in New York City: Explanations for the Emergence of Intentional Unsafe Behavior', *Archives of Sexual Behavior* 32.4 (August 2003), pp. 351–8.

Hall, Donald E., 2003, *Queer Theories*, Basingstoke: Palgrave Macmillan.

Halperin, David M., 1995, *Saint Foucault: Towards a Gay Hagiography*, New York and Oxford: Oxford University Press.

Hammonds, Evelynn, 1994, 'Black (W)holes and the Geometry of Black Female Sexuality', *Differences* 6.2–3 (1994), pp. 126–45.

Hampson, Daphne, 1996, 'On Power and Gender', in Thatcher, Adrian and Elizabeth Stuart (eds), *Christian Perspectives on Sexuality and Gender*, Leominster: Gracewing, pp. 125–140.

Han, Alan, 2006, '*I Think You're the Smartest Race I've Ever Met:* Racialised Economies of Queer Male Desire', *Australian Critical Race and Whiteness Studies Association E-Journal* 2.2 (2006), online at http://www.acrawsa. org.au/ejournalVol2no22006.htm.

Hanks, Thomas, 1997, 'A Family Friend: Paul's Letter to the Romans as a Source of Affirmation for Queers and their Families', in Goss, Robert E. and Amy Adams Squire Strongheart (eds), *Our Families, Our Values: Snapshots of Queer Kinship*, Binghampton, NY: The Haworth Press, pp. 137–50.

Hanson, Ellis, 1997, *Decadence and Catholicism*, Cambridge, MA: Harvard University Press.

Harper, Phillip Brian, 1996, *Are We Not Men? Masculine Anxiety and the Problem of African-American Identity*, New York and Oxford: Oxford University Press.

Harper, Phillip Brian, E. Francis White and Margaret Cerullo, 1993, 'Multi/Queer/Culture', *Radical America* 24.4 (1993), pp. 27–37.

Haws, Molly, 2007, '"Put Your Finger Here": Resurrection and the Construction of the Body', *Theology and Sexuality* 13.2 (2007), pp. 181–94.

Hefner, Philip J., 1998, 'Biocultural Evolution and the Created Co-Creator', in Peters, Ted (ed.), *Science and Theology: The New Consonance*, Boulder, CO: Westview Press, pp. 174–88.

Heine, Ronald E. (ed.), 1982, *Origen: Homilies on Genesis and Exodus (Fathers of the Church)*, Washington, DC: Catholic University of America Press.

Helminiak, Daniel A., 1994, *What the Bible Really Says About Homosexuality*, San Francisco, CA: Alamo Square Press.

Heschel, Susannah, 1997, 'Jesus as a Theological Transvestite', in Peskowitz, Miriam and Laura Levitt (eds), *Judaism Since Gender*, New York, NY: Routledge, pp. 188–97.

Hey, Valerie, 2006, 'The Politics of Performative Resignification: Translating Judith Butler's Theoretical Discourse and Its Potential for a Sociology of Education', *British Journal of Sociology of Education* 27.4 (2006), pp. 439–57.

Heyward, [Isabel] Carter, 1982, *The Redemption of God: A Theology of Mutual Relation*, Lanham, MD: University Press of America.

Heyward, Carter, 1984, *Our Passion for Justice: Images of Power, Sexuality and Liberation*, New York, NY: Pilgrim Press.

Hill, Renée L., 1993, 'Who Are We for Each Other? Sexism, Sexuality and Womanist Theology', in Cone, James H. and Gayraud S. Wilmore (eds), *Black Theology: A Documentary History, Volume II: 1980–1992*, Maryknoll, NY: Orbis Books, pp. 345–51.

Hilliard, David, 1982, 'UnEnglish and Unmanly: Anglo-Catholicism and Homosexuality', *Victorian Studies* 25 (Winter 1982), pp. 181–210.

Hinkle, Christopher, 2007, 'Love's Urgent Longings: St John of the Cross', in Loughlin, Gerard (ed.), *Queer Theology: Rethinking the Western Body*, Oxford: Blackwell, pp. 188–99.

Hinnant, Olive Elaine, 2007, *God Comes Out: A Queer Homiletic*, Cleveland, OH: Pilgrim Press.

Hipsher, B. K., 2009, 'God is a Many Gendered Thing: An Apophatic Journey to Pastoral Diversity', in Althaus-Reid, Marcella and Lisa Isherwood (eds), *Trans/Formations (Controversies in Contextual Theology)*, London: SCM Press, pp. 92–104.

Hollywood, Amy, 2007, 'Queering the Beguines: Mechthild of Magdeburg, Hadewijch of Anvers, Marguerite Porete', in Loughlin, Gerard (ed.), *Queer Theology: Rethinking the Western Body*, Oxford: Blackwell, pp. 163–75.

Hornsby, Teresa J., 2006a, 'The Annoying Woman: Biblical Scholarship After Judith Butler', in Armour, Ellen T. and Susan M. St.Ville (eds), *Bodily Citations: Religion and Judith Butler*, New York and Chichester: Columbia University Press, pp. 71–89.

Hornsby, Teresa J., 2006b, 'Ezekiel', in Guest, Deryn, Robert E. Goss, Mona West and Thomas Bohache (eds), *The Queer Bible Commentary*, London: SCM Press, pp. 412–26.

Horsley, Richard A., 2003, 'Feminist Scholarship and Postcolonial Criticism: Subverting Imperial Discourse and Reclaiming Submerged Histories', in Matthews, Shelly, Cynthia Briggs Kittredge and Melanie Johnson-DeBaufre (eds), *Walk in the Ways of Wisdom: Essays in Honor of Elisabeth Schüssler Fiorenza*, Harrisburg, PA: Trinity Press International, pp. 297–317.

Hull, John M., 2003, 'A Spirituality of Disability: The Christian Heritage as Both Problem and Potential', *Studies in Christian Ethics* 16:2 (2003), pp. 21–35.

Hunt, Mary E., 1996, 'Theology, Queer', in Russell, Letty M. and J. Shannon Clarkson (eds), *Dictionary of Feminist Theologies*, Louisville, KY: Westminster John Knox Press, pp. 298–9.

Hunt, Stephen (ed.), 2009a, *Contemporary Christianity and LGBT Sexualities*, Farnham: Ashgate.

Hunt, Stephen, 2009b, 'Introduction: Saints and Sinners: Contemporary Christianity and LGBT Sexualities', in Hunt, Stephen (ed.), *Contemporary Christianity and LGBT Sexualities*, Farnham: Ashgate, pp. 1–22.

Independent Radio News/London Broadcasting Company audio archive, online at http://radio.bufvc.ac.uk/lbc/ (accessed 5 February 2010).

Isherwood, Lisa and Marcella Althaus-Reid, 2004, 'Queering Theology', in Althaus-Reid, Marcella and Lisa Isherwood (eds), *The Sexual Theologian: Essays on Sex, God and Politics*, London and New York: T&T Clark, pp. 1–15.

Isherwood, Lisa and Kathleen McPhillips (eds), 2008, *Post-Christian Feminisms: A Critical Approach*, Aldershot: Ashgate.

Isherwood, Lisa and Elaine Bellchambers (eds), 2010, *Through Us, with Us, In Us: Relational Theologies in the Twenty-First Century*, London: SCM Press.

Jagessar, Michael N. and Anthony G. Reddie (eds), 2007, *Postcolonial Black British Theology: New Textures and Themes*, Peterborough: Epworth Press.

Jagose, Annamarie, 1996, *Queer Theory*, Melbourne: Melbourne University Press.

Jantzen, Grace M., 1996, 'Sources of Religious Knowledge', *Literature and Theology* 10.2 (June 1996), pp. 91–111

Jantzen, Grace M., 2001, 'Contours of a Queer Theology', *Literature and Theology* 15.3 (2001), pp. 276–85.

Jantzen, Grace M., 2007, '"Promising Ashes": A Queer Language of Life', in Loughlin, Gerard (ed.), *Queer Theology: Rethinking the Western Body*, Oxford: Blackwell, pp. 245–54.

Jeffreys, Sheila, 2003, *Unpacking Queer Politics: A Lesbian Feminist Perspective*, Cambridge: Polity Press.

Johnson, E. Patrick, 2001, 'Feeling the Spirit in the Dark: Expanding Notions of the Sacred in the African American Gay Community', in Constantine-Simms, Delroy (ed.), *The Greatest Taboo: Homosexuality in Black Communities*, Los Angeles, CA: Alyson Publications, pp. 88–109.

Johnson, E. Patrick and Mae G. Henderson (eds), 2005, *Queer Black Studies: A Critical Anthology*, Durham, NC: Duke University Press.

Jones, Serene, 2000, *Feminist Theory and Christian Theology: Cartographies of Grace*, Minneapolis, MN: Fortress Press.

Jordan, Mark D., 1997, *The Invention of Sodomy in Christian Theology*, Chicago, IL: University of Chicago Press.

Jordan, Mark D., 2007a, 'Religion Trouble', *GLQ* 13.4 (2007), pp. 563–75.

Jordan, Mark D., 2007b, 'God's Body', in Loughlin, Gerard (ed.), *Queer Theology: Rethinking the Western Body*, Oxford: Blackwell, pp. 281–92.

Kee, Alistair, 2006, *The Rise and Demise of Black Theology*, Aldershot: Ashgate.

Keller, Catherine, Michael Nausner and Mayra Rivera (eds), 2004, *Postcolonial Theologies: Divinity and Empire*, St Louis, MO: Chalice Press.

Kelly, Christopher Grant, 2010, 'The Social Construction of Religious Realities by Queer Muslims', in Habib, Samar (ed.), *Islam and Homosexuality, Volume 2*, Santa Barbara, CA: Praeger, pp. 223–46.

Khan, Mahruq Fatima, 2010, 'Queer, American, and Muslim: Cultivating Identities and Communities of Affirmation', in Habib, Samar (ed.), *Islam and Homosexuality, Volume* 2, Santa Barbara, CA: Praeger, pp. 347–72.

Koch, Timothy R., 2001, 'A Homoerotic Approach to Scripture', *Theology and Sexuality* 7.14 (March 2001), pp. 10–22.

Koch, Timothy R., 2006, 'Isaiah', in Guest, Deryn, Robert E. Goss, Mona West and Thomas Bohache (eds), *The Queer Bible Commentary*, London: SCM Press, pp. 371–85.

Kolakowski, Victoria S., 1997, 'The Concubine and the Eunuch: Queering Up the Breeder's Bible', in Goss, Robert E. and Amy Adams Squire Strongheart (eds), *Our Families, Our Values: Snapshots of Queer Kinship*, Binghampton, NY: The Haworth Press, pp. 35–50.

Kolakowski, Victoria S., 2000, 'Throwing a Party: Patriarchy, Gender, and the Death of Jezebel', in Goss, Robert E. and Mona West (eds), *Take Back the Word*, Cleveland, OH: Pilgrim Press, pp. 103–14

Koosed, Jennifer L., 2006, 'Ecclesiastes/Qohelet', in Guest, Deryn, Robert E. Goss, Mona West and Thomas Bohache (eds), *The Queer Bible Commentary*, London: SCM Press, pp. 338–55.

Kornegay, E. L. Jr., 2004, 'Queering Black Homophobia: Black Theology as a Sexual Discourse of Transformation', *Theology and Sexuality* 11.1 (2004), pp. 29–51.

Kugle, Scott Siraj al-Haqq, 2003, 'Sexuality, Diversity, and Ethics in the Agenda of Progressive Muslims', in Safi, Omid (ed.), *Progressive Muslims: On Justice, Gender and Pluralism*, Oxford: Oneworld Publications, pp. 190–234.

Kugle, Scott Siraj al-Haqq and Sarah Chiddy, 2009, 'AIDS, Muslims, and Homosexuality', in Esack, Farid and Sarah Chiddy (eds), *Islam and AIDS: Between Scorn, Pity and Justice*, Oxford: Oneworld Publications, pp. 137–53.

Kwok Pui-lan, 2001, 'The Legacy of Cultural Hegemony in the Anglican Church', in Douglas, Ian T. and Kwok Pui-lan (eds), *Beyond Colonial Anglicanism: The Anglican Communion in the Twenty-First Century*, New York, NY: Church Publishing Incorporated, pp. 47–70.

Kwok Pui-lan, 2005, *Postcolonial Imagination and Feminist Theology*, London: SCM Press.

Kwok Pui-lan, 2010, 'Touching the Taboo: On the Sexuality of Jesus', in Ellison, Marvin M. and Kelly Brown Douglas (eds), *Sexuality and the*

Sacred: Sources for Theological Reflection, 2nd edn, Louisville, KY: Westminster John Knox Press, pp. 119–34.

Lee, Jeanette Mei Gim, 2004, 'Queerly a Good Friday', in Kumashiro, Kevin K. (ed.), *Restoried Selves: Autobiographies of Queer Asian/Pacific American Activists*, New York, NY: Harrington Park Press, pp. 81–6.

Leech, Kenneth, 1988, 'Beyond Gin and Lace', in Beck, Ashley and Ros Hunt (eds), *Speaking Love's Name; Homosexuality: Some Catholic and Socialist Perspectives*, London: Jubilee Group, online at http://www.anglocatholic-socialism.org/lovesname.html (accessed 5 February 2010).

Lewis, Hannah, 2007, *Deaf Liberation Theology*, Aldershot: Ashgate.

Liew, Tat-siong Benny, 2001, '(Cor)Responding: A Letter to the Editor', in Stone, Ken (ed.), *Queer Commentary and the Hebrew Bible*, Sheffield: Sheffield Academic Press, pp. 182–92.

Liew, Tat-siong Benny, 2009, 'Queering Closets and Perverting Desires: Cross-Examining John's Engendering and Transgendering Word Across Different Worlds', in Bailey, Randall C., Tat-siong Benny Liew and Fernando F. Segovia (eds), *They Were All Together in One Place? Toward Minority Biblical Criticism*, Atlanta, GA: Society of Biblical Literature, pp. 251–88.

Long, Ron, 2002, 'A Place for Porn in a Gay Spiritual Economy', *Theology and Sexuality* 16 (2002), pp. 21–31.

Long, Ronald E., 2004, *Men, Homosexuality, and the Gods: An Exploration Into the Religious Significance of Male Homosexuality in World Perspective*, Binghampton, NY: Harrington Park Press.

Long, Ronald E., 2005, 'Heavenly Sex: The Moral Authority of an Impossible Dream', *Theology and Sexuality* 11.3 (2005), pp. 31–46.

Long, Thomas Lawrence, 2007, 'Queer Converts: Peculiar Pleasures and Subtle Antinomianism', in Gallagher, Lowell, Frederick S. Roden and Patricia Juliana Smith (eds), *Catholic Figures, Queer Narratives*, Basingstoke: Palgrave Macmillan, pp. 19–32.

Loughlin, Gerard (ed.), 2007a, *Queer Theology: Rethinking the Western Body*, Oxford: Blackwell.

Loughlin, Gerard, 2007b, 'Introduction: The End of Sex', in Loughlin, Gerard (ed.), *Queer Theology: Rethinking the Western Body*, Oxford: Blackwell, pp. 1–34.

Loughlin, Gerard, 2007c, 'Omphalos', in Loughlin, Gerard (ed.), *Queer Theology: Rethinking the Western Body*, Oxford: Blackwell, pp. 115–127

Loughlin, Gerard, 2008, 'What is Queer? Theology After Identity', *Theology and Sexuality* 14.2 (2008), pp. 143–52.

Lowe, Mary Elise, 2009, 'Gay, Lesbian, and Queer Theologies: Origins, Contributions, and Challenges', *Dialog* 48.1 (March 2009), pp. 49–61.

Luther, Martin, 1973, *Commentary on 1 Corinthians 7 [1523] (Luther's Works)*, translated by Edmund Sittler, St Louis, MO: Concordia Publishing House.

Macourt, Malcolm (ed.), 1977, *Towards a Theology of Gay Liberation*, London: SCM Press.

Macwilliam, Stuart, 2002, 'Queering Jeremiah', *Biblical Interpretation* 10.4 (2002), pp. 384–404.

Macwilliam, Stuart, 2009, 'Ideologies of Male Beauty and the Hebrew Bible', *Biblical Interpretation* 17 (2009), pp. 265–87.

Maduro, Otto, 2006, 'Once Again Liberating Theology? Towards a Latin American Liberation Theological Self-Criticism', in Althaus-Reid, Marcella (ed.), *Liberation Theology and Sexuality*, Aldershot: Ashgate, pp. 19–31

Mahaffy, Kimberly A., 1996, 'Cognitive Dissonance and its Resolution: A Study of Lesbian Christians', *Journal for the Scientific Study of Religion* 35.4 (December 1996), pp. 392–402.

Mansergh, Gordon, Gary Marks, Grant N. Colfax, Robert Guzman, Melissa Rader and Susan Buchbinder, 2002, '"Barebacking" in a Diverse Sample of Men who have Sex with Men', *AIDS* 16.4 (March 2002), pp. 653–9.

Martin, Dale B., 2006, *Sex and the Single Savior: Gender and Sexuality in Biblical Interpretation*, Louisville, KY: Westminster John Knox Press.

McCleary, Rollan, 2004, *A Special Illumination: Authority, Inspiration and Heresy in Gay Spirituality*, London: Equinox.

McClintock Fulkerson, Mary, 1997, 'Gender – Being It or Doing It? The Church, Homosexuality and the Politics of Identity', in Comstock, Gary David and Susan E. Henking (eds), *Que(e)rying Religion: A Critical Anthology*, New York, NY: Continuum, pp. 188–201.

McLaughlin, Eleanor, 1993, 'Feminist Christologies: Re-Dressing the Tradition', in Stevens, Maryanne (ed.), *Reconstructing the Christ Symbol: Essays in Christology*, New York, NY: Paulist Press, pp. 138–42.

McNeill, John J., 1976, *The Church and the Homosexual*, Boston, MA: Beacon Press

Mechthild of Magdeburg, 1998, *The Flowing Light of the Godhead*, translated by Frank Tobin, New York, NY: Paulist Press.

Miller, Randy, 1997, 'On My Journey Now', in Comstock, Gary David and
 Susan E. Henking (eds), *Que(e)rying Religion: A Critical Anthology*, New
 York, NY: Continuum, pp. 232–5.

Mollenkott, Virginia Ramey, 2000, 'Reading the Bible from Low and Outside: Lesbitransgay People as God's Tricksters', in Goss, Robert E. and
 Mona West (eds), *Take Back the Word*, Cleveland, OH: Pilgrim Press,
 pp. 13–22.

Mollenkott, Virginia Ramey, 2007, *Omnigender: A Trans-Religious Approach
 (Revised and Expanded Edition)*, Cleveland, OH: Pilgrim Press.

Monroe, Irene, 2000, 'When and Where I Enter, Then the Whole Race Enters
 with Me: Que(e)rying Exodus', in Goss, Robert E. and Mona West (eds),
 Take Back the Word, Cleveland, OH: Pilgrim Press, pp. 82–91.

Monroe, Irene, 2006, 'Response to Monica A. Coleman, Roundtable Discussion, "Must I Be Womanist?"', *Journal of Feminist Studies in Religion* 22.1
 (Spring 2006), pp. 107–13.

Moore, Stephen D., 1994, *Poststructuralism and the New Testament: Derrida
 and Foucault at the Foot of the Cross*, Minneapolis, MN: Fortress Press.

Moore, Stephen D., 2001, *God's Beauty Parlor: And Other Queer Spaces In
 and Around the Bible*, Stanford, CA: Stanford University Press.

Moore, Stephen D., 2006, *Empire and Apocalypse: Postcolonialism and the
 New Testament*, Sheffield: Sheffield Phoenix Press.

Morland, Iain and Annabelle Willox (eds), 2005a, *Queer Theory*, Basingstoke:
 Palgrave Macmillan.

Morland, Iain and Annabelle Willox, 2005b, 'Introduction', in Morland, Iain
 and Annabelle Willox (eds), *Queer Theory*, Basingstoke: Palgrave Macmillan, pp. 1–5.

Muers, Rachel, 2005, 'Feminism, Gender, and Theology', in Ford, David
 F. with Rachel Muers (eds), *The Modern Theologians: An Introduction to
 Christian Theology since 1918,* 3rd edn, Malden, MA and Oxford: Black-
 well, pp. 431–50.

Muers, Rachel, 2007, 'A Queer Theology: Hans Urs von Balthasar', in Loughlin, Gerard (ed.), *Queer Theology: Rethinking the Western Body*, Oxford:
 Blackwell, pp. 200–11.

Muers, Rachel, 2010, 'The Ethics of Breast-Feeding: A Feminist Theological
 Exploration', *Journal of Feminist Studies in Religion* 26.1 (Spring 2010),
 pp. 7–24.

Musić, Rusmir, 2010, 'Queer Visions of Islam', in Habib, Samar (ed.), *Islam and Homosexuality, Volume* 2, Santa Barbara, CA: Praeger, pp. 327–46.

Nausner, Michael, 2002, 'Toward Community Beyond Gender Binaries: Gregory of Nyssa's Transgendering as Part of His Transformative Eschatology', *Theology and Sexuality* 16 (March 2002), pp. 55–65.

Nelson, James B., 1992, *The Intimate Connection: Male Sexuality, Masculine Spirituality*, London: SPCK.

Nissinen, Martti, 1998, *Homoeroticism in the Biblical World: A Historical Perspective,* translated by Kirsi Stjerna, Minneapolis, MN: Fortress Press.

O'Malley, Patrick R., 2006, *Catholicism, Sexual Deviance, and Victorian Gothic Culture*, New York, NY: Cambridge University Press.

O'Malley, Patrick R., 2009, 'Epistemology of the Cloister: Victorian England's Queer Catholicism', *GLQ* 15.4 (August 2009), pp. 535–64.

Origen, 1979, 'Prologue to the Commentary on the Song of Songs', in Greer, Rowan A. (ed.), *Origen: Selected Writings*, New York, NY: Paulist Press, pp. 217–44.

Origen, 1982, 'Homily XVI on Genesis', in Heine, Ronald E. (ed.), *Origen: Homilies on Genesis and Exodus (Fathers of the Church)*, Washington, DC: Catholic University of America Press, pp. 214–26.

Ostriker, Alicia, 2000, 'A Holy of Holies: The Song of Songs as Countertext', in Brenner, Athalya and Carole R. Fontaine (eds), *The Song of Songs (A Feminist Companion to the Bible, Second Series)*, Sheffield: Sheffield Academic Press, pp. 36–54.

Pears, Angie, 2005, 'Riding the Storms of Change: From Reform and Reconstruction to Indecency and Queer Theology', *Theology and Sexuality* 12.1 (2005), pp. 29–50.

Perkins, Benjamin, 2000, 'Coming Out, Lazarus's and Ours: Queer Reflections of a Psychospiritual, Political Journey', in Goss, Robert E. and Mona West (eds), *Take Back the Word*, Cleveland, OH: Pilgrim Press, pp. 196–205.

Perry, Troy, 1972, *The Lord Is My Shepherd and He Knows I'm Gay: The Autobiography of the Reverend Troy D. Perry*, with Lucas, Charles L., Los Angeles, CA: Nash Publishing.

Petrella, Ivan, 2006, 'Queer Eye for the Straight Guy: The Making Over of Liberation Theology, A Queer Discursive Approach', in Althaus-Reid, Marcella (ed.), *Liberation Theology and Sexuality*, Aldershot: Ashgate, pp. 33–49.

Pippin, Tina and J. Michael Clark, 2006, 'Revelation/Apocalypse', in Guest,

Deryn, Robert E. Goss, Mona West and Thomas Bohache (eds), *The Queer Bible Commentary*, London: SCM Press, pp. 753–68.

Polaski, Donald C., 1997, 'What Will Ye See in the Shulammite? Women, Power and Panopticism in the Song of Songs', *Biblical Interpretation* 5.1 (1997), pp. 64–81.

Pollock, Griselda, 1999, *Differencing the Canon: Feminist Desire and the Writing of Art's Histories*, London and New York: Routledge.

Prosser, Jay, 1998, *Second Skins: The Body Narratives of Transsexuality*, New York, NY: Columbia University Press.

Rambuss, Richard, 1998, *Closet Devotions*, Durham, NC: Duke University Press.

Read, Nick (producer/director), 2008, *This World: Battle of the Bishops*, BBC/CTVC, broadcast BBC2, 21 July 2008.

Reay, Lewis, 2009, 'Towards a Transgender Theology: Que(e)rying the Eunuchs', in Althaus-Reid, Marcella and Lisa Isherwood (eds), *Trans/Formations (Controversies in Contextual Theology)*, London: SCM Press, pp. 148–67.

Redfearn, Caroline, 2007, 'The Nature of Homophobia in the Black Church', in Jagessar, Michael N. and Anthony G. Reddie (eds), *Postcolonial Black British Theology: New Textures and Themes*, Peterborough: Epworth Press, pp. 102–23.

Ribas, Mario, 2006, 'Liberating Mary, Liberating the Poor', in Althaus-Reid, Marcella (ed.), *Liberation Theology and Sexuality*, Aldershot: Ashgate, pp. 123–35.

Rich, Adrienne, 1980, 'Compulsory Heterosexuality and Lesbian Existence', *Signs* 5.4 (Summer 1980), pp. 631–60.

Ricœur, Paul, 1976, *Interpretation Theory: Discourse and the Surplus of Meaning*, Fort Worth, TX: Texas Christian University Press.

Rieger, Joerg, 2007, *Christ and Empire: From Paul to Postcolonial Times*, Minneapolis, MN: Fortress Press.

Riggs, Damien W., 2006, 'Editorial: "Queer Race"', *Australian Critical Race and Whiteness Studies Association E-Journal* 2.2 (2006), online at http://www.acrawsa.org.au/ejournalVol2no22006.htm.

Rivera, Mayra, 2004, 'God at the Crossroads: A Postcolonial Reading of Sophia', in Keller, Catherine, Michael Nausner and Mayra Rivera (eds), *Postcolonial Theologies: Divinity and Empire*, St Louis, MO: Chalice Press, pp. 186–203.

Rivera, Mayra, 2007, *The Touch of Transcendence: A Postcolonial Theology of God*, Louisville, KY: Westminster John Knox Press.

Roden, Frederick S., 2003, *Same-Sex Desire in Victorian Religious Culture*, New York, NY: Palgrave Macmillan.

Roden, Frederick S. (ed.), 2009a, *Jewish/Christian/Queer: Crossroads and Identities*, Aldershot: Ashgate.

Roden, Frederick S., 2009b, 'Introduction: Jewish/Christian/Queer: Crossroads and Identities', in Roden, Frederick S. (ed.), *Jewish/Christian/Queer: Crossroads and Identities*, Aldershot: Ashgate, pp. 1–18.

Rogers, Eugene F., 2009, 'Paul on Exceeding Nature: Queer Gentiles and the Giddy Gardener', in Roden, Frederick S. (ed.), *Jewish/Christian/Queer: Crossroads and Identities*, Aldershot: Ashgate, pp. 19–33.

Rouhani, Farhang, 2007, 'Religion, Identity and Activism: Queer Muslim Diasporic Identities', in Browne, Kath, Jason Lim and Gavin Brown (eds), *Geographies of Sexualities: Theory, Practices and Politics*, Aldershot: Ashgate, pp. 169–79.

Rudy, Kathy, 1996a, 'Queer Theory and Feminism', in Clark, J. Michael and Robert E. Goss (eds), *A Rainbow of Religious Studies*, Las Colinas, TX: Monument Press, pp. 81–101.

Rudy, Kathy, 1996b, '"Where Two or More Are Gathered": Using Gay Communities as a Model for Christian Sexual Ethics', *Theology and Sexuality* 2.4 (March 1996), pp. 81–99.

Rudy, Kathy, 1997, *Sex and the Church: Gender, Homosexuality, and the Transformation of Christian Ethics*, Boston, MA: Beacon Press.

Rudy, Kathy, 2004, 'Review of Stuart, Elizabeth, *Gay and Lesbian Theologies: Repetitions with Critical Difference*', *Theology and Sexuality* 11.1 (2004), pp. 107–9.

Rudy, Kathy, 2007, 'Subjectivity and Belief', in Loughlin, Gerard (ed.), *Queer Theology: Rethinking the Western Body*, Oxford: Blackwell, pp. 37–49.

Ruether, Rosemary Radford, 1985, *Women-Church: Theology and Practice of Feminist Liturgical Communities*, San Francisco, CA: Harper & Row.

Salih, Sara, 2003, 'Judith Butler and the Ethics of Difficulty', *Critical Quarterly* 45.3 (2003), pp. 42–51.

Salomon, Nanette, 1991, 'The Art Historical Canon: Sins of Omission', in Hartmann, Joan and Ellen Messer-Davidow (eds), *(En)gendering Knowledge: Feminists in Academe*, Knoxville, TN: University of Tennessee Press, pp. 222–36.

Safi, Omid (ed.), 2003a, *Progressive Muslims: On Justice, Gender and Pluralism*, Oxford: Oneworld Publications.

Safi, Omid, 2003b, 'Introduction: *The Times They Are a-Changin'* – A Muslim Quest for Justice, Gender Equality, and Pluralism', in Safi, Omid (ed.), *Progressive Muslims: On Justice, Gender and Pluralism*, Oxford: Oneworld Publications, pp. 1–31.

Schippert, Claudia, 1999, 'Too Much Trouble? Negotiating Feminist and Queer Approaches in Religion', *Theology and Sexuality* 11 (1999), pp. 44–63.

Schippert, Claudia, 2005, 'Queer Theory and the Study of Religion', *Revista de Estudos da Religião (REVER)* 4 (2005), pp. 90–9.

Schippert, Claudia, 2006, 'Turning On/To Ethics', in Armour, Ellen T. and Susan M. St. Ville (eds), *Bodily Citations: Religion and Judith Butler*, New York, NY: Columbia University Press, pp. 157–76.

Schlichter, Annette, 2004, 'Queer at Last? Straight Intellectuals and the Desire for Transgression', *GLQ* 10.4 (2004), pp. 543–65.

Schneider, Laurel C., 2000, 'Homosexuality, Queer Theory, and Christian Theology', *Religious Studies Review* 26.1 (Jan 2000), pp. 3–12.

Schneider, Laurel C., 2001, 'Yahwist Desires: Imagining Divinity Queerly', in Stone, Ken (ed.), *Queer Commentary and the Hebrew Bible*, Sheffield: Sheffield Academic Press, pp. 210–27.

Sedgwick, Eve Kosofsky, 1990, *Epistemology of the Closet*, Berkeley, CA: University of California Press.

Sedgwick, Eve Kosofsky, 1993, *Tendencies*, Durham, NC: Duke University Press.

Segovia, Fernando F. and R. S. Sugirtharajah (eds), 2009, *A Postcolonial Commentary on the New Testament Writings*, London: T&T Clark.

Shah, Omer, 2010, 'Reading and Writing the Queer Hajj', in Habib, Samar (ed.), *Islam and Homosexuality, Volume 1*, Santa Barbara, CA: Praeger, pp. 111–31.

Shaw, Jane, 2007, 'Reformed and Enlightened Church', in Loughlin, Gerard (ed.), *Queer Theology: Rethinking the Western Body*, Oxford: Blackwell, pp. 215–29.

Sheffield, Tricia, 2008, 'Performing Jesus: A Queer Counternarrative of Embodied Transgression', *Theology and Sexuality* 14.3 (May 2008), pp. 233–58.

Sherwood, Yvonne, 2000, *A Biblical Text and Its Afterlives: The Survival of*

Jonah in Western Culture, Cambridge: Cambridge University Press.

Shortt, Rupert, 2005, *God's Advocates: Christian Thinkers in Conversation*, Grand Rapids, MI: Eerdmans.

Simpson, Jennifer Lyn, 2008, 'The Color-Blind Double Bind: Whiteness and the (Im)possibility of Dialogue', *Communication Theory* 18 (2008), pp. 139–59.

Siraj, Asifa, 2009, 'The Construction of the Homosexual "Other" by British Muslim Heterosexuals', *Contemporary Islam* 3.1 (April 2009), pp. 41–57.

Sisters of Perpetual Indulgence: http://www.thesisters.org/index.html (accessed 2 December 2009).

Slee, Nicola, 2011, *In Search of the Risen Christa*, London: SPCK.

Smith, Cherry, 1996, 'What is This Thing Called Queer?', in Morton, Donald (ed.), *The Material Queer: A Lesbigay Cultural Studies Reader*, Boulder, CO: Westview Press, pp. 277–85.

Smith, Clyde, 2000, 'How I Became a Queer Heterosexual', in Thomas, Calvin (ed.), *Straight with a Twist: Queer Theory and the Subject of Heterosexuality*, Urbana and Chicago, IL: University of Illinois Press, pp. 60–7.

Spencer, Daniel T., 2004, 'Lesbian and Gay Theologies', in De La Torre, Miguel A. (ed.), *Handbook of US Theologies of Liberation*, St Louis, MO: Chalice Press, pp. 264–73.

Spivak, Gayatri Chakravorty, 1991, 'Identity and Alterity: An Interview', *Arena* 97 (1991), pp. 65–76.

Steinberg, Leo, 1996, *The Sexuality of Christ in Renaissance Art and in Modern Oblivion*, 2nd edn, revised and expanded, Chicago and London: University of Chicago Press.

Stewart, David Tabb, 2006, 'Leviticus', in Guest, Deryn, Robert E. Goss, Mona West and Thomas Bohache (eds), *The Queer Bible Commentary*, London: SCM Press, pp. 77–104.

Stone, Ken (ed.), 2001a, *Queer Commentary and the Hebrew Bible*, Sheffield: Sheffield Academic Press.

Stone, Ken, 2001b, 'Queer Commentary and Biblical Interpretation: An Introduction', in Stone, Ken (ed.), *Queer Commentary and the Hebrew Bible*, Sheffield: Sheffield Academic Press, pp. 11–34.

Stone, Ken, 2001c, 'Homosexuality and the Bible or Queer Reading? A Response to Martti Nissinen', *Theology and Sexuality* 14 (2001), pp. 107–18.

Stone, Ken, 2004, 'Queering the Canaanite', in Althaus-Reid, Marcella and

Lisa Isherwood (eds), *The Sexual Theologian: Essays on God, Sex and Politics*, London: T&T Clark, pp. 110–34.

Stone, Ken, 2005, *Practicing Safer Texts: Food, Sex and Bible in Queer Perspective*, London and New York: T&T Clark.

Stone, Ken, 2006a, '1 and 2 Samuel', in Guest, Deryn, Robert E. Goss, Mona West and Thomas Bohache (eds), *The Queer Bible Commentary*, London: SCM Press, pp. 195–221.

Stone, Ken, 2006b, 'The Garden of Eden and the Heterosexual Contract', in Armour, Ellen T. and Susan M. St.Ville (eds), *Bodily Citations: Religion and Judith Butler*, New York and Chichester: Columbia University Press, pp. 48–70.

Stone, Ken, 2007, '"Do Not Be Conformed to This World": Queer Reading and the Task of the Preacher', *Theology and Sexuality* 13.2 (2007), pp. 153–66.

Stone, Ken, 2008, 'Bibles That Matter: Biblical Theology and Queer Performativity', *Biblical Theology Bulletin* 38.14 (2008), pp. 14–25.

Stringer, Martin, 2000, 'Of Gin and Lace: Sexuality, Liturgy and Identity among Anglo-Catholics in the Mid-Twentieth Century', *Theology and Sexuality* 13 (2000), pp. 35–54.

Stuart, Elizabeth, 1993, *Chosen: Gay Catholic Priests Tell Their Stories*, London: Geoffrey Chapman.

Stuart, Elizabeth, 1995, *Just Good Friends: Towards a Lesbian and Gay Theology of Relationships*, London: Mowbray.

Stuart, Elizabeth (ed.), 1997a, *Religion is a Queer Thing: A Guide to the Christian Faith for Lesbian, Gay, Bisexual and Transgendered People*, London: Cassell.

Stuart, Elizabeth, 1997b, 'Sex in Heaven: The Queering of Theological Discourse on Sexuality', in Davies, Jon and Gerard Loughlin (eds), *Sex These Days: Essays on Theology, Sexuality, and Society*, Sheffield: Sheffield Academic Press, pp. 184–204.

Stuart, Elizabeth, 2003, *Gay and Lesbian Theologies: Repetitions with Critical Difference*, Aldershot: Ashgate.

Stuart, Elizabeth, 2004, 'Queering Death', in Althaus-Reid, Marcella and Lisa Isherwood (eds), *The Sexual Theologian: Essays on God, Sex and Politics*, London: T&T Clark, pp. 58–70.

Stuart, Elizabeth, 2007, 'Sacramental Flesh', in Loughlin, Gerard (ed.), *Queer Theology: Rethinking the Western Body*, Oxford: Blackwell, pp. 65–75.

Sturgis, Alexander, 2000, discussion of Campin's *The Virgin and Child in an Interior*, in Finalde, Gabriele (ed.), 2000, *The Image of Christ*, London: National Gallery Company Limited, pp. 56–57.

Sugirtharajah, R. S., 2003, *Postcolonial Reconfigurations: An Alternative Way of Reading the Bible and Doing Theology*, London: SCM Press.

Sweasey, Peter, 1997, *From Queer to Eternity: Spirituality in the Lives of Lesbian, Gay and Bisexual People*, London and Washington: Cassell.

Swicegood, Thomas L.P., 1974, *Our God Too*, New York, NY: Pyramid Books.

Taylder, Siân, 2004, 'Our Lady of the Libido: Towards a Marian Theology of Sexual Liberation?', *Feminist Theology* 12.3 (2004), pp. 343–71.

Taylder, Siân, 2009, 'Shot From Both Sides: Theology and the Woman Who Isn't Quite What She Seems', in Althaus-Reid, Marcella and Lisa Isherwood (eds), *Trans/Formations (Controversies in Contextual Theology)*, London: SCM Press, pp. 70–91.

Thomas, Calvin (ed.), 2000a, *Straight with a Twist: Queer Theory and the Subject of Heterosexuality*, Urbana and Chicago, IL: University of Illinois Press.

Thomas, Calvin, 2000b, 'Straight with a Twist: Queer Theory and the Subject of Heterosexuality', in Thomas, Calvin (ed.), *Straight With a Twist: Queer Theory and the Subject of Heterosexuality*, Urbana and Chicago, IL: University of Illinois Press, pp. 11–44.

Tiemeyer, Tracy Sayuki, 2006, 'Retrieving "Asian Spirituality" in North American Contexts: An Interfaith Proposal', *Spiritus* 6.2 (2006), pp. 228–33.

Toft, Alex, 2009, 'Bisexual Christians: The Life-Stories of a Marginalized Community', in Hunt, Stephen (ed.), *Contemporary Christianity and LGBT Sexualities*, Farnham: Ashgate, pp. 67–86.

Tolbert, Mary Ann, 2000, 'Foreword: What Word Shall We Take Back?', in Goss, Robert E. and Mona West (eds), *Take Back the Word*, Cleveland, OH: Pilgrim Press, pp. vii–xii.

Townes, Emilie M., 1995, *In a Blaze of Glory: Womanist Spirituality as Social Witness*, Nashville, TN: Abingdon Press.

Trible, Phyllis, 1973, 'Depatriarchalizing in Biblical Interpretation', *Journal of the American Academy of Religion* 41.1 (March 1973), pp. 30–48.

Trible, Phyllis, 1984, *Texts of Terror: Literary-Feminist Readings of Biblical Narratives*, Minneapolis, MN: Fortress Press.

Trzebiatowska, Marta, 2009, 'Common Pathways, Different Lives: The "Coming Out" Narratives of Catholic Nuns and Lesbians in Poland', in Hunt, Stephen (ed.), *Contemporary Christianity and LGBT Sexualities*, Farnham: Ashgate, pp. 51–65.

Valentine, Gill, Robert M. Vanderbeck, Johan Andersson, Joanna Sadgrove and Kevin Ward, 2010, 'Emplacements: The Event as a Prism for Exploring Intersectionality; a Case Study of the Lambeth Conference', *Sociology* 44.5 (October 2010), pp. 925–43.

Vasey, Michael, 1995, *Strangers and Friends: A New Exploration of Homosexuality and the Bible*, London: Hodder and Stoughton.

Voas, David and Rodney Ling, 2010, 'Religion in Britain and the United States', in Park, Alison, John Curtice, Katarina Thomson, Miranda Phillips, Elizabeth Clery and Sarah Butt (eds), *British Social Attitudes: The Twenty-Sixth Report (National Centre for Social Research)* London: Sage Publications, pp. 65–86.

Walker, Alice, 1983, *In Search of Our Mothers' Gardens: Womanist Prose*, New York, NY: Harcourt Brace Jovanovich.

Walters, Suzanna Danuta, 1996, 'From Here to Queer: Radical Feminism, Postmodernism, and the Lesbian Menace (or, Why Can't a Woman be More Like a Fag?)', *Signs* 21.4 (1996), pp. 830–69.

Walton, Heather, 2004, 'The Gender of the Cyborg', *Theology and Sexuality* 10.2 (2004), pp. 33–44.

Warner, Michael, 1991, 'Fear of a Queer Planet', *Social Text* 9.4 (1991), pp. 3–17.

Warnke, Georgia, 2001, 'Intersexuality and the Categories of Sex', *Hypatia* 16.3 (Summer 2001), pp. 126–37.

Webster, Alison, 1995, *Found Wanting: Women, Christianity and Sexuality*, London: Cassell.

Webster, Alison, 1998, 'Queer to be Religious: Lesbian Adventures Beyond the Christian/Post-Christian Dichotomy', *Theology and Sexuality* 8 (1998), pp. 27–39.

Weeks, Jeffrey, 1995, *Invented Moralities: Sexual Values in an Age of Uncertainty*, New York, NY: Columbia University Press.

Weeks, Jeffrey, 2000, *Making Sexual History*, Cambridge: Polity Press.

West, Gerald and Ujamaa Centre staff, 2007, *Doing Contextual Bible Study: A Resource Manual*, The Ujamaa Centre for Biblical & Theological Community Development & Research (formerly the Institute for the Study of the

Bible & Worker Ministry Project), online at www.ukzn.ac.za/sorat/ujamaa/ ujam123.pdf (accessed 2 December 2009).

West, Mona, 1997, 'The Book of Ruth: An Example of Procreative Strategies for Queers', in Goss, Robert E. and Amy Adams Squire Strongheart (eds), *Our Families, Our Values: Snapshots of Queer Kinship,* Binghampton, NY: The Haworth Press, pp. 51–60.

West, Mona, 2000, 'Outsiders, Aliens, and Boundary Crossers: A Queer Reading of the Hebrew Exodus', in Goss, Robert E. and Mona West (eds), *Take Back the Word,* Cleveland, OH: Pilgrim Press, pp. 71–81.

Williams, Rowan, 1988, 'Introduction', in Beck, Ashley and Ros Hunt (eds), 1988, *Speaking Love's Name; Homosexuality: Some Catholic and Socialist Perspectives,* London: Jubilee Group, online at http://www.anglocatholic-socialism.org/lovesname.html (accessed 5 February 2010).

Williams, Rowan, 1996, 'Review of Stuart, Elizabeth, *Just Good Friends: Towards a Lesbian and Gay Theology of Relationships', Theology and Sexuality* 4 (1996), pp. 123–6.

Wilson, Nancy, 1995, *Our Tribe: Queer Folks, God, Jesus, and the Bible,* San Francisco, CA: HarperSanFrancisco.

Wilson, Nancy, 2000, *Our Tribe: Queer Folks, God, Jesus, and the Bible, Millennium Edition: Updated and Revised,* Tajique, NM: Alamo Square Press.

Woodhead, Linda, 2007, 'Sex and Secularization', in Loughlin, Gerard (ed.), *Queer Theology: Rethinking the Western Body.* Oxford: Blackwell, pp. 230–44.

Yep, Gust A., Karen E. Lovaas and Alex V. Pagonis, 2002, 'The Case of Riding "Bareback": Sexual Practices and the Paradoxes of Identity in the Era of AIDS', *Journal of Homosexuality* 42.4 (July 2002), pp. 1–14.

Yip, Andrew K.T., 1999, 'The Politics of Counter-Rejection: Gay Christians and the Church', *Journal of Homosexuality* 37 (1999), pp. 47–63.

Yip, Andrew K.T., 2000, 'Leaving the Church to Keep My Faith: The Lived Experiences of Non-Heterosexual Christians', in Francis, Leslie J. and Yaacov J. Katz (eds), *Joining and Leaving Religion: Research Perspectives,* Leominster: Gracewing, pp. 129–45.

Yip, Andrew K. T., 2002, 'The Persistence of Faith Among Nonhetero-sexual Christians: Evidence for the Neosecularization Thesis of Religious Transformation', *Journal for the Scientific Study of Religion* 41.2 (2002), pp. 199–212.

Yip, Andrew K. T., 2003, 'Spirituality and Sexuality: An Exploration of the Religious Beliefs of Non-Heterosexual Christians in Great Britain', *Theology and Sexuality* 9.2 (2003), pp. 137–54.

Yip, Andrew K. T., 2004, 'Embracing Allah and Sexuality? South Asian Non-Heterosexual Muslims in Britain', in Jacobsen, Knut A. and P. Pratap Kumar (eds), *South Asians in the Diaspora: Histories and Religious Traditions*, Leiden: E.J. Brill, pp. 294–310.

Yip, Andrew K. T., 2005, 'Queering Religious Texts: An Exploration of British Non-Heterosexual Christians' and Muslims' Strategy of Constructing Sexuality-Affirming Hermeneutics', *Sociology* 39.1 (2005), pp. 47–65.

Yip, Andrew K. T. and Michael Keenan, 2009, 'Transgendering Christianity: Gender-Variant Christians as Visionaries', in Hunt, Stephen (ed.), *Contemporary Christianity and LGBT Sexualities*, Farnham: Ashgate, pp. 87–102.

Yorukoglu, Ilgin, 2010, 'Marketing Diversity: Homonormativity and the Queer Turkish Organizations in Britain', in Habib, Samar (ed.), *Islam and Homosexuality, Volume 2*, Santa Barbara, CA: Praeger, pp. 419–44.

Yoshino, Kenji, 2007, *Covering: The Hidden Assault on Our Civil Rights*, New York, NY: Random House.

Zimmerman, Barry E. and David J. Zimmerman, 1996, *Killer Germs: Microbes and Diseases That Threaten Humanity*, Chicago, IL: Contemporary Books.

Index of Biblical References

Index of Names and Subjects